Advanced Praise for
Becoming Unbelievably Successful

Stu Heinecke
Author, Host, Marketer, and Wall Street Journal Cartoonist

"Becoming Unbelievably Successful is a 'What I Wish I Knew Then' kind of book. It is a thorough review of best practices and advice for young adult readers."

Selvi Aurora
Founder and President of Youth Engineers

"John Knotts' book – Becoming Unbelievably Successful is a must-read. Once I began to read it, I couldn't stop until I finished! Extremely powerful novel, I highly recommend this to high school and college students, especially because it can change our perspective on life and provide us with the entrepreneurial tools we need to lead the future of tomorrow. As always, John's extensive business experience has led him to publish an influential book for our generations! So excited for all that's to come in the future John!"

Gina Riley
Career Coach & Creator of Career Velocity

"Becoming Unbelievably Successful cuts to the heart of where costly organizational breakdowns occur and prescribes methodical ways to circumvent or overcome these challenges with clear foundational concepts, models, and frameworks. Simultaneously, Knotts breaks down, to the micro-level, practical techniques each person can use to create a plan to become personally and professionally successful. What makes this book unique is how Knotts intersects the personal, professional, organizational development and planning aspects into one tidy, easy-to-understand guide. In short, you bring the motivation and Knotts' brings a plan for you to follow. This book would make a great addition to an MBA course curriculum. If you have the drive to become unbelievably successful, this book should be a ready reference in your back pocket."

Becoming Unbelievably Successful

John Knotts

Copyright © 2022 John Knotts
All rights reserved.

This book or any portion thereof may not be reproduced or used in any manner whatsoever without the express written permission of the publisher, except for the use of brief quotations in a book review or scholarly journal.

ISBN-13: 978-1945151040
ISBN-10: 1945151040

Crosscutter Enterprises
www.crossctr.com
John.Knotts@crossctr.com
All images are property of Crosscutter Enterprises.

Special discounts are available on quantity purchases by corporations, associations, educators, and others. For additional details, contact the author at the email address listed below.
John.Knotts@crossctr.com

10 9 8 7 6 5 4 3 2 1

Dedication

To my parents who always told me that I could do anything I put my mind to. Especially my mom!

To my wife, Lori, who has supported me through my journey of becoming unbelievably successful.

To those leaders over the years who have inspired and supported me in some way to be better than I was.

To the poor role models who taught me more than they will ever know.

"Hard work always pays off, whatever you do." Dustin Lynch

"With hard work and dedication, anything is possible." Timothy Weah

"There are no shortcuts to any place worth going." Beverly Sills

"When you truly dedicate yourself to your goals, there is no way not to achieve them." Max Moreno

"Dedication is belief transitioned into action which is transformed into change." Byron Pulsifer

"Genius is one percent inspiration, ninety-nine percent perspiration." Thomas Edison

"Only those who dare to fail greatly can ever achieve greatly." Robert F. Kennedy

"Who you are tomorrow begins with what you do today." Tim Fargo

"Self-belief and hard work will always earn you success." Virat Kohli

"Whenever you do a thing, act as if all the world were watching." Thomas Jefferson

Table of Contents

Foreword 2
Preface 3
Acknowledgments 5

Part 1 – Foundations of Unbelievable Success 6
   Chapter 1 – Introduction 7
   Chapter 2 – How To Use This Book 11
   Chapter 3 – My Story 15
   Chapter 4 – Success Defined 23
   Chapter 5 – Self-Actualization 32
   Chapter 6 – The Universal Laws 38

Part 2 – Personal Strategic Plan to Becoming Unbelievably Successful 50
   Chapter 7 – Creating the Plan 51
   Chapter 8 – Implementing the Plan 60
   Chapter 9 – Staying on Plan 71

Part 3 – Leading Yourself Towards Unbelievable Success 78
   Chapter 10 – Self-Efficacy and Locus of Control 79
   Chapter 11 – Moving from Victim to Creator 87
   Chapter 12 – Emotional Intelligence 91
   Chapter 13 – Mastering Mindsets 97
   Chapter 14 – Structured Lifelong Learning 103
   Chapter 15 – Shuhari 111
   Chapter 16 – Memory Mastery 116
   Chapter 17 – Interpersonal Relationships 120
   Chapter 18 – Agile Perfectionism 125

Part 4 – Stress Management and its Importance in Unbelievable Success. 134
   Chapter 19 – Self-Care 135
   Chapter 20 – Health and Fitness 142
   Chapter 21 – Financial Management 146
   Chapter 22 – Spirituality 150
   Chapter 23 – 5S Your Life 154

Part 5 – Business Transferable Skills of Unbelievably Successful People .. 162
   Chapter 24 – Time Management 163
   Chapter 25 – Strategy and Culture 172
   Chapter 26 – Leadership and Management 178
   Chapter 27 – Change Management and Change Readiness 185
   Chapter 28 – Personal and Professional Communication 189
   Chapter 29 – Program and Project Management 195
   Chapter 30 – Process Management and Process Improvement 200
   Chapter 31 – Business Insights 208

Part 6 – Personal Motivation to Unbelievable Success 222
    Chapter 32 – Understanding Motivation 223
    Chapter 33 – Personal Goal Setting 231
    Chapter 34 – Confidence 236
    Chapter 35 – Overcoming Fear 240
    Chapter 36 – Creativity 244
    Chapter 37 – Persistence 248

Part 7 – Volunteerism Leads to Unbelievable Success 258
    Chapter 38 – Volunteering and Self-Actualizing 259
    Chapter 39 – Acceptable Environment to Fail Forward 263
    Chapter 40 – Being Active versus Being Present 267
    Chapter 41 – Leading versus Participating 271

Part 8 – Becoming A Recognized Unbelievable Success 278
    Chapter 42 – Social Networks 279
    Chapter 43 – Professional Organizations 284
    Chapter 44 – Published Author 289
    Chapter 45 – Public Speaker 296
    Chapter 46 – Awards and Recognitions 300

Part 9 – Becoming Unbelievably Successful 306

Becoming Unbelievably Successful Glossary 310
Becoming Unbelievably Successful Index 315
Becoming Unbelievably Successful Bibliography 318
Becoming Unbelievably Successful Acronyms 324
About the Author 326
Related Works 328

Foreword

Robyn Tresnak, PhD
Educator; President and Founder of Robyn's N.E.S.T. – Nurturing Early Success & Teaching

When John first asked me to write the Foreword for *Becoming Unbelievably Successful*, my first thoughts were, "Why me?" Afterall, I am not a famous author or psychologist who speaks to self-help. Yet I know, and have experienced, the wisdom that John shares in his writing. More importantly, I know his wisdom needs to be shared with learners of all ages.

As an educator, I am appreciative of the format of this book. Whether it is read by a high school student or a middle-aged individual seeking to find success, the brief chapters accompanied by thought-provoking questions, create a simple way for the reader to move through the book. Concepts presented in the reading are critical to building a successful path in life. Additionally, it is incredibly helpful to see ways to prepare, stay on, and assess the path. Not only are there suggestions, but there are samples. This allows the reader to implement the concepts with ease.

Our lives offer a journey filled with twists and turns, ups, and downs. John, through his experiences and daily work impacting successful steps in the lives of those around him, displays how to make that day-to-day and year-to-year journey successful. People who pick up this book are not guaranteed success. People who pick up this book, spend time focusing on the reflection questions, then execute each step of the process, will definitely embark on a reliable journey of *Becoming Unbelievably Successful*.

I am privileged to serve learners of all ages, in various facets of education. Through two readings of John's book, once after the initial writing and another recently, following final edits, I continually say this book is about building a deliberate path to success for ALL. This should begin early in life ... or NOW. I am beyond honored to share the Foreword for John's book. As an educator and lifelong learner, I read a lot of books. In fact, John and I are both board and faculty members with Executive Book Review (EBR), in San Antonio, where we are exposed to all manners of business and self-help books. John's advice and direction in Becoming Unbelievably Successful gives the reader an easy-to-follow roadmap of how to become unbelievably successful. I encourage everyone to use this book as a guide, plus give copies to those of all ages who you know, lead, mentor, or coach.

Success is not a hope, it is an intricate journey.

Preface

Why did I want to write a book about success?

For years, I wrote books and articles on business challenges. Specifically, I focused on driving to the root causes of major operational excellence issues and presented ways to systematically overcome these challenges. The writing I have done in the past has been primarily focused on growing, scaling, and improving business operations.

However, I am a personal and professional business coach and consultant. My focus is not only on promoting a businesses' success, but also on developing individuals' personal success in business. In fact, I consider myself to be a "Success Incubator." What this means to me is that I provide both personal and professional business coaching and consulting to help you and your business succeed in today's ever-changing world.

I have read many different self-help and success books. Some of them are good, but most of them tend to provide theory without application. I want to do more than that. Over the last 57 years of my life, I have learned not only what you should do to become unbelievably successful, but how you should do it.

Thus, I decided to create a book – no, a guide – that anyone can follow to become unbelievably successful.

As I wrote this book, the world was dealing with one of the most dramatic crises of current times. COVID-19 gripped the world with sickness, death, fear, and dread. In addition to the sickness and catastrophic loss of life, with over 40 million people unemployed in the United States alone, the need for positive and simple instructions to achieve unbelievable success was never more necessary.

As I thought about putting together this book on success, I really had to think about what would have benefited me most in my journey. My journey has not been the best, or as easy as it could have been. But it has been an incredible one, which over the years, has taught me a great deal about what it takes to become unbelievably successful in life and in business.

When I thought about the audience for this book, which is something that every author should do before putting pen to paper (or fingers to keys), and I wondered who would benefit from it, I thought about how I wished that I had been given a step-by-step blueprint for success as a teenager. So, the first person I wrote this book for was the high school student, who has their whole life in front of them, and is eager to be unbelievably successful in their life. But this book can also be valuable to someone in many phases of life. I was 35 when I finally put my life on the path to deliberate success and it would have been a lot easier if I had had this book.

Deliberate Success

Deliberate success is what this book is all about – making a concerted effort to constantly focus on building yourself, and your successes, every day. There are no magic pills for success in this world. If the stories of others' successes are not encouragement enough, this book makes it clear that you can become unbelievably successful, regardless of how you start out in life. There have been many incredibly successful people in this world (Thomas Edison, Walt Disney, Stephen King, Elvis Presley, and even Albert Einstein) who started out humbly. This is not a theoretical book of habits of successful people. No! This is a book of no-nonsense, easy-to-apply strategies and thought-patterns that will put you on the road to unbelievable success.

The earlier in life you read this book, the more successful you can become. So, I welcome you today to take the first step on your journey to becoming unbelievably successful!

Acknowledgements

First and foremost, I want to recognize my wife, Lori. Not only has she supported my dreams of success, but she has become my strongest editor when it comes to writing.

My parents – maybe not unbelievably successful in life – were still happy. My mom instilled a belief in me that I could be anything I put my mind to.

To The Skippers … specifically Kevin, Jeff M., Jeff F., Mark, and Greg. They say you are the byproduct of your five closest friends, and these five have been close to me since junior high school.

For greatly broadening my mind, I would like to personally thank the faculty of the EBR, and all of those with whom I regularly converse on LinkedIn. Both have provided me with new avenues of learning, ideas, and enlightenment.

My wife turned to me, as she was editing this book, and asked, "Do you believe that you are unbelievably successful?" My reply was simple. "Of course not, but I am on the journey."

Part 1
Foundations of Unbelievable Success

"Life's most persistent and urgent question is, what are you doing for others?"
~ Martin Luther King, Jr.

Chapter 1
Introduction

What are some of the greatest books about becoming successful that you have read? Do you encourage your kids to read these books?

In high school, we were required to read the classics, like: *Catcher in the Rye*, *Animal Farm*, *The Great Gatsby*, and *Lord of the Flies*. Honestly, the only book I remember was, *Lord of the Flies*.

When I was a kid, I devoured fantasy and science fiction. I remember the *Shannara* and *Forgotten Realms* series were big on my list. Also, I loved all *The Hardy Boys* books. I owned nearly every one of the original hardcover releases – collected them in fact

It was not until much later in life that I started to read success-related books. In fact, I did not read *Think and Grow Rich*, or *How to Win Friends and Influence People* until a few years ago. Both books were published 40 years before I was even born. However, they are still considered classic success books today and I learned a lot from reading them.

Today, I have well over 300 business and success-related books in my library. At any given point, I have probably 10 to 20 books waiting to be read.

Have you read these books?

- *Think and Grow Rich*
- *How to Win Friends and Influence People*
- *The Law of Success*
- *Rich Dad Poor Dad*
- *The Total Money Makeover*

Well, my parents did not read them. Maybe if they had, they would have encouraged me to read those books along with what I was already reading. How different my life might have been if I had read those books when I was in my teens?

Becoming Unbelievably Successful is one of those books that you should read early in life. It should accompany the classics from high school and the diversions from reality today. This book provides a step-by-step blueprint of how to become unbelievably successful in your life. All you need to do is read and apply the principles of this book!

Probably one of the biggest points that I want to make, in the introduction for this book, is that you are going to have to step out of your comfort zone to become unbelievably successful. Stepping out of our comfort zone is scary and always represents a change (see Chapter 27 on Change Management). This means that when you step out of your comfort zone you immediately enter what is known as the fear zone. Many people stop at this point in their journey of self-discovery and improvement. Thus, they return to their comfort zone.

If you are able to push through that zone of fear and take risks, you will begin learning. Throughout this book, I will consistently and constantly discuss treating failure as a learning tool. If you cannot step out of your comfort zone and accept and face your fears (Chapter 35), then you will struggle to become unbelievably successful. However, when you fail forward and learn from your mistakes, you enter what is known as the growth zone.

This entire book is focused on pushing you out of your comfort zone, through the fear zone, into the learning zone, so that you can explore your growth zone.

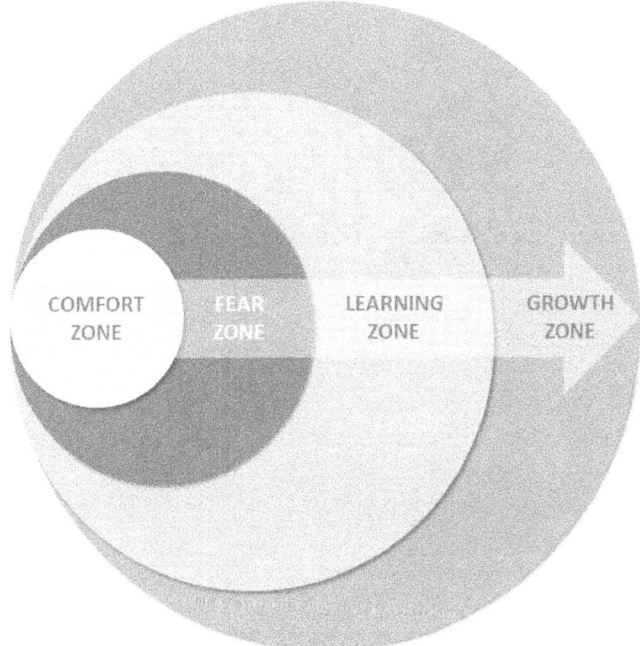

But this is not a book that will simply tell you that you need to do something. No, there are too many self-help books on the shelves today that will give you theory without step-by-step guidance. This book will provide specific actions on how to become unbelievably successful.

Chapter 1 Questions

1. What was one book that the author remembered from high school?

2. How many business and success-related books does the author have in his library?

3. What will *Becoming Unbelievably Successful* provide you with?

4. What is the title of one of the books that the author listed, but did not read in his youth?

Essay Question

Why do you feel reading success-related books is good early in your life?

Chapter 1 Notes Page

Use this page to capture notes in each Part and Chapter

Chapter 2
How To Use This Book

Becoming Unbelievably Successful is broken down into 9 Parts, with 46 Chapters.

Part 1, which includes the Introduction and this chapter, provides the foundations of unbelievable success. In this part of the book, I share the story of how I ended up on my journey to my own unbelievable success. Throughout this book, I share additional points about that story and stories from others to accentuate the point. I provide my story so you can better understand the road I took to discover the lessons in this book.

Also, in Part 1 of this book, are three fundamental lessons that have stuck with me since the moment I learned them. First, is how to define your success as I did. This concept of ikigai is deceptively simple yet will be incredibly important when you get to Part 2 of the book.

The second fundamental lesson is founded in Abraham Maslow's foundational work, *A Theory of Human Motivation*, published in 1943. This groundbreaking work in human developmental psychology resulted in what is known today as Maslow's Hierarchy of Needs. Self-actualizing – or reaching the top of the needs pyramid – is critically important to understand while on the journey to becoming unbelievably successful.

The last fundamental lesson in Part 1 of this book is how to obtain a strong understanding of the 15 universal laws. Many people, while on the road to success, have heard of the Law of Attraction – some have even stumbled upon the Law of Vibration. However, the 15 universal laws are very important to success, as is how they work together. You will not find a more comprehensive study of all these laws at once anywhere else.

Part 2 of this book is the most important. In Part 2, we will go through the detailed steps of creating and implementing your Personal Strategic Plan. This plan will be the single most important thing in your life after reading this book. Everything else in this book will support you in the creation and implementation of this plan. Specifically, Chapter 9 in Part 2 covers the challenges you might encounter as you implement your plan. That chapter is designed to help you stay on your plan, regardless of what might happen to you.

There are nine core understandings that you must master to become unbelievably successful. These are discussed in the nine chapters in Part 3, Leading Yourself Towards Unbelievable Success. It is important for you to spend the time you need to understand these concepts, as failure to master these areas will significantly hamper your journey. Remember, these pages contain not only concepts and ideas, but specific actions that you can take to master those concepts and ideas. These are crucial when creating and implementing your Personal Strategic Plan!

Parts 4 through 8 are all helpful along your journey. Becoming unbelievably successful requires resilience and determination. By working to become unbelievably successful, you will experience considerably more stress than someone going through their life on autopilot. So, Part 4 discusses specific actions you can employ to deal with the stresses that you will face.

Part 5 highlights the transferable business skills that I found most useful to becoming unbelievably successful. These skills are designed to be applicable to any situation or career in life. All too often, we are only taught the skills we need for our job, and how to complete the tasks associated with that job. Unfortunately, in our changing world today, jobs are being phased out, outsourced, automated, and adjusted, sometimes faster than people can even learn them. In fact, about 65 percent of children in grade school right now will end up working in jobs that do not even exist today. To prepare for this ever-changing business landscape, this part of the book covers eight broad transferable skills that are crucial to you becoming an unbelievable success.

As said, becoming an unbelievable success requires resilience and determination. Some might call it "Moxy." You will need a very high level of personal motivation. In Part 6 of this book, we will explore what motivation is, and how to feed and protect your personal motivation.

In Part 7, I share with you why it is inherently important to get involved early and often with volunteer activities. I became an involved volunteer in 1992, and the lessons on success from my volunteer activities I learned were priceless. Today, I have founded and run three nonprofit organizations of my own. This part of the book shares why volunteerism is critical to becoming unbelievably successful.

The final Part of this book, before the Summary, focuses on the five things you should start doing today to become a "recognized" unbelievable success. It is one thing to be unbelievably successful, but a totally different thing to be recognized as someone who is unbelievably successful. This last part of the book is dedicated to five ways to establish your success across your industry and the community as a whole.

If you read nothing else in this book, make sure it is Part 2. It contains the foundation of becoming unbelievably successful. Everything else in this book is only good information without that specific guidance.

Enjoy your journey to becoming unbelievably successful!

Chapter 2 Questions

1. What is the most important Part of this book to read?

2. What is one of the three fundamental lessons found in Part 1 of this book?

3. Which Part of this book will focus on personal motivation?

4. How many different ways will you learn to become a recognized unbelievable success?

Essay Question

Why do you feel it is important to know how a book is laid out before you read it?

Chapter 2 Notes Page

Use this page to capture notes in each Part and Chapter

Chapter 3
My Story

I have been relating my story for several years. That is what prompted me to finally write this book. Working with my coaching clients over the last several years, I have used my story over-and-over again to emphasize the importance of having a Personal Strategic Plan. I will discuss more about that in Part 2 of this book. But, by sharing my own story, I can better show you how actions taken today will pay dividends in the future. I will continue to reflect on my story to emphasize a point or activity throughout this book.

Now, I want to start off by telling you that this is not a story of overcoming insurmountable adversity. I was born healthy and into a stable middle-class home. Anything and everything bad that ever happened to me, happened because of me. This also is not a story of unfathomable success. I am not going to share stories of how I slayed dragons and demons, became a multimillionaire, own fabulous things, and describe something I am not.

My journey to unbelievable success did not start until I was 35 years old. This demonstrates two things: 1) you can start your journey at any age, and 2) the earlier you start your journey, the greater your success can become.

As I said, I was born healthy and grew up as an only child in a well-adjusted middle-class family. I lived the first 22 years of my life in the suburbs of Detroit, Michigan. My father was a police and firemen working for Beverly Hills Public Safety – not the Beverly Hills in California. He was not overly strict, even though he spent his entire life working in public safety just five miles outside of the Detroit city limits. My mother was a bookkeeper and accountant. She was always good at managing money – much better than me! She worked with a university for several years and eventually worked for herself.

My parents liked to travel and camp, and we always had a travel trailer or motor home. I saw most of the continental United States before I even graduated high school. We also had a summer place in the upper part of the lower peninsula of Michigan. It was a good spot to visit in the middle of the year. And, as you can see, my life was not isolated to the Detroit area.

We lived in Berkley – the city in Michigan, not Berkeley, California – until my last year in elementary school. The summer before my last year, we moved to Beverly Hills. There was one problem. Math. When I lived in Berkley, I was in old math, but the elementary school in Beverly Hills had already transitioned to new math. The ramifications of this little challenge in my life did not become overly apparent, though, until I started junior high school.

When we started junior high, we were tested for our aptitude in core studies, like English, science, and … of course, math. These tests placed you into a "social standing" in school. It was not until years later that I discovered the true impact of this placement strategy. I was placed in "slow math." Now, if I had never been placed in this math program for special students, I might never have realized the effect it had on me throughout junior and senior high school. So, this was a good thing – it just did not feel like it at that time.

That first year of math was great! Mainly, because I had a teacher who really cared about my scholastic development. Also, the class size was much smaller so that the students could receive special attention. I excelled and was back in normal math class the next year. Obviously, this program had to retrain my brain in new math – something I missed in my last year of elementary.

Two other major things happened in junior high. The first thing was that I gave up my dream of being a big rig driver. The second was I met "The Skippers." More about those things below.

When you were young, what did you want to be? Astronaut, doctor, lawyer, President? Not me; I wanted to drive a big rig like Jerry Reed, who played Cledus Snow (Snowman), in the television show *Smokey and the Bandit*. I think my uncle was also driving a truck at the time, but all that traveling across the country with my parents and the romanticization of truck drivers during that era really had me mesmerized.

In junior high, I took a course in architectural drawing – I really liked that course. The course was clearly designed using William Heard Kilpatrick's, 1918, *The Project Method* (at the time, I did not know this). I learned about this method while reading *Prepared*, by Diane Tavenner many years later). Our class project was to research the career we wanted in life – specifically the salary – and design a house based on a budget derived from that career's salary. Using what we learned, we designed our future homes, created elevation drawings, and built a model of our houses. All was cool, until I compared my two-bedroom cabin in the woods to some of the fabulous homes my fellow students had designed – students who wanted to grow up to be astronauts, doctors, lawyers, or the President.

You can imagine that my life's direction changed at that point! The problem was that while I realized big rig driving might not be for me, my interest in driving a big rig was never replaced with another dream. This became my biggest lesson – a lesson that I did not learn until much later in life – but one I share with you now!

Lesson #1. If you are going to become unbelievably successful in life, you need to define where you are going!

The second major thing that happened to me in junior high was meeting "The Skippers." We were not called that in junior high, it was not until we were in senior high, at Groves

High School, that the name settled upon us. The Skippers were – are – a fairly close-knit group of guys that I am still friends with today. In all honesty, I went on to become probably the worst influence on this little group possible (Chapter 17)! However, even today, at 57 years old, I am still friends with the core group: Kevin (Bogo), Jeff M. (Mards), Jeff F. (Franz), Mark (Animal), and Greg (Coobird). This brings me to my next lesson.

Lesson #2. You have heard this before, I am sure. You are the product of those you allow closest to you. To all The Skippers, I am sorry, but I am probably better for knowing you, than you are for knowing me! I was the worst influence on the group when we were in high school.

If you are in high school and you are reading this book – now is the right time. If it is later in your life, please give a copy of the book to your son or daughter as they enter high school. If I had read more books like this, instead of just *Catcher in the Rye* and *Lord of the Flies*, things would have been so incredibly different in my life!

Obviously, you can see that I was totally set up for unbelievable success going into senior high school – Not! I was still behind everyone else in math, regardless of being back on track. I had lost my singular focus of what I wanted to be when I grew up (no more big rig driver for me). I was part of a group of friends that eventually would be called The Skippers, and I was the worst influence of that group!

I was doomed!

What does it mean when you are not one of the smarter kids in school, but you are also not one of the slower kids? You end up in, what I call, "the movable middle." You are in a population in which the general teacher is not going to take any specific interest in your scholastic development – you are essentially on your own! If you are smart, you move up to the smart classes. If you are slow, you move back to the slow classes. In both situations, small class sizes mean more focused attention by more talented teachers. The rest – the movable middle – must learn to fend for themselves.

I was essentially, "in population" – a proverbial prison of my own making. I treated senior high school like I was in a daily episode of *Hogan's Heroes* – a comedy television show with American, English, and French prisoners of war (POWs), being held in a German POW camp during World War II. The POWs were constantly escaping the camp through a series of tunnels and escape routes. My senior high experience was overshadowed by me constantly determining new ways to skip class and not get in trouble!

What I learned was that I could get away with just about anything. I also learned that I could skip class and still graduate. Granted, I did not have a great grade point average (GPA) when I graduated, but I really did not care. I was in school because you were supposed to be in school, and I did just enough to get by. See what happens when you do not have a direction in your life?

While I was in high school, personal computers started to appear. I owned the Texas Instrument TI-4A, one of the first personal computers released to consumers in 1981. I fell in love with computers. I took every computer class that was offered. I could not get enough. One subject still haunted me though – math! When it came to hypothetical statistics in Algebra, I just could not get it! I still struggle with some of these concepts today. This means that I never went on to courses like Calculus and Trigonometry. You will see why this is important in a moment. However, I knew everything there was to know about computers!

Or so I thought…

Not having a stellar GPA and still lacking direction, I ended up going to Northern Michigan University in Marquette, Michigan. For those who do not know, Marquette is one of the most northern cities in the state, situated on Lake Superior across from Ontario, Canada. My degree program was computer science, of course. After all, I knew everything there was to know about computers. Why Marquette? They were one of the few schools that would accept me.

Why did I go to college? My parents thought going to college was important and they were paying. Even though they never got a degree themselves, they still believed, like many, that you were supposed to get a degree after high school and then get a job!

Nothing was going to go wrong here!

So, I showed up in northern Michigan. The first thing I learned was that, while I may have taken every available computer class in high school, I did not know squat! I was surrounded by a freshman class that was programming in Assembly Language. What was more, they were in Calculus and Trigonometry classes and – you guessed it – I was back in remedial Algebra I.

Lesson #3. There are always going to be people who are better at something than you. The moment you think you are better than everyone else is the moment the universe lets you know that you are wrong!

Funny thing about college. As long as you were paying, they cared less if you attended class. I did not need to be inventive to skip class this time, I just did not go! Results; however, were not the same as they were in high school. My first semester was a complete and utter failure – I received Fs or incomplete grades in every class!

So, I went home on winter break, with my tail between my legs, to quit college and go to work. My parents, still footing the bill, convinced me to give it another try. So, I went back after the break and proceeded to repeat my failure all over again. No joke! The road to success had completely eluded me. I returned home to live in my parents' basement and flitted from job-to-job until I was 22 years old.

Lesson #4. Never rely on anyone else to motivate you! All my failures were my fault – no one caused me to fail. I chose my path and circumstances. Take control of your success today and never give up that control!

As I said, for several years after my college failure, I jumped from job-to-job. I always excelled at whatever I did, and I would quickly be promoted. Then, I would run into someone with seniority who would stop my promotion in my tracks. It did not matter what job I had, without a degree I simply struggled to advance far in any company. I also still did not have any direction for my life.

Finally, late in 1987 – four years after graduating high school – I started to explore entering the military. Since I loved photography, I initially wanted to go into Combat Camera in the Air Force. However, the wait to get in under that career field was up to two years. Instead, I decided to go in right away as a Security Policeman. So, I officially enlisted in the Air Force on January 4, 1988.

My start in the Air Force was a little rocky. You can imagine what it might be like to be completely undisciplined and going into the military. It really took me about three years to fully adapt to the military way of life.

Adapt I did! I was excelling again. I won two major awards at my first base, and new opportunities just kept opening up for me. My understanding of computers made a world of difference as well. I also developed a new outlook on college and education in general – I learned to love school (I'm not kidding). All in all, my first 13 years of my military life were pretty successful.

But I was not unbelievably successful!

Why was I not unbelievably successful? Mainly, because I still was without direction! I had risen to the top jobs for my rank in every assignment. I was involved with nonprofits always in leadership roles. I was constantly winning awards for this and that. I was selected for a prestigious special duty assignment as a Security Police Officer guarding the Commander of the United States Air Forces in Europe (USAFE). I was selected as the Top Noncommissioned Officer for USAFE and was among 40 finalists that competed for Twelve Outstanding Airmen of the Year! But I did all this without direction.

In the late 80s to early 90s, I started to realize my true passion. The Air Force had embarked on its Total Quality Management movement. Being at a closure base when this first started, I was able to take a lot of different "Quality Air Force" training classes. I continued to immerse myself in understanding the quality movement until I finally retrained into the Manpower and Quality career field in 1998 – ten years after enlisting in the Air Force.

It was about two years later when it happened. I had joined Toastmasters at Ramstein Air Base in Germany. And, by this point in my life, I did not just join a nonprofit organization, I usually got very involved in the leadership of it. That is when it happened, what I often refer to as my "light bulb" moment.

There was a retired senior noncommissioned officer who lived in Germany and was an active member of the local Toastmasters club. He had been involved with Toastmasters for a long time, and he had achieved the highest level in the organization – Distinguished Toastmaster. We were in a planning meeting, and he told us he and his wife would be on a cruise the next week, so they would miss the next meeting. I made an offhand comment about my interest in cruising. He told me that the cruise line they went on gave him free cruises, and all he had to do was give a couple of presentations during the cruise.

The idea intrigued me – someone paid him to speak on a cruise! This is when my Personal Strategic Plan started to formulate (see Part 2 for more details on my Personal Strategic Plan). The question I started to ask myself was, "How could I get someone to pay me to do the things I loved: travel, sightsee, take pictures, and play golf?

Chapter 3 Questions

1. Where was the author born and raised?

2. What did the author consider the "movable middle?"

3. What was the author's first lesson?

4. When did the author have his "light bulb" moment?

Essay Question

Of the author's four lessons, which one do you feel is the most powerful for you and why?

Chapter 3 Notes Page

Use this page to capture notes in each Part and Chapter

Chapter 4
Success Defined

Dr. Benjamin Hardy, in a 2016 Inc. article, shared these key words, "Success is continuously improving who you are, how you live, how you serve, and how you relate."

Success is defined as the accomplishment of an aim or purpose. Being unbelievably successful is about consistently achieving everything you have set out in life to achieve – a life lived with true purpose.

Sydney J. Harris once said, "The greatest enemy of progress is not stagnation, but false progress."

Just "being busy" is not moving forward – it is just moving. Action without a plan is no action at all – it is just noise. A plan without a direction is fruitless. If you happen to go in the right direction without a plan, it is just luck!

Your life might seem like it is going in the right direction … but is it?

For 35 years of my life, I was moving, and I felt like that direction was forward. I thought I was successful. But I did not have a direction – I was only moving on autopilot, reacting to every change and opportunity without purpose. I did not realize it at the time, but I wasted a great deal of my life just being busy!

What was it that Lewis Carroll's Cheshire Cat said? "If you don't know where you are going, any road will take you there."

Do you know where you are going – where your North Star lies?

In the late 90's (98/99), I was researching process improvement tools. I was new to my career field (Manpower & Quality) in the military, and I wanted to understand the tools I had read about. One was called a Venn Diagram, conceived by John Venn in 1880. I stumbled across a Venn diagram with four overlapping circles. What I did not realize is that Venn Diagrams can have many applications. Your life is a Venn diagram. In the center of those four circles lies your purpose. Many years later I discovered that this Venn diagram was now being referred to as an ikigai, which is a Japanese concept known as "a reason for being." The word ikigai refers to having a direction or purpose in life. In Simon Sinek's work, this would be known as your "Why." The image below represents the Japanese concept known as ikigai.

According to Akihiro Hasegawa, an Associate Professor at Toyo Eiwa University, the origin of the word, "ikigai" goes back to the Heian period (794 to 1185). "Iki" roughly meaning Life; and "Gai" roughly meaning value.

There are other similar concepts to the Venn Diagram and Ikigai. The Purpose Diagram first appeared in the 2012 book, *What Would You Do If You Weren't Afraid?* by Borja Vilaseca. Andrés Zuzunaga officially took credit for the Venn diagram. But, like I said, I discovered the simple diagram in 98/99. The "Ikigai Venn Diagram" was born when entrepreneur Marc Winn thought it would be a good idea to merge the Purpose Venn diagram with the word, Ikigai, and share it in a blog post.

For the purposes of this book, I will continue to use the term ikigai to refer to the life purpose in the center of the diagram.

This simple depiction became instrumental in the creation of my Personal Strategic Plan. As you might remember from the previous chapter, my ultimate goal in 2000 was to find a way for someone to pay me to speak so that I could travel, sightsee, take pictures, and play golf on someone else's dime. This Venn diagram helped me think through the actions and behaviors that might make that a reality.

How to find your ikigai – your purpose.

Although, this ikigai diagram appears deceptively simple, it is not. Things are never really that easy. Thus, I will provide you with a series of simple-to-follow steps.

1. It is always easiest to start with something we personally know. So, let us start by making a list of everything we are capable of doing today. This could take some

time, as we want it to be exhaustive. Also, add things to the list that you do not do today, but you might like to do. Put each of these items in a list with five extra columns to the right. Using a spreadsheet works great, but you can do this on paper as well.

Listing everything you do or are interested in doing might take a while – do not rush this process. This is very important! Do not be afraid to talk to family, friends, and coworkers to get ideas from them. There are a couple of websites that also can help you create your list:

- www.mymajors.com
- www.careerplanner.com

If you started later in life, perhaps you are already in a career field, but do not be afraid to explore other possibilities. Those who are looking to "pivot" or "reinvent" themselves during a crisis will find this exercise particularly helpful!

What I Do and Would Like To Do

Process Improvement
Change Management
Strategic Planning
Coaching
Consulting
Speaking
Writing
Recruiting
Mentoring
Teaching

2. Once you have your list complete, it is time to score each item on your list. On the top of each column, write down (or enter) the following statements:

- I do this today
- I am considered good at this
- I enjoy doing this
- I believe people would pay me to do this
- I believe this solves a need in the world

You may be tempted to simply answer each statement with a basic yes or no, but you will get much more value out of giving each statement an actual score of 1 to 5. An answer of 1 means that you completely and wholeheartedly agree with the statement. An answer of 5 means that you absolutely disagree with the statement. An answer of 3 means that you could go either way depending on the situation. Of course, you should be able to figure out what a score of 2 and 4 means based on this guidance.

By the way, this is called a Likert scale. The Likert scale is a psychometric scoring methodology, typically used in scoring survey responses. Likert Scales have the advantage that they do not expect a simple yes or no answer, but rather allow for degrees of opinion, and even no opinion at all. The number of responses normally varies from 5 to 7. Psychologist Rensis Likert created the system of scoring in 1932.

For each of your items on your list, score them against each statement in its respective column.

What I Do and Would Like To Do	I Do This Today	I Am Considered Good At This	I Enjoy Doing This	I Believe People Would Pay Me To Do This	I Believe This Solves A Need In The World
Process Improvement	Absolutely Agree				
Change Management	Absolutely Agree				
Strategic Planning	Agree / Somewhat Agree / Somewhat Disagree / Disagree / Absolutely Disagree				
Coaching					
Consulting					
Speaking					
Writing					
Recruiting					
Mentoring					
Teaching					

3. Once you have each item on your list completely scored, total up the five scores for each item. You will end up with scores between 5 and 25. This is a good range of scores that will help you analyze in Step 4.

What I Do and Would Like To Do	Final Score	Do	Good	Enjoy	Pay	Need
Process Improvement	10	1	4	2	2	1
Change Management	14	3	4	2	3	2
Strategic Planning	7	2	2	1	1	1
Coaching	13	3	4	3	2	1
Consulting	12	3	4	2	1	2
Speaking	16	3	3	4	3	3
Writing	14	4	3	3	2	2
Recruiting	13	2	2	5	2	2
Mentoring	13	2	2	2	5	2
Teaching	12	3	3	2	2	2

4. Now comes the time to analyze your scores. You might think that the lowest scores are the best, but that is not always true. This is because you listed things you do not do today, and why you use scores versus a simple yes or no answer. Obviously, items with the lowest scores should be the primary focus of your attention. But you might have listed something you did not do today (5 points), and since you do not do it, you are not good at it and you do not love doing it (5 points for each).

However, this item might have scored very low on the last two statements: people will pay for it, and it solves a need. Your total score could be high (e.g., 17 points out of 25) and you might not actually consider this.

What I Do and Would Like To Do	Final Score	Do	Good	Enjoy	Pay	Need
Process Improvement	10	1	4	2	2	1
Change Management	14	3	4	2	3	2
Strategic Planning	7	2	2	1	1	1
Coaching	13	3	4	3	2	1
Consulting	12	3	4	2	1	2
Speaking	16	3	3	4	3	3
Writing	14	4	3	3	2	2
Recruiting	13	2	2	5	2	2
Mentoring	13	2	2	2	5	2
Teaching	12	3	3	2	2	2

Now, you should look at your scoring and your list. This is the time to start making some decisions. If nothing else, this will help you create a short list of potential items to take into Part 2 of this book.

When I stumbled upon this original Venn diagram, I kind of already knew that I wanted to improve organizations. Besides, I was already doing that in the Air Force, and I really liked everything I was doing with the Quality Air Force movement. I knew enough by this time to know that this field was lucrative enough, and every business in the world needed it – some much more than others. For me, I had validated my purpose – my ikigai.

Internal and External Success

Chris Croft, educator, writer, and keynote speaker looks at success as either external or internal. He explains how success and happiness go hand-in-hand. Externally successful people might have fame, money, and power, but they might still not be happy. If you appear to be successful, but you are not happy, then how successful are you? Any amount of fame, money, or power is pointless if it does not make you happy. There are many examples in the world of people who thought that these things would make them happy, and, in the end, they did not.

Internal success is much more likely to make you happy. Because this type of success is much more likely to be closer to what you really value. The types of internal success are things like personal and professional achievement, successful use of skills, and accomplishing worthwhile tasks. This is the kind of stuff that I will talk about in the next chapter on self-actualization. Of course, these things may also lead to fame, money, and power, but you will be happy because you enjoy the successes.

Success Strategies

Also, Chris Croft highlights in his training six key life strategies to success. Two of them require being self-employed. The other four apply equally to people in organizations so I hope you find it relevant to your current situation.

1. His first life strategy is to build your own company and then sell it.

2. His second life strategy is to create a "lifestyle business." This is a business where you earn a decent living doing whatever it is you enjoy doing. How this life strategy is different from the first life strategy is that you cannot sell it because the business depends on you and your ability.

3. Chris' third life strategy is to have a plan for retiring early. This life strategy probably requires you to pay a pretty big price during your working years in order to be able to retire early. The question is, is this price worth paying.

4. The fourth life strategy is to have a very easy job that allows you to pay your bills and have maximum fun in your life outside of work. I often see people in the horse business who are attracted to this type of strategy. For the most part, horse businesses do not provide a lot of money because horses can be very expensive. However, many people simply enjoy being around horses and working outside.

5. His fifth life strategy is working in a job that you really love, enjoy, and believe in. Even if you do not make a lot of money from it – or any money from it. There are many people who dedicate their lives to nonprofit activities and might not make any significant money.

6. The last life strategy that Chris outlines is to have a job and work hard, doing whatever it takes to climb the corporate ladder. This strategy requires you to work long hours, make life sacrifices, and generally do whatever is necessary to become a senior employee and retire with a big pension.

Success and Golf

Focusing on the worst first feels kind of negative. When I think about envisioning something I think of golf. And I love to play golf!

When you look at this golf hole above, what do you see first? That deep rough in front of you? The forest encroaching on each side? Or the sand trap almost hidden down range?

Or do you focus on that big, open, and beautiful green, where your ball will land solidly and slowly roll down to the right toward the pin with the white flag?

Let me tell you this ... golfers that focus on the hazards always end up in the hazards. Food for thought.

You will have to find the strategy that fits best for your vision of success. As I said in the beginning of this chapter, becoming unbelievably successful is about achieving everything you have set out in life to achieve. Thus, you must determine your own direction; never let anyone dictate what your success looks like.

Chapter 4 Questions

1. What is an ikigai?

2. What is the potential scoring spread of the five columns?

3. How many steps are listed in the book to build your ikigai?

4. When you are doing something you are good at and that you love, what is that according to the ikigai Venn diagram?

Essay Question

Using the guidance and steps outlined in this chapter, what is your top ikigai?

Chapter 4 Notes Page

Use this page to capture notes in each Part and Chapter

Chapter 5
Self-Actualization

Abraham Maslow was an American psychologist. He was born in 1908 to first-generation Jewish immigrants, and grew up in Brooklyn, New York. Maslow was one of Sigmund Freud's early colleagues. In 1943, Maslow published a paper in the *Psychology Review* called, *A Theory of Human Motivation*. In this paper, he explored his concept of a "Hierarchy of Needs." Later, in 1954, the concept was expanded upon in his book, *Motivation and Personality*.

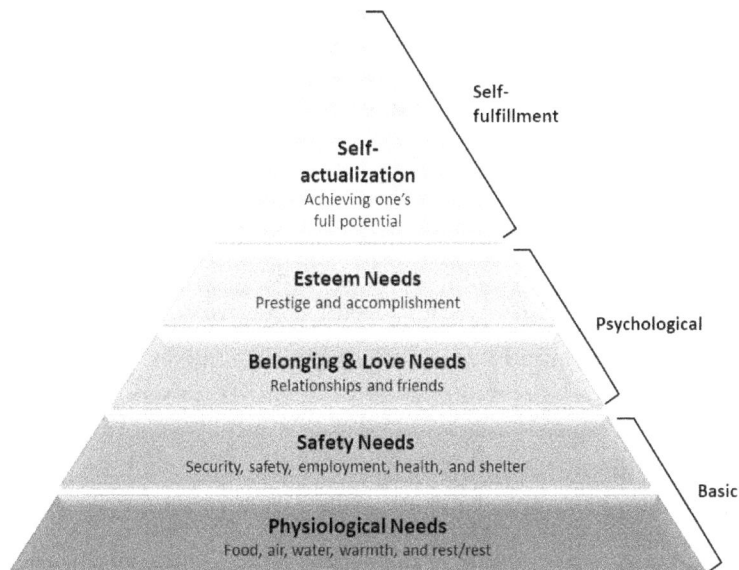

Maslow's Hierarchy of Needs was a study of intrinsic motivation. His pyramid-shaped model was used to depict how humans behave based on the intrinsic factors of physiological needs, safety needs, belonging and love needs, esteem needs, and self-actualization. Maslow proposed that a person could not move up the pyramid from one level to the next until the previous level had been satisfied.

Self-actualization is at the highest point of the pyramid of needs. Self-actualization means that someone has achieved their fullest personal potential. If someone is still struggling with fulfilling the needs below self-actualization, then they cannot easily reach this pinnacle of performance.

The two lowest levels of the pyramid are considered the basic needs. The physiological needs include things like food, water, breathing, and sleep. Without these, the body simply cannot function, thus the person cannot perform. Safety needs include things like shelter, physical safety, and security. Imagine being homeless and hungry with very little money – being able to do much more than survive would be impossible.

The second set of needs, as you move up the pyramid, are the psychological needs. The psychological needs, according to German researcher, Clouse Grau, fall into one of four categories: attachment, control, pleasure, and self-enhancement.

The concept of attachment aligns with Maslow's love and belonging needs tier. This is our human reliance on others. It is a basic and powerful psychological need. Whenever you start a new job, have you noticed how ineffective you are in that job, until you feel like you fit in? Bruce Tuckman outlined this behavior in his famous group development model. When new teams form (or when a new team member joins an existing team), the team goes through the stages of forming, storming, norming, and performing. This behavior is based on Maslow's love and belonging tier, or the attachment need. Chapter 17 explores this concept in more detail.

It was this important realization that led to me publishing, *Overcoming Organizational Myopia: Breaking Through Siloed Organizations*. I realized that this importance of belonging is one of the reasons that "breaking or tearing down silos" in business does more harm than good.

The fourth tier of Maslow's pyramid is the most difficult for people to master. Specifically, to master so they can self-actualize. This tier is the one containing the esteem needs. This level of the pyramid is so challenging, that most parts three through eight of this book are designed to help you master these needs.

According to Grau, the intricate psychological needs of control, pleasure, and self-enhancement all reside in the realm of esteem. One of the most critical areas of control is rooted in the concepts of self-efficacy and locus of control (see Chapter 10). As I related in my story earlier in this part of the book, I said, "Anything and everything bad that has ever happened to me, happened because of me." If you go around blaming others and other things for your misfortunes, you will never become unbelievably successful in life. When you do this, two things happen: 1) you never take personal actions to fix the situation, and 2) you lack the belief that you are in ultimate control of becoming an unbelievable success!

Why is this important to becoming unbelievably successful?

Most people function for much of their life on a lower level – Maslow referred to this as the "psychopathology of normality." When you have met the four needs (physiological, safety, love and belonging, and esteem), you still might struggle to self-actualize in your life. Remember, self-actualization is the achieving of one's fullest potential. Many people never achieve this in their life. Some only achieve it in moments. If you are not clear on your direction in life, it is hard to consistently achieve self-actualization. However, those who are unbelievably successful in their lives live in a near-constant state of self-actualization.

Maslow was not the only person to use this term of self-actualization. Kurt Goldstein, a German psychiatrist, discussed the concept in a 1939 book called, *The Organism: A Holistic Approach to Biology Derived from Pathological Data in Man*. Exciting stuff, huh? Goldstein saw the concept as the realization of one's "essence" in real life. Carl Rogers, an American psychologist, also proposed a definition of self-actualization as an ongoing process of maintaining and enhancing one's self-concept.

Have you ever had an extreme feeling of success and accomplishment? Perhaps you were volunteering with a beneficial charity, and you just completed a tremendous effort. Maybe you just completed a really challenging project at work and received praise. It could be the end of a phenomenal speech where you received a standing ovation. That feeling – that experience – is what I recognize as self-actualization. It can include standing on a stage, receiving recognition for something you worked hard for, or building and creating something amazing with your own hands. We can self-actualize repeatedly if our lower needs are met. So, this means that unbelievably successful people focus first on meeting the lower needs and ensuring they stay met.

When I first started volunteering, my supervisor and mentor at the time, Master Sergeant Matt Pollock, was the one who got me involved. He took me, as a young Airman, to an Air Force Sergeants Association (AFSA) chapter meeting. It turns out that I was the only Airman who had attended one of their meetings in a long time. A new position had recently been created in AFSA called the Airman Activities Coordinator (AAC). No one really knew what this position was supposed to do, but I was quickly appointed into the role – after all, I was the only Airman who had come to a meeting. It was like my college experience all over again – I completely failed in the role! I did not do anything with the role I was given. What was weird is that everyone celebrated my effort (I did try) and wanted me to continue a second year.

I remained an incredibly active member of AFSA into my retirement from the Air Force, and I am still a lifetime member of this professional military association. I went on to lead large local chapters and AFSA's largest division. I even sat on the International Council as a trustee for one year. There were many times, working with this volunteer organization, where I felt like I had reached self-actualization. Even if it was only for a little while. However, I did not regularly start to experience this feeling until the early 2000s, after I had found my purpose and built my Personal Strategic Plan.

One of my goal areas in my Personal Strategic Plan (learn more in Part 2), was to increase my personal and professional networks. Working and growing with AFSA became an important part of my strategy towards achieving self-actualization more-and-more often.

If you wish to become unbelievably successful, your aim should be to achieve self-actualization in your life on a near-constant basis. This means that you must ensure your lower needs remain constantly met. Otherwise, you will be too focused in your life on meeting the lower-level needs to ever achieve your full potential. The first step to achieve self-actualization; however, is to define your purpose and develop a Personal Strategic Plan. If your needs are not being met when you build your plan, then that should be your first goal to rectify.

Understanding this concept of self-actualization and Maslow's Hierarchy of Needs is foundational to becoming unbelievably successful. I implore you to continue to deepen your knowledge and understanding of this subject. Much of Parts 3 through 8 are designed to help you with these mid-tier needs of this hierarchy.

The only thing you need to do now is to work towards consistently self-actualizing in your unbelievably successful life.

Chapter 5 Questions

1. Who created the Hierarchy of Needs?

2. What are the basic needs in the Hierarchy of Needs?

3. Becoming unbelievably successful in life means that you are self-actualizing how often?

4. When people function much of their life on a lower level of the Hierarchy of Needs, what is this referred to as?

Essay Question

Why do you feel that self-actualization is a good goal for becoming unbelievably successful?

Chapter 5 Notes Page

Use this page to capture notes in each Part and Chapter

Chapter 6
Universal Laws

In the world there exists what some might call universal truths. If you research the subject, you can find a whole host of laws that people consider to be universal laws. For instance, Murphy's Law – something will always go wrong – might be considered a universal law. In fact, there is a book on Amazon that lists 442 cosmic and universal laws. I believe I have even seen a list once of over 1,000 universal laws.

The most popular universal law, the Law of Attraction, was made famous by Napoleon Hill in *The Law of Success*, and then later by Rhonda Bernie in *The Secret*. But this is just one of the many universal laws. In this book, and for the purpose of becoming unbelievably successful, we will discuss 15 of these laws. They are as follows:

1. The Law of Divine Oneness.
2. The Law of Vibration.
3. The Law of Action.
4. The Law of Correspondence.
5. The Law of Cause and Effect.
6. The Law of Compensation.
7. The Law of Attraction.
8. The Law of Perpetual Transmutation of Energy.
9. The Law of Gestation or Divine Timing.
10. The Law of Relativity.
11. The Law of Reciprocity.
12. The Law of Polarity.
13. The Law of Rhythm.
14. The Law of Belief.
15. The Law of Gender.

Some believe that the universal laws govern all life on Earth, and that if you master these laws, you will master life itself. This is because everything that happens is interconnected to these laws.

1. **The Law of Divine Oneness.** This law states that everything is connected to everything else. Your actions, thoughts, and words influence yourself, others, and the world you live in. Specifically, the Law of Divine Oneness means that we are all connected to one source – one energy. This is the universal law that binds all other laws together. This is important because all the laws interact with one another and cannot exist without that oneness.

2. **The Law of Vibration.** This law states that everything is energy, and all energies vibrate at certain frequencies. It is believed that living a poor and unsuccessful life will cause your energy to vibrate slowly and lowly. In contrast someone who is becoming unbelievably successful is increasing their vibrations through positive thoughts, actions, and experiences. Have you ever met someone and "got a feeling" about them (good or bad)? According to this law, you are sensing their vibration. Bioscience believes that horses are very "tuned into" energy and vibration in the world. Working with our equitherapy program since 2017, has led me to agree. We can increase (or raise) our vibration by focusing on positive activities like expressing gratitude; living a life of joy, love, and passion; walking in nature; grounding; yoga and exercise; and eating healthy. Have you ever noticed when you water the garden, two things grow? The stuff that you planted and the weeds that you did not. Why is that? See, the water is the same – it is indifferent – wherever the water lands it has the same effect. In a similar way, our thoughts are a form of energy and where we direct our thoughts energy flows. You might have heard the saying from Tony Robbins, "Energy flows where thought goes." In a similar way, when we start thinking negative thoughts, we are sending our negative energy in that direction, and we are thickening that negative effect. The same goes for positive thoughts. To leverage the Law of Vibration towards becoming unbelievably successful, cultivate the habit and understanding that your thoughts are energy. Just like you would not waste energy in your house, stop wasting it by directing it at negative thoughts. By being mindful, you can recognize each time that you are directing negative energy into your life, and you can refocus that energy towards positive thought. Those positive thoughts can become cumulative, and you will witness more positive results in your daily life. Another interesting note, when it comes to energy, is how you derive your energy. If you are extroverted, then you draw your energy from others around you. Presenting in front of an audience, going to a networking event, and having fun at a party are all energy boosters for the extrovert. If you are an introvert, then you derive your energy from within. Thus, introverts would feel very drained after a presentation, a networking event, or a party. Instead, introverts fill their energy bank by spending time alone, reading a good book, exercising, meditating, and the like. Understanding where you draw your energy from helps you better harness the Law of Vibration.

3. **The Law of Action.** This law states that you must take action for action to occur. Simply dreaming about becoming unbelievably successful will not make it happen. To achieve what you want out of life, you must act. In the immortal words of Yoda, from *Star Wars*, "Do or do not. There is no try." Regarding the 15 laws, this one is of particular importance. For instance, if you do not read this book, you will not know how to become unbelievably successful. If you do not implement the guidance in this book, you will not become unbelievably suc-

cessful. Basically, you can want something all day long, but if you do not take action on the thing you want, it will only happen by luck.

4. **The Law of Correspondence.** This law states that there is an equal relationship (mirror) between the positive and negative world. Basically, our current reality (what is happening in our outer world) reflects what is going on inside of us. If you harbor negative thoughts inside your mind, you will exhibit negative actions outside of you.

5. **The Law of Cause and Effect.** This law states that nothing happens without an equal reaction. For every cause, there is an effect. For every effect, there is a cause. Your thoughts, behaviors, and actions manifest life as you know it. Nothing happens by chance. Change your actions ... change your life. Everything within the universe is relative and nothing is separate (Law of Oneness). If you move your hand, you are moving the space that surrounds your hand and that space is connected to all space within the universe.

6. **The Law of Compensation.** This law is the Law of Cause and Effect applied to blessings and abundance, which provide the visible effects of your deeds. Often, this is called, "you reap what you sow." Your efforts come back to you in different forms matching the same energy with which we performed the actions. If you want to increase your compensation, you must increase the value of your contribution – essentially do more of what you have been asked. What you do in life will dictate how you will get compensated – what you give will determine what you get in return. This does not always mean money or financial gain; if you give more love to the world, you will get more love in return. If you help others, you may get happiness, financial rewards, or fulfilling relationships. The Law of Compensation can relate to money, relationships, happiness, thoughts, ideas, or any other important aspect in your life.

7. **The Law of Attraction.** This law states that your actions (positive and negative) will bring about equal experiences. The Law of Attraction is, perhaps, the most publicized universal law. There have been books, videos, workshops, etc. ad nauseam on the subject. The book, *The Secret*, was born out of this concept, as was *The Law of Success*. The important thing to remember is that all the laws are interconnected – refer to the Law of Divine Oneness – so just mastering this law pales to mastering all the laws. Many people refer to this as "manifestation." Remember that without the Law of Action, the Law of Attraction only occurs in happenstance. Thinking, dreaming, and pondering something does not make it happen – you must speak it, do it, and make it happen. Therefore, vision boards can be so effective. If you have a vision (an image) in front of you every day, then every day you will probably consider what action you might take that

day to get closer to that vision. Consider Gary Keller's book, *The ONE Thing*, where he advises doing one thing every day that makes everything easier. When you are fixated on a specific thing, your actions fixate on that one thing – Law of Vibration.

8. **The Law of Perpetual Transmutation of Energy.** This law states that everyone has the power to change the conditions within their life. By understanding the universal laws, a person can manipulate the very energy around themselves to become unbelievably successful. This law proposes that the energy around and within you is always moving and always changing. Thus, by accepting this law, you accept that change is a constant in everything. Accepting this, you make the decision to harness change and control that energy. In Part 2, you will build and implement your Personal Strategic Plan. This plan is a structured methodology of harnessing energy toward beneficial change (more on change in Chapter 27).

9. **The Law of Gestation.** This law states that everything must go through a period during which it is conceptualized and actualized. "There is no such thing as an overnight success." This quote has been used so much that it is impossible to trace its origins. In Malcolm Gladwell's book, *Outliers*, he introduced his "10,000 Hour Rule." Basically, becoming an expert at something takes 10,000 hours of dedicated effort. How long do you think it would take you to walk up 1.8 billion steps? That is 1,800,000,000 steps! It would probably depend on things like your walking pace, your fitness level, the number of people doing the trek, and how often you stop and rest. If you were able to walk straight from the base of the steps to the very top without stopping, it should take you 10,000 hours – One Billion Eight Hundred Million Steps!!! That is what it takes to be an expert. If you worked full time, 8 hours a day, at something -- nonstop -- you would become an expert at it in 1,250 days. That would be 3 years and 155 days. But no one works at the same thing non-stop, just like no one climbs 1.8 billion steps all at once. Becoming an expert at something is much like walking up those steps – it depends on your pace, your capability, who you encounter along the way, and how often you stop and rest. However, in your journey, you do not have to become an expert in just one thing. You can work on many related things at once.

Everything in the universe has a gestational period to manifest from thoughts and feelings into actions. This is core to your Personal Strategic Plan and becoming unbelievably successful. Today, we live in a "need and want it now" society. This is especially true of the United States, where at any time of the day or night you can get something that you want. On a lark, I posted on social media, "I just ordered a chicken and an egg from Amazon. We shall see." Even in a world that operates at the speed of Amazon, everything takes time to become. When you build your Personal Strategic Plan in Part 2, you will see how this law unfolds in your implementation strategy.

10. **The Law of Relativity.** This law states that everything in the physical world is made real by its relationship to something else. Light exists because you can compare it to dark. Hot exists because you can compare it to cold. Over the years, I have visited all but eight of the U.S. states – it is my goal to visit all of them. I have lived in four of them. Outside of the U.S., I have lived in 2 countries and visited a total of 25. This gives me a broader perspective on things, but I still have a long way to go before I would call myself "worldly." But this is what this law is all about. We are the sum of our experiences in life and how relevant they are to each other. If you have always lived in a hot climate and never been cold you could not imagine the winters in Fairbanks, Alaska, or Moscow, Russia. To you, 40°F might be your "cold." This is true for success as well. We measure success based on our relativity to success. If you earn $15 per hour ($31,200 annually), then having a lot of money might mean $100,000 to you. By expanding our understanding through experiences, we expand our relativity. When I first created my Personal Strategic Plan, my relevant experiences were limited, but I accepted that and made my initial goals to increase my understanding of the things I wanted to improve upon. More than likely, for your first Plan, your field of comparison will be narrow, but if you accept that and embrace what you do not know, you are on the path to becoming unbelievably successful.

Essentially, the Law of Relativity is all about looking at things from your unique perspective. This law is a primary reason why I wrote this book. Everyone wants to become successful, but in the game of success, the closer you get to the goal line, the further it is away. This is because of the Law of Relativity. When you are just starting out in the world, your world-perspective is very small. As you grow and develop (getting closer to your goals) your world-perspective grows too. You soon realize that those old goals become small and insignificant and need to grow as well. Thus, you never "achieve success;" you are always on the journey of becoming unbelievably successful. Therefore, having a documented Personal Strategic Plan (Part 2) and a rigorous process in place (Chapter 9) is critically important. These allow you to look back at your strategic achievements and really see what you have accomplished and how far you have come. Without a documented plan, you do not remember the path that got you to where you are today.

11. **The Law of Reciprocity.** This law states that when someone does something nice for you, you have a deep-rooted psychological urge to do something nice in

return. An emphasis of the law, when it comes to success, is to practice the belief of giving more than you get. In Part 7 of this book, I will talk about the importance of volunteering when it comes to success. That whole section is focused on giving. The true reciprocity of volunteering is typically self-actualization (see Chapter 5). As a business professional, my vision (different from my personal vision I discuss in Chapter 7) is to "leave nothing in my wake but success." What this means to me is that I always want to leave an interaction with someone feeling that they have really got something out of it. I believe the true success-based application of this law is to give without expectation of reciprocity. When you expect reciprocity, then you tend to stop giving when not reciprocated.

12. **The Law of Polarity.** This law states that everything is on a continuum and has an opposite. There cannot be positive energy without negative energy. There is not an up without a down, no hot without a cold, and no love without hate. Understanding that everything operates on a continuum helps you develop the goals of your Personal Strategic Plan. In my plan, I knew that I needed to achieve a PhD, but, aside from a high school diploma, I did not have any degrees at the time. I was at one end of the spectrum and a PhD was far to the other. In between were steps and stages to achieving my ultimate goal. Your goal areas will also exist on the same types of continuums. Since the Law of Polarity states that everything has an opposite, that means there is always a negative and a positive. We are much like batteries that will not work without a negative and a positive. Just because the negative or the dark side of things exists does not necessarily mean you want to hang out there. It is good to know and be aware that it exists, but not to linger. A common understanding of this law is depicted in the concept of Yin and Yang.

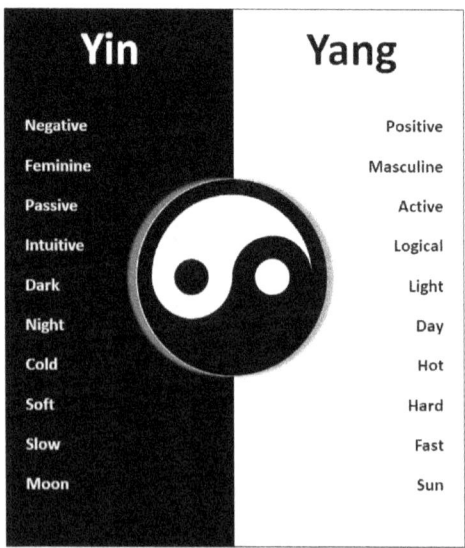

13. **The Law of Rhythm.** This law states that energy is like a pendulum, flowing left and right. In Chapter 5, we talked about self-actualization. One does not live in a constant state of self-actualization. They flow in and out of this state with the ebbs and flows of success along their journey.

14. **The Law of Belief.** This law states that whatever we fully believe in, eventually becomes our reality. I believe that anything I put my mind to, I can accomplish. This belief was instilled in me by my parents – specifically my mother. When you believe in something strongly enough, it will eventually happen. The number one thing for you to believe in is that you will become unbelievably successful. If you do not believe, you will fail. Belief is the first step in your reality.

15. **The Law of Gender.** This law states that everything has its masculine and feminine energies. Gender is manifested in everything. This law is like the Law of Polarity, as that law is about polar opposites. If we know that both masculine and feminine traits exist in everything, then we can look for their existence in all things. This book, itself, presents things from a Law of Gender perspective. Some of the book is very logical and well laid out (right brain), and some of this book is very focused on esoteric and creative thoughts (left brain). Your ability to look for and recognize gender in all things helps you on your Shuhari journey, discussed in Chapter 15.

The study of universal laws can go very deep. This chapter was designed to enlighten you about the existence of these laws and broaden your perspective with a brief explanation of 15 of them. Some of these laws can be directly manipulated or employed, while others simply exist. Becoming unbelievably successful is not possible without understanding that these laws exist. As you read through this book, look for the application and applicability of these laws.

Chapter 6 Questions

1. Which of the 15 universal laws is considered the most popular and well known?

2. Which law tells us that increasing the value of our contribution will increase our compensation?

3. Which law highlights that success will not occur overnight?

4. Which law causes things to adjust as we learn more about the world?

Essay Question

Of the 15 universal laws outlined in this chapter, which do you feel is most important to your success and why?

Chapter 6 Notes Page

Use this page to capture notes in each Part and Chapter

Part 1 Questions

1. What is one of the books that the author recommended everyone read to become more successful?

2. How old was the author when he developed his Personal Strategic Plan?

3. What is the most important Part of this book?

4. Why is the Law of Divine Oneness so important to all the universal laws?

Essay Question

Why do you feel that a foundation of knowledge is important to the overall learning process?

Part 1 Notes Page

Use this page to capture notes in each Part and Chapter

Part 2
Personal Strategic Plan to Becoming Unbelievably Successful

"He who fails to plan is planning to fail."
~ Sir Winston Churchill

Chapter 7
Creating the Plan

If it has not become abundantly clear to you that, to become unbelievably successful, you must have a plan, then let me hammer this point in a little harder.

Benjamin Franklin might be considered an unbelievably successful person, but his successes in life did not come without challenges, mistakes, and a few failures. He stood up a failed newspaper and created an alphabet that was never adopted. He knew about failure – but he also knew about planning. And, he was famously known to say, "Failing to plan, is planning to fail." Later, Winston Churchill repeated these famous words during World War II.

I have studied business failures for many years. I specifically look for the root causes of these failures. This led me to writing, *Overcoming Organizational Myopia: Breaking Through Siloed Organizations* and *Business 2020: The Business World After COVID-19*.

However, the number one root cause of business failure is lack of planning, lack of an effective plan, or a lack of following an effective plan. Nine times out of 10, the plan does not even exist! Going through life without a plan is akin to driving your car across the country with a blindfold on – just plain stupid!

But I was stupid for 35 years of my life, so I get it. Today, that changes for you!

How do you create a Personal Strategic Plan? How do you live the rest of your life with purpose and direction?

Building a Personal Strategic Plan starts by simply thinking about who you want to be when you grow up. You might feel this is much like answering the question, "What is the meaning of life," but it is not that hard.

Let us go back to the four-step activity in Chapter 4. You remember, the one where you were trying to determine your ikigai. From that activity you should have at least a short list of potential expectations for your life. With this list in hand, answer some additional questions to narrow your ikigai down to one or two ideas – maybe even combining some of the ideas into one.

What is it from this list that you would most like to do? Of the items on this list, which ones excite you the most – give you the most energy? This is where you self-actualize – reach the top of Maslow's pyramid. If you love doing something; you are good at it; you get great energy from it; and people need it and will pay for it; then let us figure out how you can do that for the rest of your life!

With that in mind, let us take some next steps.

Step 1. Determine what you really want to do in your life – the thing you really enjoy. For me, I wanted to travel, sightsee, take pictures, and play golf. You might want to be able to spend time with your kids and grandkids. You might want to sail around the world. You might want to own a huge mansion and throw elaborate parties. You might even want to ride and train horses on your own 100-acre horse farm, just like my wife.

Be very clear about what you want out of your unbelievably successful life. Discuss it with your friends and family – remember the Law of Attraction.

Step 2. By this time, you should already have your ikigai defined from Chapter 4 and solidified from the questions above. But this is the next question to answer. Now that you know what you want to do in your life, how can you get someone to pay you to do that?

When I learned that a cruise line would pay someone to speak on a trip, it hit me. My goal was to get companies to pay me enough for a daylong visit of coaching, speaking, and training on solving business problems and improving their organization. They would pay me enough to travel first class, do all the sightseeing that I wanted to do, take a bunch of photographs, and golf in the local area all week long. I calculated the price tag of this one-day visit at a minimum of $10,000.

Now, you might be thinking, "Who would pay someone $10,000 to visit their company for a day?" The better question to ask yourself should be, "What would that person have to look like, to get paid $10,000 for a one-day visit of business improvement?" Because, I am here to tell you, companies pay that all the time!

But that is a great question that leads us to Step #3.

Step 3. Determine what you must look like for someone to pay you what you need to live the life you want. Put yourself in the shoes of your future client, customer, or business.

These are the things I came up with nearly 20 years ago – go ahead and validate my list. To get a company to pay $10,000 for a one-day visit of coaching, speaking, and training on business improvement, I would have to look like the following.

They would pay for someone…

1. With a strong educational background – educated people are considered smart and should be listened to.
2. Who had a great deal of experience improving organizations.
3. Who was a proven expert at improving organizations.
4. Who is a published author – authors are clearly experts in their field.
5. Who is very personally and professionally connected – has a strong network.

6. Who was a great and accomplished presenter, trainer, coach, and speaker.

Would you agree with that assessment? However, we still must quantify these six areas a little bit better. We need to find exactly what people would pay for.

1. Higher Education. The highest level of professional education is a doctorate. Specifically, in this case, I determined they would pay for a PhD. I had no idea what that PhD would be in at the time I formulated my plan, but I was pretty sure that was the right level.

2. Business Experience. This person would need a broad range of business experience – the broader the better. I knew I was going to need to significantly expand my experience, because I was not even sure what it looked like at this point.

3. Proven Expert. I knew that I would need to be recognized as a proven expert. For this, I knew I could obtain certifications that demonstrated my abilities. At the time, the Air Force did not care much about certifications when it came to its military personnel. So, I did not know exactly what I wanted or needed, but I knew I needed to find out.

4. Published Author. I was going to have to figure out how to do something like this. I did not know what I would write about, but I knew I needed to publish a book on business improvement – that I was sure of.

5. Established Network. I was involved in several professional military organizations by this time. So, I knew the inherent value of having strong connections. However, I knew I needed to branch outside of the military if I was really going to build a strong network.

6. Accomplished Speaker. I was already in Toastmasters, so I knew I needed to climb to the highest level in the organization. But I also learned that there was a level higher than Distinguished Toastmaster. Once you achieve Distinguished Toastmaster you can work for Accredited Speaker status in Toastmasters. This puts you on a list where people can contact you to speak. I knew I was going to need a lot of education and experience to get where I needed to be in this area.

Now, you need to do the same thing. Do not worry about exactly what each thing looks like, or how you are going to get there. Just picture in your mind what you have to look like for someone to fully pay for the life you want to live in the future.

At this point, when working with clients, they often start to second-guess their future. They start to downplay what they can achieve. Stop! Just write down what someone would expect and pay for – we will worry about the details in a minute.

Okay, my list above was probably scary right? Getting a PhD in 2000 was a big deal – only 8.6 percent of people even had an advanced degree (masters or doctorate) back then. Today, the percentage has doubled, but 13.1 percent is still low, and for just a PhD, the percentage is even lower. But what if you do not even have an associate degree – it could feel insurmountable.

Step 4. With your realistic expectations in hand, now is the time to establish the gap. Gap analysis is something we do every day, but seldom do people recognize how they do it when it really matters. If you are driving to work, you determine the route to travel and the potential things that you must deal with along that route – this is gap analysis in a nutshell.

For this step, determine (pretty easy really) where you currently exist with each major item on your list. Then, make an initial list of the things that you would have to do to get where you need to be. Right now, you might not know the specifics, so just generalize where you need to be. As you implement and get closer to your goals, the exactness will come more into focus.

I will share my gaps from my original plan and share what steps I knew I needed to take at that time.

1. Higher Education. I had decided I needed a PhD. I did not have a clue what it would be in, or what school it would be from – I just knew I needed to have a PhD. However, I did not even have an associate degree yet. I had been working on one, but I did not have it yet. In order to complete a PhD, I needed to complete my associate degree, get a bachelor's degree, get a master's degree, and then get a PhD.

2. Business Experience. This is an area that I was not very clear on at the start. I knew what I needed, but I was not sure what that actually looked like. I just needed broad experience and knew the military alone was not going to cut it. So, I would need to expand my experience when I retired from the Air Force. I left it at that.

3. Proven Expert. Since I did not know much about certifications, my list was pretty much blank. Over time, with focused effort, I determined what I needed. Over the last several years, this has become a much more important consideration than it was in 2000.

4. Published Author. Well, this one was simple. I needed to publish a business book. So, I would need to figure out what to write about; I would need to find

out how to write and publish a book; and then I would be set. Easy, right? In fact, over 80 percent of the population wants to publish a book and less than 10 percent ever do so.

5. Established Network. I knew I was going to have to expand past the professional military associations I belonged to. But I did not know enough at the time to know what to look for. For now, I would grow these networks and look for more opportunities.

6. Accomplished Speaker. Well, I was in Toastmasters and on my way to my first level – Competent Toastmaster. I researched the requirements to get to Distinguished Toastmaster, and then to Accredited Speaker. This was not going to be easy either.

Take your list and define your gaps and major steps to get where you need to be. Do not get overwhelmed! You will not have all the answers, but as you can see, that is okay – go with what you know.

Step 5. We have come to the final step of your plan – timing. To complete each goal, each step will take a certain amount of time. By looking at each goal, and creating a timeline, you can determine about how long your plan will take. Find the one goal that will take the longest and use this to guide the rest of your plan.

I will use my education goal area as an example.

I was almost done with my associate degree, so I expected to be done within a year. I actually completed two associates that first year. Since I was working and distance education was not big in 2000, I planned on four years to finish my bachelor's degree. In fact, it took me seven years to get my Bachelor's Degree in Management. I had to determine what and where, in regard to my Masters, I was going to study. I figured that out in 2007, but I did not finish my master's degree until 2011. In 2007, I also had figured out what I wanted to get my PhD in – Industrial and Organizational Psychology. However, I had no idea where I would get it from until much later. In 2014, I finally started my PhD program, but opening our horse farm in 2016 derailed my timeline.

After I laid out all my expectations across my plan, I expected to finish my goals by 2022 – this would be 20 years after I built the final plan. Yes, it took me two years to develop my plan after I first determined what I wanted to do with my life.

Now you have your plan – hopefully much faster than it took me to create mine. Do not worry if it still has a lot of holes, you will refine it as you go.

So, how have I done with implementing my plan?

Regarding education, I completed about three years of my PhD program. I plan to finish it but opening our horse farm set me back.

From a business perspective, I retired from the Air Force after 21 years in 2008. I had some very good learning opportunities in the military that helped my goal areas. I opened my coaching and consulting practice when I retired, but it was more of a side hustle for several years. For three years after retirement, I worked strategy and organization with the prestigious management consulting firm, Booz | Allen | Hamilton. Then, I drove four strategic transformations, over seven years, with Fortune 100 United Services Automobile Association (USAA). I have been a full-time and Fractional Chief Operating Officer (COO) as well as an independent coach and consultant for 15 years. Founding seven businesses of my own, I still run five of them today.

When it comes to becoming a proven expert, I have numerous training programs under my belt and a string of designations. If I were to list everything today, my signature block would look like alphabet soup. It looks something like this:

BS, MS, LSSGB, LSSBB, LSSMBB, PROSCI, CMAP, ITIL, MSW, PMP, PgMP, SAFe SA, SAFe SP, and SAFe POPM. Soon, I will have my CoachU, Coaching certification.

Whew! That was a lot of letters. Let us suffice it to say, I have distinguished my capabilities with many certifications over the last 20 years. In addition to this, I have been an adjunct professor for two colleges, and I am an invite-only member of Forbes Coaches Council with over 100 publications.

My plan was to publish one business book. In 2012, I published, *One Dead Marine*, a post-apocalyptic sci-fi fantasy. This was my pilot effort in self-publishing. It is available in paperback and on Kindle. It took me ten years to publish my first business book. *Overcoming Organizational Myopia: Breaking Through Siloed Organizations*, was finally published in paperback in May 2019. I have yet to release it on Kindle or Audible, but I plan to. Following that book, I have at least 16 more titles in some level of completion other than the book COVID drove me to write and publish, *Business 2020: The Business World After COVID-19*. You can request your free copy of this book from https://bit.ly/GetBusy2020. I wanted as many people as possible to have access to it. That book took me four months to write, edit, format, and publish. Also, I put all my other books (16) aside when I decided to write, *Becoming Unbelievably Successful*, on July 11, 2020. As mentioned above, I have been published with Forbes over 100 times; I have written for the Global Business Playbook, and now Authoritti 5.0, releasing an article every month; and I have also been a prolific blogger and active poster on social media.

My involvement on social media has been a large part of my strategy. Building a strong network is a slow and arduous process – especially when you do it right. I also have cultivated memberships with several active professional organizations. This includes standing up an organization in San Antonio, Texas, which now the University of Texas, San Antonio, runs. Before COVID, I was very involved with many face-to-face business networking groups. This included establishing my own social business networking group called, "Whiskey Bid'ness, And Cigars."

Lastly, I still have some work to do when it comes to Toastmasters designations and my ultimate goal of Accredited Speaker status. Although, I do have an extensive background in speaking, teaching, mentoring, and coaching. Over the years, I have created several new Toastmasters clubs and helped turn failing clubs around – in total, I have belonged to 13 different Toastmasters clubs. Today, I am a board and faculty member of the EBR. Aside from my adjunct faculty positions, I created and taught many different training programs over the last 20 years.

Now you have your Personal Strategic Plan completed. This one thing is the most important step to becoming unbelievably successful!

The next step is to implement this plan. A plan that sits on the shelf (or on a hard drive) and collects dust, does you no good.

So, let us implement the plan.

Chapter 7 Questions

1. What good does a Personal Strategic Plan do for you if it sits on your shelf?

2. How many steps does it take to create a Personal Strategic Plan?

3. Do you have to know exactly what steps will be required to reach your vision when you start?

4. What item will you start your planning process with from Part 1?

Essay Question

Describe your vision and goal areas you created for your Personal Strategic Plan.

Chapter 7 Notes Page

Use this page to capture notes in each Part and Chapter

Chapter 8
Implementing the Plan

Now that you have a Personal Strategic Plan, what do you do with it?

Implement it of course!

This is a lot easier said than done. People and businesses struggle every day to implement the strategies they create. The good thing is that the plan you have created, following the guidance in Chapter 7, should be solid enough to implement.

Staying true to form for this book, I will provide you with step-by-step guidance on successfully implementing your Personal Strategic Plan and becoming unbelievably successful.

The first thing you need to do, now that you have your plan, is to document it so it is in a structured manner. This does not have to be detailed like a business strategic plan – it can be a simple one-page document. In fact, I recommend you keep it to only one page, so that you can use the back of it to document your annual action plans.

At the top of the page, write out your purpose – the ikigai you created in Chapter 4, and built your entire plan around in Chapter 7. This is what you do – your mission.

Below that, write down why you are doing this. This is the thing you wanted people to pay you for that we discussed in the previous chapter. This is your vision.

Here are mine below.

Mission: Help companies improve their operations by coaching, speaking, and training during a one-day visit for a minimum of $10,000.

Vision: Travel first class, sightsee, take pictures, and play golf around the world, while someone else pays for it.

Your mission and vision will be entirely different from mine, based on what interests you and what you discovered in your ikigai. However, writing it down helps you focus on it. It makes it more real.

Below your mission and vision statements, list out each of the major goal areas that you created in the last chapter. It might take some work to organize your thoughts.

As you remember, I had six goal areas that I built for my plan.

- Higher Education

- Business Experience
- Proven Expert
- Published Author
- Established Network
- Accomplished Speaker

You do not want too few goal areas, otherwise you will probably pack too much stuff in each goal area, and it will get confusing and become unclear. Also, you do not want too many goal areas, because they will be too hard to track. I recommend four to six goal areas, if possible.

I recommend you make your goal areas broad. If you noticed from the previous chapter, being an accomplished speaker – Toastmasters Accredited Speaker – was only part of that goal area of mine. I also included teaching, mentoring, and coaching in that goal area. These things relate closely to public speaking. Being a published author meant more than just publishing a book. It included writing content on social media, blogging, and writing professional articles for magazines.

Now you have your one-page Personal Strategic Plan documented. Yours might look like this.

John Knotts – Success Incubator

Mission
Help companies improve their operations by coaching, speaking, and training during a one day visit for $10,000.

Vision
Travel first class, sightsee, take pictures, and play golf around the world, while someone else pays for it.

Goals

Education: Complete professional degrees through a PhD in Industrial and Organizational Psychology.

Business: Obtain broad industry-wide experience helping for-profit, non-profit, and service-based companies from startups to Fortune 100 size improve their business operations using holistic systems-thinking approaches to operational excellence.

Expert: Complete highest levels of training and certification in professional Operational Excellence disciplines.

Author: Become a successfully published author with at least five solid business books published.

Network: Recognized by a large network across professional and social channels as an industry expert in the areas of Operational Excellence.

Speaker: Completed all levels of Toastmasters certification through DTM, earned Accredited Speaker status, and garnered significant speaking experience.

The next step is to flip the page over and break it into equal sections to correspond with the number of goal areas you have. Only use the back of your plan, no more paper than that. Then, break each goal area box into four separate boxes – one for each quarter of the year.

The back page of your plan should look something like this.

Education		Business	
Q1	Q2	Q1	Q2
Q3	Q4	Q3	Q4
Expert		Author	
Q1	Q2	Q1	Q2
Q3	Q4	Q3	Q4
Network		Speaker	
Q1	Q2	Q1	Q2
Q3	Q4	Q3	Q4

This becomes your simple two-page (front and back) planning document. Save this document on your computer with today's year – every year you will make a new copy and keep the old one – this way you will have a record of your journey.

Now is the time to create and document actions for the rest of your calendar year.

1. Print out the two-page plan.

2. Place an "X" in every Quarter that has already occurred for the year – no sense in trying to go back in time, now is there?

3. In the Q4 block of each goal area, I want you to write down the key accomplishments that you want to complete that further that goal area for the year. For instance, in the Q4 block of my published author space, I might write down, "Publish two books." At this point, in planning, I do not need to know which

books I plan to publish – I just want to publish two books by the end of the year.

Make these big and broad accomplishments. Some people like to use the term "BHAGs," Big Hairy Audacious Goals. Try to keep your list of annual goals for each year relatively short, maybe two to five. If I had 3 BHAGs for all 6 of my goal areas, that would be 18 BHAGs for the year! I probably would not complete them all because I would be spread too thin. Also, by using one sheet, you do not have a lot of room to write down very much – this helps prevent you from getting crazy with your goals.

Now, backwards plan each goal area and write down the major accomplishments that you need to complete each quarter to achieve each BHAG for the year. You do not need to be specific and list out all the activities – just the major steps or actions.

Let us say that I am filling my plan out for the entire year. I listed, as I stated above, that I wanted to publish two books by the end of the year. Then, I might plan to publish the first book by the second quarter and the second one by the end of the year. By the end of the first quarter of the year, I will have the outline and initial draft done for the first book. By the end of the second quarter, I would complete editing, cover design, and publishing of the first book. By the end of the third quarter, I need to have the outline and initial draft of the second book done. And I would finish editing, cover, and publishing of the second book by the end of the year. This gets me to two books published for the year.

If you are just starting out maybe just one book for the year is too much of a stretch. Maybe, you just want to research your first book for the first year. Be realistic but think big. As you really start thinking about all the things it might take to achieve your BHAGs for the year you have left, you might have to rethink your BHAGs. It is okay to stretch yourself and aim high, but do not get crazy – you will only frustrate yourself.

Remember, just complete the plan for the rest of the calendar year. If you are building your first plan and it is already the fourth quarter of the year, the plan should be for the entire next calendar year.

Once you have your plan completed for the year, type it up on the computer and save it. Then create a copy and call it your "Working Copy." Throughout your implementation, things will change – none of us planned for COVID – and your plans will change with it. You might complete something sooner, while other BHAGs might be abandoned altogether. By having your original and working copy, you can see how good or bad your initial planning was, and you can adjust for the next year.

Looking at your next quarter, break the goals down into major activities for each of the three months in that quarter. Only focus on those three months. However, seeing as this is your first action planning activity, you can include any remaining months from the current quarter as well. Using my BHAG example of publishing two books in the year, this is what my first quarter plan might look like.

| January | February | March |
| Complete Ideation of First Book | Complete Outline of First Book | Finish Initial Draft of First Book |

Here is a template that I use for my quarterly planning. It is self-explanatory.

	January	February	March
EDUCATION			
BUSINESS			
EXPERT			
AUTHOR			
NETWORK			
SPEAKER			

Now is the time to turn your plan into action. I am going to give you a recommended approach to getting your plan accomplished, but you need to find the way that works best for you. Not everyone creates to-do lists the same or prioritizes things as I do. So, I suggest following my approach for a month or so, and then trying out some of your own changes. Essentially, what we are doing here is turning your strategy into daily action.

Every week, break a sheet of paper into four equal squares. It is best to do this on lined paper – I use a computer-generated weekly planning sheet as my template. See below.

Goal Area Actions	Must Do Actions
Try To Do Actions	Fun To Do Actions

In the top left box, list out the major things you plan to accomplish this week that move you closer to achieving your goals for this month. These are the most important tasks to complete this week. Many people like to use the four-quadrant prioritization approach created by Stephen Covey in, *7 Habits of Highly Effective People*. But that would make this box urgent and important (Quadrant I), which is bad in his book. However, strategically these are the most urgent and important tasks that you should accomplish. If you have ever read or heard about the concept of The ONE Thing in Gary Keller's book, *The ONE Thing*, you will understand. These are the few things that, if you complete this week, will move you closer to becoming unbelievably successful.

In the top right block, list out the things that you must do this week. These include mundane, but required things, like grocery shopping, getting a haircut, etc. You do not have to list daily things, like making meals, going to school, or going to work – these things will occur regardless. This block should only include those things that you must get done this week that are not standard day-to-day activities. They might also include a major work project, or some required schoolwork that you have. You get the idea. Essentially, everything on the top half of your page should be accomplished by the end of the week.

The bottom half of the page is what I call "below-the-line" activities. In business, you may have heard of the concept of below-the-line budgeting. These are budget items that you currently do not have the money to invest in, but if the money does become available, these items are listed in the order that you would invest in them. In the left box, list actions that you want to try to get done, but do not have to get them done this week. On the right side, list some fun things you would like to do this week.

I personally use this sheet throughout the week to guide my actions. I would suggest you fill this out on Sunday and put it in a notebook that you keep all your weekly planners in. As you complete items, cross them off the list. You are welcome to add items throughout the week – I even add items I have completed just to cross them off the list.

If something did not get done last week that was in one of the top two boxes, it should be carried over to the next week. Unless, of course, it was overcome by events (e.g., you missed the deadline, and it is too late). Evaluate the remaining items in the bottom two boxes. If something was a try to do item, but now is a must do item, move it up to the appropriate top box. If it is something that was overcome by events, or you just decided not to do it, then remove it from the list. If you still want to get the thing done, then carry it over to the next week.

Most of all, do not get discouraged when starting out. This is a whole new strategic planning and implementation muscle that you are exercising – you are going to be a little sore when you start out. You must make this a habit.

Putting this into regular practice

Everything in this chapter has focused on building your first plan – from a long-term strategy, all the way down to weekly implementation. If you have learned anything about Agile, this approach mimics an Agile implementation process. You might even consider creating a daily Kanban board, with To-Do, Doing, and Done columns. However, this might be too much for some people.

Now is the time to create a routine around this approach. I am going to use a United States calendar suggestion, but you can adjust based on your own calendar, wherever you are in the world.

Between Thanksgiving and Christmas, draft up your annual plan for the next year. This should be a must-do action on one of your weekly planning sheets. Also, I suggest you plan out January, February, and March, at the same time. You might be tempted to do this the week between Christmas and New Year's Day, but things can get a little hectic during that time of the year, so I like to get it done before Christmas. This is a whole lot more powerful than coming up with some New Year's resolutions that you will quit a couple months into the year.

In the middle of the third month of the first, second, and third quarter, you should create your next quarter's plan. Again, make this a must-do action item on your weekly plan. Adjust your working annual plan as required at the same time.

As I already said, every Sunday create your weekly plan and use it every day.

This is continuous planning.

I keep all these documents in one planning binder for easy reference. I also have an electronic backup of the documents, should I lose the binder, or in case it gets damaged.

This will become your roadmap to becoming unbelievably successful.

Rebluing!

I was very active in AFSA, while in the Air Force. Every year, I would go to their annual conference and convention. It was a very high energy few days and everyone would come back pumped with ideas. There would typically follow a few months of a flurry of activities. We called this experience "Rebluing," as the formal uniform in the Air Force was blue. I have experienced this after attending other professional conferences, like the American Society for Quality (ASQ). However, it was interesting that this feeling of excitement only lasted for about three months.

You can still capitalize on this type of feeling. Want to get yourself in the right frame of mind for your quarterly and annual planning sessions? Create a day-long, planned event for yourself every quarter. In this event, line up positive and supportive articles and presentations – like videos of motivational speakers. Then, dedicate the entire day to positive motivation and structured lifelong learning. Basically, you set up your own personal rebluing event, focused on things related to your Personal Strategic Plan. Then, the next day, do your planning for the next quarter or year.

Becoming Unbelievably Successful and The Maze of Life

For 35 years, I followed what I call now, "Aimless Goals." Later in those first 35 years, I had become successful in the military. Opportunities presented themselves and I went after them. However, they were hollow efforts because I lacked structure. I was always searching for what was next.

See, we are all in this endless maze called "Life." Have you ever been in a maze? All we can see are the walls around us and the twists and turns ahead of and behind us. We often make choices in life based on gut, instinct, and luck. At the end of the day, they are all guesses.

Enter the Plan.

Imagine lifting yourself high (30,000 feet) out of the maze for a short period and giving yourself a glimpse of this endless maze. With that view, you establish a direction and a plan to get there.

Now, your choices are more purposeful and strategic. You start to recognize signposts in the maze that you never really paid attention to before – now they matter. With every twist and turn you feel more confident.

That is having a Personal Strategic Plan.

Now imagine regularly raising yourself up out of that maze to check your bearings and ensure you are heading in the right direction. Weekly, you only rise up about 50 feet. Monthly, you climb to about 500 feet to check. Quarterly, you climb to 5,000 feet to take a good look around. Once a year, you fly back to 30,000 feet to ensure everything is still as it was from that height.

This is your Personal Strategic Planning Process at work.

Chapter 8 Questions

1. How many pages do you need to use to document your Personal Strategic Plan?

2. What are BHAGs?

3. Which one of the four boxes on the weekly planning sheet is the most important?

4. What do you do with items on your weekly planning sheet that you do not complete that week?

Essay Question

What do your personal annual plan, next quarter plan, and next week plan sheets look like for your Personal Strategic Plan?

Chapter 8 Notes Page

Use this page to capture notes in each Part and Chapter

Chapter 9
Staying on Plan

Creating and implementing your Personal Strategic Plan is, by far, the most important part of this book. It is <u>an absolutely critical step</u> for you to becoming unbelievably successful.

However, sometimes you might find it challenging to stay on your plan. This can be especially true when you first start out. In the previous chapter, I shared several tools and template examples that might help you as you create and implement your plan.

What do you do when life throws you a curveball? How do you handle it? When you are following a plan, you can expect something to come along and attempt to mess with everything. How you handle it will impact how quickly you become an unbelievable success.

Mike Tyson once said, "Everybody's got a plan, until they get punched in the face." While I do not agree that everyone has a plan, I do agree with Mike's assessment of plan adversity. In the military – I was a warplanner for seven years – we lived by the mantra that "No plan survives first contact." The fact is your ability to adjust to unforeseen challenges will define your ability to become an unbelievable success.

Obviously, COVID has been one of the most massive curveballs that we have had to deal with in a very long time. But we have all had other curveballs to deal with and will experience more in the future. In fact, COVID is the very reason that I have written this book! If it had not been for COVID, I would have probably stayed on the book writing and publishing path that I created along with the publishing of *Overcoming Organizational Myopia* in 2019. Associated with that book, I had 16 related books planned, each that delved deeper into sections of that first book. I also would not have published *Business 2020* and given it away for free if it were not for COVID!

Five years ago, the lady that managed the horse stables, where my wife kept her horses, passed away from cancer. Her entire family owned the property, but her uncle had the controlling interest. He flew in from California for the funeral and proceeded to give all the horse owners a 30-day notice to remove their horses, so that he could sell the property to a cement plant. Surprisingly enough, there were not a lot of places to relocate 40 horses, even though we live in South-Central Texas.

Five months later, we ended up purchasing a rundown, 100-acre, horse property. Seven months after that, we opened Fine Print Farms – a premier equestrian destination in the Texas Hill Country.

At the time, I was three years into my PhD program. My wife and I both had full-time careers. We owned a beautiful home, situated in a golf course community about 30 minutes away. Initially, we identified someone to house on property and run the entire operation. Within a month, we realized this person was not the right fit. We were faced with a decision – stop the effort or move on to the property and run the operation ourselves.

We chose to do the latter.

We bought a fifth wheel recreational vehicle (RV) and put it on our property. We moved from our 5,000 sq. ft. home to a 360 sq. ft. RV. We figured we would sell the house within six months. It took us over two years to sell the house!

None of this was in my plan. But it was very important to my wife, and we adjusted. At the same time, we also created two equestrian-related nonprofits. Working full time, opening a horse farm, moving into a fifth wheel, and starting two nonprofits, destroyed my attempts to continue my PhD work. Working on a PhD is easily a 40-hour a week job! Also, a horse farm was not anywhere in my plans.

How do you handle curveball like this?

Many people feel that planning is worthless because of unforeseen events like this.

I disagree.

Yes, my PhD program has moved to the right. I am now researching the possibility of restarting and finishing this massive goal. However, opening the farm and starting two nonprofits, although not in my initial plan, fit very nicely in my business experience goal area. Not only do I have deep experience as a business coach and consultant, but now I am gaining exceptional experience as an active business owner – a true entrepreneur.

What I found was two things.

1. Just because something in your plan does not happen when you expect it to, it does not mean it will not happen. Plans can be adjusted – dates can be adjusted. If you get something done earlier than planned, you do not complain. So do not worry if something has to take a little longer.

2. When something unexpected happens, look at how it supports, or fits into your plan, versus being upset about it. Our horse farm and COVID were not on our radar, but I used my plan to align activities and make the best of it.

This is what unbelievably successful people do.

To stay on track and better respond to life's curveballs, you might want to get someone to become your accountability partner. My recommendation is that you find someone that is going to be 100 percent honest with you and not sugarcoat things – you do not need that. They should be talented enough to coach you on building and implementing your plan, so they best have read and understood this book. They also should be skilled enough to help you deal with challenges and adversity along your journey.

You should engage this person to help you build your annual and quarterly plans. Also, they should check up on you once a month, between quarters, to ensure you are on track and help when you are slipping. This level of engagement should not require much involvement over the year – three to four hours for the annual and quarterly planning sessions, and one to two hours a month, tops.

If you do not have someone in mind to help you as an accountability coach, contact me at John.Knotts@crossctr.com. I can offer you an annual planning and coaching package with monthly, quarterly, or annual payment options. I am here to help you become unbelievably successful.

Also, I welcome you to join my Success Incubator groups on Facebook and LinkedIn. Here, everyone shares and discusses the successes, challenges, and ideas they have around becoming unbelievably successful. Both groups are free for you to join.

Chapter 9 Questions

1. What is the role of an accountability partner in your Personal Strategic Plan implementation?

2. What two major setbacks (curveballs) did the author discuss in this chapter?

3. What are the two major ways you can deal with the unexpected during plan implementation?

4. What is the name of the social media group on Facebook and LinkedIn that is free for you to join?

Essay Question

What major setback have you experienced in your life and how did you deal with it?

Chapter 9 Notes Page

Use this page to capture notes in each Part and Chapter

Part 2 Questions

1. Who said, "Failing to plan is planning to fail?"

2. What is the first step in developing your Personal Strategic Plan?

3. How many goal areas does the author recommend you have in your Personal Strategic Plan?

4. Who can help you stay on track when implementing your Personal Strategic Plan?

Essay Question

Now that you have developed your Personal Strategic Plan, how confident does this make you feel about becoming unbelievably successful and why?

Part 2 Notes Page

Use this page to capture notes in each Part and Chapter

Part 3
Leading Yourself Towards Unbelievable Success

"Always be a first-rate version of yourself, instead of a second-rate version of someone else."
~ Judy Garland

Chapter 10
Self-Efficacy and Locus of Control

Perhaps one of the most important concepts to becoming unbelievably successful is self-efficacy and locus of control. Earlier, in Part 1 of this book, I touched on the subject when discussing esteem needs.

I will repeat this, "Anything and everything bad that has ever happened to me, happened because of me." However, I will also add, anything good that ever happened to me was also my fault as well.

These two statements above represent my self-efficacy and locus of control. Although these are two different psychological terms, which mean two different things, they are very important together. As we discussed, in Chapter 5, part of your esteem needs on Maslow's pyramid are based in the psychological need for control. We have a high sense of control when we have a large number of options available to us. The lower the number of options, the lesser sense of control we have. When we feel like we have less control in our lives this negatively impacts our esteem.

So, what does control, self-efficacy, and locus of control have to do with each other?

"If you think you are too small to make a difference, try sleeping with a mosquito." Dalai Lama.

Self-efficacy is inherently your belief in your own abilities and capabilities to perform a specific task or activity. Specifically, according to Albert Bandura, who originally proposed the concept, it reflects our confidence in our ability to exert control over our own motivation, behavior, and social environment. When you are faced with solving a problem, reaching a goal, completing a task, or basically achieving anything you set out to do, your self-efficacy takes control.

In Chapter 4, I asked you to determine your ikigai. In Part 2, I asked you to establish a plan to achieve your vision, using that ikigai. I am sure you probably had some self-doubt about your ability to implement your plan to become unbelievably successful. That is your self-efficacy at work.

The thing is, you do not just read this chapter and suddenly change your self-efficacy. It is not a switch that can be flipped or a lever that can be thrown. There are ways to increase your self-efficacy, but it is not going to be easy.

The first step is to honestly measure your own self-efficacy. In all things, you need to learn to measure before improving. Below are eight statements for you to score your self-efficacy. There is also a tool that can help you improve your self-efficacy over time. Let us talk about the tool first.

At the end of every week, write down at least ten major things that happened to you that week. Record each item in this format:

Name: Provide a short name for the thing that occurred.
Description: Fully describe what happened.
Results: Describe the positive and negative results of what happened.
Self-Efficacy: Using "high," "medium," or "low," rate your own self-efficacy feelings going into this situation.
Next Steps: List out things that you could do to improve this type of situation and your self-efficacy in the future. Below are the four areas to consider when listing the next steps. Incorporate the steps into your personal strategic planning activities.

Over time, you will see how your self-efficacy and confidence in your abilities improve, as you focus on them.

About every six months, no more than once a year, you should analyze your self-efficacy, using these eight statements below. Score each statement with the following Likert responses:

1. Strongly Disagree.
2. Disagree.
3. Neither Agree nor Disagree.
4. Agree.
5. Strongly Agree.

Here are the statements:

1. I can achieve the goals that I set for myself.
2. When facing difficult tasks, I am certain that I will accomplish them.
3. I can obtain results that are important to me.
4. I can succeed at anything I set my mind on completing.
5. I can successfully overcome challenges I face.
6. I can perform effectively on many tasks.
7. I can do most tasks better than others.
8. I perform quite well, even when times are tough.

Really up for a challenge? Complete this self-efficacy survey; then have someone who is really close to you complete it about you as well. Scoring yourself high, while those around you score you low, could be a result of overconfidence or a refusal to see the truth – self-delusion. Toba Beta said, "Arrogance is a creature. It does not have the senses. It has only a sharp tongue and the pointing finger." Scoring yourself lower than others can help you recognize something they see that you do not. Higher esteem – here you come!

As mentioned earlier, self-efficacy can be improved in four different ways. The first way is based on the tool I shared above – through experiencing major positive and negative experiences. The key to effectively leveraging this way of improving, is to record, track, and analyze the major experiences in your life. Otherwise, your learning from these experiences will be haphazard at best. Best to treat this like a structured lifelong learning exercise, like I will talk about in Chapter 14.

The other three ways to improve your self-efficacy revolve around building your mastery through task completion, living vicariously through close connections, and establishing and looking up to role models.

Mastery

When I was enlisting in the Air Force, my father (who was drafted into the Army for three years) gave me a great piece of advice. He said, "Never volunteer for anything." Like a good rebellious son, I did exactly the opposite. In the military, I was the first person to step forward when someone asked. The way I looked at it, I could do anything I set my mind to do. And what was the worst thing that could happen? I volunteered after all – so they could not expect much from me. What I learned was, most of the work was easy, but since no one liked doing it, people felt the work was hard. Four years into my military career, I learned that volunteering with nonprofits provided even more opportunity to improve my self-efficacy.

The term you might be looking for is "failing forward." Stepping up and taking on difficult tasks will build your confidence. Of course, how you respond to failures can also affect your self-efficacy. Because you will fail – but will you learn from the failure?

Several years ago, my wife and I bought our "forever home" in a gated golf course community. This near-5,000 sq. ft. home was beautiful, albeit a little dated. A month after moving in, the water heater in the second story attic (it is common to put water heaters in attics in Texas I guess) failed. I had just finished unpacking all the upstairs the day before. That morning, I was walking up the stairs to my office, with coffee in hand, and I heard the dripping. In Chapter 11, I will talk more about how unbelievably successful people respond to these situations. But for now, I use the story to emphasize my self-efficacy.

We had good insurance, and it paid to replace a major amount of carpeting. When we bought the house, we knew we wanted to put down wood flooring upstairs. So, we decided to install the flooring ourselves, so we could do the entire upstairs – well, I convinced my wife that we could do it. As we bought all the bamboo flooring, underlayment, nails, and tools, my wife asked, "Have you ever done this before?" Of course, the answer was, "No." So, she questioned if we should hire a professional. What do you think someone with a high self-efficacy would be thinking – "I got this!" A little way into the project, my wife woke up to me creating a drawing on some graph paper. I had designed a built-in bookshelf for my office. I showed her what I was going to build, as I worked on the flooring in that room. She just shook her head. Below is a photograph of the flooring and bookshelf that I built with zero experience. Do you think this built my confidence?

Learning From Others.

More so today, than in years past, people are learning more and more from others than they do from formal education. Today, there are more podcasts that interview people than one might think possible. This format of discussing one's successes and failures has almost become overused and trite. However, many people enjoy tuning into their favorite shows to learn through others. The self-help industry today is dominating the world – researchers predict the industry will be worth $41 billion by 2030. Self-help gurus are pushing self-education these days over formal education.

I agree with the concept of learning from others. Although, I think the industry has become overwhelmed with bad actors who profess their own success, and their success at making others a success. When, in reality, they have achieved very little in their lives.

So, who do you trust? How do you find the right people to learn from who are not part of formal education? Research their background. For instance: When someone claims to be awesome at social media marketing, I always look at their profile. Do they have a great deal of connections? Do they post regularly? Do they generate a lot of engagement? What do their posts look like – content marketing, or just marketing content?

Being a personal and professional business coach and consultant with over 25 years of experience, I am regularly amazed when someone shamelessly approaches me offering to sell me business coaching. The first thing that goes through my mind is, "Did they even look at my profile?" Do not get me wrong – I have coaches, but it still makes me wonder. Then, I look at their background. Who knows? They might be incredible – remember my third lesson from Chapter 3? The minute you think you are better than everyone else, the universe steps in to let you know that you are wrong.

Regardless, the first thing you do is research them. In Manpower in the Air Force, we called this, "Trust but verify."

The second thing to look for is how they portray themselves. Do you remember the Law of Compensation (Chapter 6)? You will also read about an abundance mindset (in Chapter 13). Unbelievably successful people freely give away knowledge to make other people smarter. What are they giving away for free? These are the kind of people you want to learn from.

Role Models.

Although modeling is similar to learning from others, it is slightly different. A role model is someone you follow, admire, and want to emulate. You do not necessarily learn directly from them – you learn from their behaviors and actions.

In the Air Force, a popular book to read was *Lincoln on Leadership*, by Donald Phillips. When I worked at USAA, this was also a popular book among leaders there. Lincoln, through his depiction by Phillips in his book, is a role model to many leaders.

When looking for those to learn from – those to become your role models – pay particular attention to how they exhibit their self-efficacy and locus of control (see more on this subject below).

So, as you can see, unbelievably successful people live with an extremely high sense of self-efficacy.

As I said before, one cannot really talk about self-efficacy without talking about locus of control. The word, locus, means position, point, or place – thus locus of control means, where your control stems from. It is measured from internally to externally. Have you ever met someone who always blamed everything (good or bad) on someone or something else? That was a person with a highly external locus of control.

Stephen Covey, in *7 Habits of Highly Effective People*, talks about the circle of concern, circle of influence, and the circle of control. Basically, he emphasized that we should focus on the things we can influence and have control over and not worry about what we cannot – the circle of concern. The more we believe we are in control – internal locus of control – the more control we have in our lives overall. This increases your esteem needs (see Maslow's Hierarchy of Needs in Chapter 5), helps you self-actualize more often, and leads you to becoming unbelievably successful.

Using the same Likert scale as we used with the self-efficacy test, respond to these eight following statements:

1. My heredity determines my personality.
2. When I make plans, something unexpected always interferes with them.
3. My intelligence is set, and it cannot be increased or decreased.
4. I cannot change my destiny.
5. There is nothing I can do about the politics in this country.
6. Doing well on tests and projects means that they were easy.
7. My academic success is a result of my socio-economic background.
8. My successes in life were all because of chance and luck.

When trying to improve your locus of control, let me take you back to the tool I shared earlier. Modify your sheet just a little bit. Right after the self-efficacy column, create a locus of control column. Using "IN" or "EXT" note what type of control you felt you had going into the situation – internal or external. Use the next steps column to list things you can do about this in the future. Do not forget to incorporate the steps into your Personal Strategic Plan.

Trust me, when I was in high school and my first college, I blamed everyone but myself. I sucked in math because I felt I was not capable of learning the subject. Yes, my parents always told me that I could do anything I set my mind to – I just needed to believe in it myself.

Now that you have a better understanding of self-efficacy and locus of control, I suggest pulling out your Personal Strategic Plan. Give it a critical eye analysis. Do you believe you can achieve unbelievable success with this plan? Do you believe that you are in control of achieving unbelievable success? If your answers are "Yes," you are on the right track to becoming unbelievably successful.

Chapter 10 Questions

1. Define self-efficacy.

2. Define locus of control.

3. To track and improve your self-efficacy and locus of control, how many things should you write down each week?

4. How is self-efficacy measured?

Essay Question

Why do you feel that self-efficacy and locus of control are important to becoming unbelievably successful?

Chapter 10 Notes Page

Use this page to capture notes in each Part and Chapter

Chapter 11
Moving from Victim to Creator

In the last chapter, we talked a lot about control and its impact on your esteem needs. Probably one of the biggest things you can control is how you respond to bad things that happen to you.

When COVID hit in early 2020, how did you feel? How did you respond? Did you feel like you were the victim of something not in your control?

The drama triangle is something I recently learned about. I remember that the triangle was explained to me as, when bad things occur, we end up in one of three roles: the victim, the rescuer, or the persecutor. At the time that I learned about the concept, I did not like it.

Why?

Because I did not want to play the drama game! I did not want to find myself in any of those three roles – none of them were good. I knew there had to be another answer!

Along came *The Power of TED*, by David Emerald – you may notice that I read a lot (you will learn more about that in Chapter 14). My biggest concern was the victim role. This is the "poor pitiful me", played by animated characters like Pig Pen, Schleprock, and Eeyore. People stuck as the victim in the drama triangle have given up control and how they respond to their situations. *The Power of TED* talks about a new way to look at the problem you are facing, so that you do not become the victim. If you change the problem into an opportunity – look for that silver lining – you move from a victim to a creator!

Several years ago, during a quality improvement conference, I attended a workshop on inventive problem-solving. In this workshop, the presenters revealed a Russian problem-solving approach called TRIZ. TRIZ is a Russian acronym for the *Theory of Inventive Problem-Solving*. I found the story behind the creation of this problem-solving approach to be so interesting that I continued to research and follow it over the years. In the workshop, we went through an exercise where could save the Titanic. We were all part of the crew, and we were given a list of all the things available to us. With that list, we all came up with super-inventive ways to stop the Titanic from sinking and protect the passengers from freezing in the water and drowning. Like the Titanic crew, we raced against the clock to invent solutions.

One of the inventive teachings of TRIZ is to use your problem as your solution. After presenting all our solutions – some very inventive – the workshop presenter drew our attention to the iceberg that the Titanic hit, and which had ripped open her hull. When the ship hit the iceberg, it continued to sail on – it was considered an unsinkable ship after all. Well, it turns out that the iceberg that the Titanic struck was large and had a very flat surface above the waterline. If the Titanic had turned around and gone back to the scene of the accident, the crew and passengers' salvation might just have been the very thing that doomed them – the iceberg itself.

When COVID struck like a world-ending meteorite, how do you think most people responded? As I shared in my book, *Business 2020*, I had accepted a full-time COO position with a former client six months before the pandemic. I had thrown myself into the success of that company 100 percent – resigning from teaching, stopping writing for Forbes, and canceling all my coaching and consulting engagements. The success of that company was forefront in my mind, and I dedicated long days, evenings, and even weekends, to working to improve and grow that company. That is what a good COO does. As COVID reared its ugly head in the United States, the Chief Executive Officer (CEO) and owner became concerned about cash flow. They started considering layoffs. I offered myself up to be laid off to help ease the cash crunch. The CEO told me, "I would never be let go and that I was too valuable to the company – my job was safe." A month later, I was the first person the CEO and owner called to layoff. I was one of the millions who became part of the statistics of COVID-unemployed.

Finding any type of substantial work turned out to be nearly impossible while on lockdown. This was true for many on unemployment. However, I did not look at COVID as a problem – I looked at it as an opportunity. The day after being laid off, I started researching and writing *Business 2020*. I published it four months later, as a free downloadable PDF for anyone that wanted to benefit from its knowledge. In addition to my other books, once I published *Business 2020*, I almost immediately started working on this book. This time afforded me the opportunity to resume writing with Forbes; I joined the Global Strategist Team and started writing with the Global Business Playbook; I returned to Hallmark University as an advisor to their business school; I posted my Facebook Marketing Workshop online and worked on improving it; I started working on ideas for a podcast and a magazine; and I took a more active role in our farm as our COO.

Problems are how you look at them – you control how you respond to adversity. On your road to becoming unbelievably successful, you will run into many different roadblocks. How you respond to them will affect whether you ever reach your destination or not.

Chapter 11 Questions

1. What are the three roles in the Drama Triangle?

2. What book did the author highlight that tells you to look at problems as opportunities?

3. What is the name of the Russian problem-solving method mentioned in this chapter?

4. What role should you focus on transitioning into to become unbelievably success?

Essay Question

Why do you feel it is important to look at problems as opportunities?

Chapter 11 Notes Page

Use this page to capture notes in each Part and Chapter

Chapter 12
Emotional Intelligence

Emotional Intelligence (EQ) is perhaps one of the most talked about concepts in success today. I personally know several coaches who strictly focus on improving their client's EQ, but almost every professional and personal development coach talks about it. I almost did not include this topic in this book because it seems so well-known. However, I still find people who do not know about the concept, or who have a very low EQ.

Whereas your Intelligence Quotient (IQ) can be improved with education; reading; puzzles and thinking games; and learning languages and how to play musical instruments, improving EQ is not as easy. However, your success in life will be significantly impacted by both your IQ and EQ. Throughout this book, you will learn ways to improve yourself, which will impact your IQ. This chapter; however, focuses on what EQ is and how to improve it.

A lot of credit for the creation of EQ goes to Daniel Goleman, and he has authored several books on the subject. However, the psychological theory was originally created by Peter Salovey and John Mayer in 1990. Prior to that, in 1985, a graduate student, named Wayne Leon, wrote a doctoral dissertation that included the term. Although the concept of EQ is rather new, it has been deeply studied. It has become recognized as a crucial factor in becoming unbelievably successful. As you embark on your journey, remember to continually focus on improving your EQ.

EQ falls into four categories: self-awareness, self-management, social awareness, and relationship management. The concept is typically depicted in a Boston Square like the one shown below.

	Recognition	Regulation
Personal Competence	Self-Awareness	Self-Management
Social Competence	Social Awareness	Relationship Management

Self-awareness is about understanding yourself on a deep level. You actively recognize your personality, your feelings, what motivates you, and what you believe in. I like to think about self-awareness as three things. They are:

- Why we do what we do
- Why we feel what we feel
- Blind spots

We do things in our life based on impulses from within our body. The basic requirements, like eating, drinking, and breathing are driven by our internal systems. What we eat and drink is driven by us – we choose those items. The actions that we choose are based on our personality, feelings, motives, and beliefs. Our body encourages us to eat when we are hungry, in order to survive. Our mind encourages us to eat when we are not hungry as a response to an external stimulus. For instance, binging on ice cream when sad. Self-awareness is understanding why we do what we do. It is purposefully asking our conscious self, "Why am I doing that?" This trains us to understand the triggers and drivers and how we react and why. This goes the same for feelings. Why are you happy, sad, or mad? Something happens and we react. Knowing what makes us react with action or feeling is being self-aware.

So, what are blind spots?

Your level of self-awareness is based on what you know and what you do not know. We often do things or feel things that just do not register in our consciousness. They have become so routine that we are not even aware when they are happening. These are blind spots. The fewer blind spots you have, the higher your self-awareness will be.

Improving your self-awareness starts with recognizing what you are doing or feeling and exploring why. The most impactful way to do this is through daily journaling. At the end of every day, write down what you did, what you felt, and why (i.e., the external triggers and drivers and internal motivators). Over time, you will recognize the why behind your actions and feelings. However, blind spots require outside assistance. Since these are things that you do not recognize, you need honest brokers around you to call out your behaviors and actions, bringing them to light. These people can be your family and friends, or you can hire a coach to help you. To identify your blind spots, you need to allow or employ people to be honest with you.

Being self-aware is the first step to increasing your EQ, but it hardly stops there. Knowing why you do what you do and feel what you feel is great, but useless if you do not regulate it. If you know that you binge on chocolate ice cream when you are sad and upset, but do not stop yourself, you have poor self-management. Where self-awareness is something you reflect upon, self-management requires action in the moment. Self-management is recognizing triggers and drivers as they occur and managing your responses (actions and feelings) to them.

Using your daily journal, identify the triggers, drivers, and responses. Once you have identified them, the next step is to develop ways to hijack them. This is done in the moment; you recognize what is going on and actively change your behavior. In typical situations, where these triggers and drivers appear, you can control the situation. Sometimes, when I get really upset it feels like I just downed an entire pot of coffee. My body is super-amped up and I want to respond by lashing out. Recognizing the reasons I am upset and managing the emotions, prevents me from acting on impulse. I am not one who often deals with road rage, but that is because I try not to put myself in the position where road rage appears. I give myself ample time to get somewhere. I plan out my route to avoid traffic when possible. I stay in the right lanes and drive safely. By managing my own actions and behaviors, I normally avoid the triggers and drivers that could upset me on the road.

Once you have become very self-aware, you can create your own formalized set of instructions on how you will behave. These are called values or principles. They are a set of rules that you desire to live by. For instance, one of my personal values is integrity – doing the right thing even when no one is looking. When I retired from the Air Force, I briefly sold oil and gas with a brokerage. I was told I would be paid a salary plus commission, although I had expected the job to be 100 percent commission based. After training and certification, I went to work. In my first two weeks, I had three sales lined up. When I received my first paycheck, I found out it was a "salary draw." Basically, they were paying me out of my future commissions – not a real salary. I approached the vice president who had hired me with my concerns. He said, "What's the big deal, you'll make $300,000 your first year here." The big deal was that they had lied to me to get me to work for them. If they lied to their employees, then they would lie to their customers. I quit on the spot – I responded with my integrity.

Become highly self-aware, create solid values or principles, and stick to them. This will ensure high self-management. Add these values or principles to your Personal Strategic Plan.

Being socially aware means that you are tuned into what is happening around you and with others. A lot of social awareness is grounded in the Law of Vibration, covered in Chapter 6. Having a high social awareness allows you to recognize potential drivers and triggers in social situations. This allows you to respond or avoid in an appropriate manner (self-management) faster and easier.

You can build your social awareness by really paying attention to the room and the people in it. If you constantly become self-absorbed in your own thoughts, you will not recognize what is going on around you. In our Reckless Rangers program, we provide free equine-based learning and therapy to veterans who are dealing with post-traumatic stress. Horses are incredibly socially aware animals. Plus, they release soothing pheromones when groomed. Working with horses has helped me slow down and pay attention to the world around me.

The last category in EQ is relationship management. In a nutshell, this is getting along with others through strong social awareness and self-management. When you consistently apply these two effectively in interpersonal relationships, you operate with a high level of relationship management. Again, use your journal to help you identify your actions and then the responses of others. This will help you improve this category.

As you can see, possessing a high EQ is not easy to obtain, but it is very important to your success. As you recognize areas for improvement, ensure you are leveraging your Personal Strategic Planning Process to hold yourself accountable. If you struggle with a low EQ (there are many free tests online), I recommend getting professional assistance from a coach or even a therapist. Do not let a low EQ hold you back from becoming unbelievably successful.

Chapter 12 Questions

1. What is the abbreviation for Emotional Intelligence?

2. How is your Emotional Intelligence different from your Intelligent Quotient?

3. What are the four areas of Emotional Intelligence?

4. What is the primary tool, presented in this chapter, to assess, evaluate, and improve Emotional Intelligence?

Essay Question

What do you feel is the easiest thing to improve about one's Emotional Intelligence and why?

Chapter 12 Notes Page

Use this page to capture notes in each Part and Chapter

Chapter 13
Mastering Mindsets

These days, the term, "mindset," appears in practically every conversation I have. The word has become so cliché these days, in many ways, it has become meaningless.

A mindset is a set of attitudes, assumptions, methods, or notions held by someone. When I retrained in the Air Force from Security Police to Manpower and Quality, I was presented with a term called, "paradigm." A paradigm is considered a typical example, model, or pattern of something. I have come to recognize mindsets are mental paradigms.

As I said, people seem to want to attribute the term mindset to the many actions of a person these days – "Oh, that's just his mindset." Depending on where you are in your journey to becoming unbelievably successful, you may or may not have ever heard of this term. The reason I hear this term so much these days, is because of the type of people with whom I commonly hang out and collaborate (see Chapter 17).

I think it was Carol Dweck, and her 2006 book, *Mindset: The New Psychology of Success*, that really kicked off the mindset movement. Dweck introduced her readers to the concept of fixed versus growth mindsets. Mindsets tend to be viewed as representing an "either-or" relationship in your mind. (Remember the Law of Polarity in Chapter 6). The light switch is either on, or off; the temperature is either hot, or cold; etc. In reality, your mindset is a sliding scale from one side of the spectrum to the other. As you embark on your journey to becoming unbelievably successful, recognize that everything in this book, or in your mind, does not have to change overnight – you will learn into it.

Some of the more documented mindsets are as follows:

- Fixed versus growth mindset
- Scarcity versus abundance mindset
- Defensive versus productive mindset

There are other identified mindsets, and someone was probably dreaming up a new one as I wrote this book. However, I have found these three to perhaps be the most important, when becoming unbelievably successful.

The most powerful of these three mindset concepts is the fixed versus growth mindset. People with a fixed mindset believe that their capabilities, intelligence, and talents are set in stone and cannot be changed. Unbelievably successful people realize this is complete hogwash! They believe that their abilities, intelligence, and talents can be developed through effort. In fact, to become unbelievably successful, that effort must be structured and aligned with your Personal Strategic Plan. Therefore, the next chapter focuses on structured lifelong learning.

Many people think in finite amounts. They believe there is only so much pie. These people operate from a scarcity mindset. Stephen Covey coined this mindset of scarcity versus abundance. Those with a scarcity mindset never think they have enough and never want to share anything with others. You remember, as a little kid, being asked to share your toys. You might have had 50 toys, but you were not willing to part with any of them! We grow up with these vicious thoughts of comparing ourselves and what we have, to those around us. An abundance mindset flips an individual's thinking to one where giving away means getting more in return. You might remember me discussing the Law of Cause and Effect, the Law of Compensation, and, specifically, the Law of Reciprocity highlighted in Chapter 6.

The last of these three crucial mindsets is defensive versus productive. A defensive mindset exists when someone has a low self-efficacy and an external locus of control (remember from Chapter 10). A defensive mindset is self-protective and self-deceptive in nature. Imagine the information hoarder at work – after all, information is power. They protect themselves, and their jobs, by not letting people know what they do and what they know. Someone with a defensive mindset, like a fixed mindset, will not seek additional learning, because additional knowledge forces them into the unknown – and the unknown is scary. Ever hear the abrupt comment, "I don't want to hear about it!" People cut you off because they are afraid of change that comes from "hearing about it." Productive people, on the other hand, openly share and seek out additional knowledge to expand their mind and surroundings.

If you struggle with a fixed, scarcity, or defensive mindset, there are four steps to take to overcome this challenge. They are:

Step 1 – Recognize. You may have heard of the term, "mindfulness." This means to be very self-aware of where you are and what you are doing at this very moment. In the previous chapter, we discussed self-awareness, so you should have a good idea of what I mean here. However, this step is focused on being self-aware in the moment – being mindful. When faced with a challenging or difficult situation, what is your inner voice telling you? Remember the tool I described in Chapter 10? This will help you look back on what you were telling yourself.

"I'm not good enough."

"I'm not smart enough."

"I don't have enough money."

"I can't deal with this right now."

These are your negative mindsets at work, trying to prevent you from becoming unbelievably successful. This is a psychological phenomenon known as "The Imposter Syndrome." It is psychological because it is all in your mind. Once you recognize your mind is playing tricks on you, how do you deal with that?

Dr. Wayne Scott Anderson, the architect behind the *Habits of Health Transformational System*, emphasizes an effort to combat these thoughts – in the moment. This is called: Stop, Challenge, and Choose.

Step 2 – Stop. The moment you realize your mind is feeding you with negative self-talk, you need to stop and examine the situation. The more that you have recorded and analyzed your thoughts and actions, using the tool from Chapter 10, the better and better you will become at this.

Step 3 – Challenge. Compare your current thoughts with those of the obverse mindset. If you have fixed mindset thoughts, compare them with growth mindset thoughts. Examine these in the open light and determine which thought you prefer.

I work with a lot of startups and small business owners. The first thing all future and current business owners should do is establish a strategic business plan – I bet you are not surprised I would say that! I initially work with them on developing the expressed purpose of their company. Your business purpose, much like a business ikigai, is why you exist, written from the perspective of your stakeholders (customers, employees, partners, and suppliers). Purpose is what gets people up in the morning – and becoming unbelievably successful only occurs when you live life with purpose. After establishing the business purpose, we discuss the vision of the company – I call this their What Vision. Typically, startups and small businesses think small in their vision. They think with a scarcity mindset. I ask them to repeat the purpose to me. Then, I ask, "Wouldn't you want everyone in the world to have that?" The answer always starts the same, "Yes, but…" My follow-up question is, "But, what if you could?"

Step 4 – Choose. You are faced with options every day, all day long. Your response to these options can be easy, normal, or hard. When we let negative mindsets take over our thoughts, we give into the "easy." Now is the time to choose how you will live your life every day. I do not think I need to tell you how someone who is becoming unbelievably successful thinks. But I will assure you that it tends to be the "hard" response. I will cover more about this concept in Chapter 37.

As I said above, I work with a lot of businesses, helping them develop and implement their strategic business plan. As with you, I do not want to see them fail. In fact, I recognize that the root cause of most business failure is a lack of effective planning. I had recognized this several years ago, working with Booz | Allen | Hamilton. Over the ensuing years, I have watched failure after failure, all a result of poor or no planning. But I am a "Success Incubator," so how can I prevent this? My idea is simple: Every single business in the world should have an effective strategic business plan that they use every day to improve and grow their business. Can you imagine what would change in this world if most businesses were successful versus failures?

Of course, my mindset tried to play tricks on me. "You don't have enough bandwidth to develop a plan and coach every business in the world through implementation! Besides, all businesses can't afford your services to build a plan and have you coach them." Oh, I entertained these thoughts – I listened to them. But then I rallied back, "But what if I could? What if they could?" The answers are in accepting the problem as an opportunity. What if my capability could be built into an automated program? What if I could partner with a lender that invests in the companies if they create and follow the plan?

These are the questions unbelievably successful people ask of themselves every day.

Chapter 13 Questions

1. What are the mindsets discussed in this chapter?

2. What are the three options we are faced with when making decisions?

3. What was Dr. Anderson's three-step approach presented in this chapter?

4. What two mindsets did Carol Dweck make popular?

Essay Question

Describe a situation where you dealt with one of these mindset situations and how you handled it.

Chapter 13 Notes Page

Use this page to capture notes in each Part and Chapter

Chapter 14
Structured Lifelong Learning

One clear thing that unbelievably successful people all have in common is that they are lifelong learners. Lifelong learners continuously pursue knowledge for their personal and professional reasons. Lifelong learning is an ongoing and constant effort that successful people embark upon willingly and of their own volition.

Malcolm Knowles produced a book in 1975, titled, *Self-Directed Learning: A Guide for Learners and Teachers*. His work outlined the creation of a mutual learning environment, where educators are no longer seen as teachers, but as facilitators. The learner becomes their own teacher directed by the "guidance" of a facilitator (the teacher).

Although published in 1975, I did not learn of this book until 25 years later. My mentor at the time, Master Sergeant Jerry Peña, was scheduled to teach an all-day workshop at a government housing conference. Due to personal issues, he had to travel home – we were stationed in Germany – and he would not be able to lead the workshop.

Master Sergeant Peña asked me if I would lead the workshop. Scared and unsure, but despite myself, I agreed. The first step was to read the book, which was luckily very short. I also had to design the workshop – great mentor, huh?

As I have shared, I was not the best student in my youth. I did not find the value of education until I entered the Air Force – an education I was involuntarily pursuing. I learned, reading that book, and conducting the following workshop, that I had been practicing self-directed learning since I entered the Air Force.

Recently, I conducted a poll. I asked if people considered themselves to be lifelong learners. Nearly everyone agreed that they felt that they were a lifelong learner. Perhaps this opinion is because every day we learn something new about our life, our family, our friends, our jobs, even our environment. Simply picking up a magazine in a waiting room can lead to reading and learning.

This approach; however, is haphazard and disjointed. Although you are learning, you are not learning in a purposeful and structured manner. Structured lifelong learning is about purposefully establishing a methodical self-directed learning approach. Learning is no longer some random act. This is how someone becomes unbelievably successful. Structured lifelong learning should be treated as a doctoral dissertation research project.

When I decided on my strategic direction, I recognized that I needed to look and be a certain way – this was embodied in my vision. That created a journey of purposeful discovery. For instance, I knew I wanted to become a recognized expert in process improvement. At the time, I did not even know what Lean and Six Sigma were. However, I did know the Air Force's seven-step continuous improvement process. I learned most of what I knew from the 1994 publication, *Process Improvement Guide, Second Edition: Quality Tools for Today's Air Force*.

I dog-eared and tape-flagged that entire book. For several years, it was my Bible. I would further research every approach, model, and tool presented in the book. Eventually I was given *The Memory Jogger II*, by GOAL/QPC. This book began to expand my mind even further. Like the previous book, I was again deeply researching topics within the book – learning a little more every day. One concept, expanded on several more. I was slowly mastering my "Shu," which you will read about in the next chapter.

As my learning expanded and the field of knowledge became more popular and, born out of my desire to become an expert in the field, I learned of Lean, Six Sigma, business process management, and many other process improvement ideas. This led me on a structured path of constant learning and discovery. Today, I have earned certifications as a Lean Six Sigma Green Belt, Lean Six Sigma Black Belt, and culminating in the highest level – Lean Six Sigma Master Black Belt. I also have a Master's Degree from the National Graduate School in Quality Systems Management.

This all was a result of focused and structured lifelong learning. It all started with my focus on process improvement and one single book. This constant immersion bled over into my work, what I write and speak about, and eventually my whole being. But every day I am continually learning, exploring, and discovering – growing.

So how do you establish a path of structured lifelong learning?

The first step is to determine your North Star – your purpose and your vision. Basically, where you are going in life. Your direction guides your actions and your learning. This is why we discussed developing your strategy early in this book.

With your purpose in mind, you can establish paths to learning that will allow you to grow along those paths. Remember, I only knew I had to have certifications and become a recognized expert in process improvement. I did not really know much about the subject at all. All journeys start with the first step.

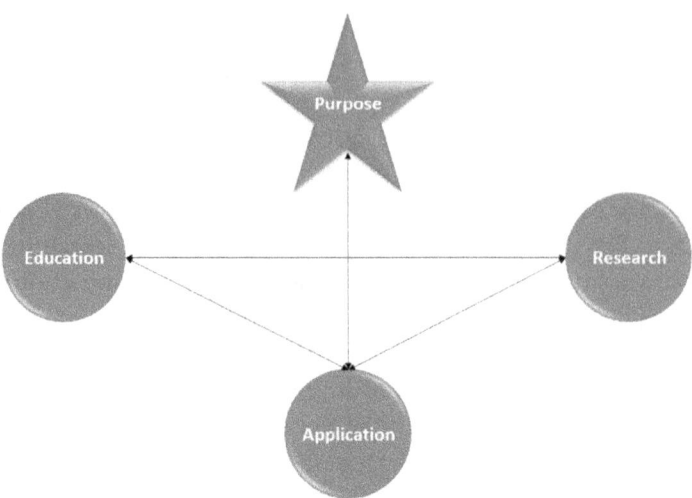

Lifelong learning occurs when you engage in three basic things: Education, Research, and Application. When you know your direction, you start to see what resources are available to you. Thus, learning becomes purposeful and structured versus absently watching a National Geographic special on dinosaurs.

Formalized Education and Training

There is a movement in the world today that promotes the idea that a formal college education is worthless, and in today's economy one should simply start working. I bought into this mindset when I was younger – after failing out of college. "Who needs college," I thought. Today there are many self-help gurus out there who will tell you that you no longer need a formal education.

I disagree.

What you do not need is an education that someone tells you that you must have. This is not self-directed learning – you are not learning on your own volition. You are simply gaining a degree because society tells you that you need a degree.

Education – whether it is formal schooling or informal training – is never a bad thing when you are learning for the right reasons. I failed in college, partially because I did not have the drive to learn. I was only there to get a degree and for no other reason than to get a degree.

A friend of mine, Jeff, was a different story. His father was a dentist and Jeff knew he was going to do something medical with his life too. Maybe partially because his family wanted it, but Jeff wanted it as well. Jeff excelled in college – maybe he screwed off a little bit, but he still excelled! Jeff did not stop at becoming a dentist. He went on to become a well-respected professional oral surgeon. Jeff has been recognized by major publications and imparts his knowledge to students as an adjunct professor. Jeff, knowing his direction early in life and following it, has become very successful.

With your plan in hand, plot your educational journey. Maybe you will be like me and recognize the importance of a doctorate in your future, but still be without even an associate degree. But formal education is not the only way to learn. There are learning opportunities everywhere you look. I approach all training today as an opportunity to learn something new, even if I have taken the training course before. Using LinkedIn Learning, I try to complete one course a month on a subject that furthers my success.

Most of my education in the areas of process improvement came from training programs and not formal education. In fact, I had my black belt certification before I even started my master's program in quality systems management.

Focused Educational Research

Have you ever read a book because it sounded interesting, someone recommended it, or the cover caught your eye? Of course, you did – we all do. Have you ever gone to a conference or attended a seminar because work dictated it, it was expected in your career, or someone suggested it? I am sure the answer is yes – I know it has been for me. Do you read random articles in a magazine because they are simply there? We all do it.

However, these days things are a bit different for me. I seek out books that will expand my understanding in very specific areas. Seldom do I randomly pick up a book just to read it. I read purposefully to learn. I attend conferences, seminars, and speeches that cover topics that further my development. When I attend a conference, I plan out session attendance with specific results in mind. I specifically subscribe to publications that produce content aligned to my path. I tend to read research papers that expand my mind and explore new subjects. Even on social media, content that typically stays my swiping finger is that which is aligned with my learning strategies.

To this end, I seldom waste time on mindless television, and I listen to fiction books on Audible only prior to going to sleep – because it is relaxing.

But consuming information from books, magazines, articles, and presentations is only surface based. To become unbelievably successful, I propose you take a different and more methodical approach to your information consumption.

In school, we took notes and studied. Do you have a system, or do you simply read one book and then move on to the next?

I have coached several executives regarding more effective reading of business books. Two things normally are going on:

1. They think reading more is better. They proudly tell me how many books they have read.

2. They think every book is the best one they have ever read, and the ideas from the book should be implemented immediately.

Slowing down, reading to learn, and incorporating the ideas into your Personal Strategic Plan, helps the eager lifelong learner make solid use of their reading.

How do you do this?

As you complete a chapter, record your thoughts about that chapter in a separate document. For each thought entry, list the page and paragraph that triggered that thought or idea. Next, copy the specific section word-for-word – committing it to memory. Then, write out the actions you plan to take as a result of that section – what you plan to do with this new knowledge. When you are done with the book, rewrite all the actions into one list.

Then, incorporate these actions into your short and long-term strategies in your Personal Strategic Plan.

Obtaining knowledge from education and research is like getting into the shallow end of a big pool, but then getting right back out again. Your proverbial mind gets all wet, but quickly you dry off and forget much of what you have learned. To really experience the pool and everything it has to offer, you need to swim around!

Purposeful Application of Knowledge

Learning loss is a phenomenon where a student experiences specific or general losses of knowledge due to extended gaps or discontinuation of education. In fact, researcher Youki Terada determined that the normal rate of knowledge loss is particularly alarming. Based on his research, students lost approximately 56 percent of knowledge gained after only one hour of learning it. Additionally, he determined that students lose up to 75 percent after only six days!

By following the previous recommendations of capturing key points from formal and informal learning, and incorporating this learning into your ongoing strategy, you undoubtedly will slow down this rate of learning loss. However, the immediate application of knowledge learned is the best way to prevent learning loss.

When I worked at Booz | Allen | Hamilton, we had a very specific way of writing annual development goals related to learning. If we identified a specific growth area, the development path was always the same. The employee would enroll in some type of course, workshop, or seminar. Then, they would teach-back what they learned to the team – either through a presentation, training, or trip report. Lastly, they would apply what they learned in a real-world client engagement. All this would be under the watchful eye of a mentor or coach.

This structured approach to purposeful application proves extremely effective for lifelong learners. Requiring the learner to teach-back what they learned forces them to fully understand the material and commit it to memory. Research has proven that when you teach something to someone else, you learn more about the subject.

As an adjunct professor with Hallmark University's Business School, I was asked to teach a business intelligence and data analytics course. Although I had a fair amount of knowledge on the subject because of my operational excellence experience, I decided it was best to up my game on the subject. It was a good thing I did too. When I received the course material for my first class, we realized the actual course had not been built yet. Thus, I had to develop the entire course as I taught it. I literally was teaching content one week while creating content for the following week.

I went on to teach a few other business analytics courses over the following year. Coming into the teaching role, I was forced to learn a particular subject more deeply than I had ever done in the past. If it did not beat all, I even had to get better at hypothetical statistics to teach the course. You might remember, in Chapter 3, the difficulty I had with math.

So, as you can see, do not just learn something in a class or from a book and move on. Teach what you learned back to people in some way that helps you remember the material and learn more about it.

Do not stop there. Take what you have learned and apply it! To emphasize this to my students in our analytics courses, we would collect data, assess the data, and report the data. This hands-on learning activity helped solidify the subject with my students. Then, I would ask the students to apply what they were learning in the class, either at work or at home.

By recording what actions you plan to take, as a result of what you have learned, and then incorporating those actions in your Personal Strategic Plan, you are purposefully and strategically applying what you learn. By following this three-step process of education, research, and application, you will be a structured lifelong learner. Structured lifelong learners become unbelievably successful!

You can learn more about lifelong learning in EBR's, *Lessons in Life Long Learning*.

Chapter 14 Questions

1. What is structured lifelong learning?

2. What are the three aspects of structured lifelong learning?

3. What is one way to apply knowledge learned?

4. What is the first step in structured lifelong learning?

Essay Question

Explain the difference between lifelong learning and structured lifelong learning.

Chapter 14 Notes Page

Use this page to capture notes in each Part and Chapter

Chapter 15
Shuhari

When you think about success, what comes to mind? A new house, a new car, happy family, travel? Or is it being recognized for your abilities – fame? Success might mean all these things and more to you.

There was a time when I measured my success in life by accumulation of some of materialistic things mentioned above. However, I look at success in a new light these days. All of this came fully into focus about seven years ago when I learned about Shuhari.

Shuhari is an ancient Japanese martial arts term that was westernized by Alistair Cockburn in his 2001 work, *Agile Software Development*. Primarily used in the Aikido martial arts style, Shuhari is an approach to learning and growth.

Becoming unbelievably successful is about following Shuhari.

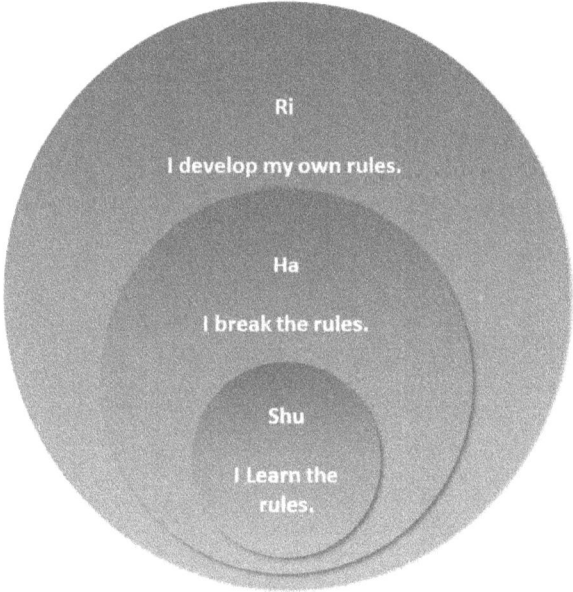

Shuhari is portrayed as three concentric circles. These represent the three stages of gaining and applying knowledge.

"Shu" is at the very center of the three circles. Shu represents the stage when we are just beginning to understand something. When you are in this first stage, you are learning from one master – be it a person, school, book, etc. The focus, in this stage, is on learning how to perform a task a certain way without worrying about the reasons behind accomplishing that task.

Many of us can relate to certain classes that we were required to take in school. It did not matter why we needed to complete these classes, just that we had to do it. When I started out my journey in process improvement, as mentioned in the last chapter, my master in Shu was the first book that I discussed.

Many people – unsuccessful people – never progress past Shu. It is not that they are not good at what they do. It is that they have become comfortable doing something the way they were taught. These people are like a hammer and, to them, everything they look at looks like a nail. Mainly, because they know no other way to look at things.

Previous generations – less today – lived by the guiding principle that you obtained a degree, got a job, stayed with that company for most of your life, and then retired. These are people stuck in Shu!

As we move outward from the center, the second circle is known as "Ha." This is the second stage of learning and growth. This is all about broadening one's knowledge and experiences.

People who enter this stage expand from their single source of education and understanding. Not only do they learn new ways to do something, but they learn the reasons why it is done. Moving through Shu and Ha is like progressing from high school through a doctorate program.

Those who are in the Ha stage of their lives now have many masters to learn from. When I retrained from Security Police to Manpower, in the Air Force, I pretty much existed in Shu. In fact, if I had not created my Personal Strategic Plan in 2000, I might never have moved to Ha. My journey into Ha probably began with a certain college course in my bachelors' program. At that time, I was completing my degree, as a step along my educational journey. I was learning – sure – but I was taking the required courses of a set degree program. That is when I took a fourth-year course in Industrial and Organizational Psychology. I did not know what this course was all about, but it looked like an interesting elective.

What a difference a course can make in someone's life! I realized, with that course, that process improvement was just a part of a system of operational excellence thinking. I did not officially finish my bachelor's degree until two months after retiring from the Air Force. But my eyes were wide open by that time.

Booz | Allen | Hamilton is really where I "cut my teeth" on my craft. I was pretty good at what I was doing after retirement, but my experiences while there really opened my eyes to everything.

While different from Shu, people in the Ha stage are not unbelievably successful either. In fact, while in this stage, you might be fooled that you have reached the pinnacle of what you can achieve.

You may have heard the phrase, "The student becomes the master." This does not simply mean that the student starts teaching others. No! This means, the student begins to teach the master from whom the student learned. This is "Ri."

When you have learned all that you can from everything and everyone around you, where do you go? How do you continue to learn? Who will teach you?

Those few who traverse this barrier, move into the third and final stage – Ri. With the absence of others to teach you, you must begin to learn from yourself. Those unbelievably successful people create their own approaches to their craft. They adapt and adjust everything they have learned to respond to their particular circumstance. Those in Ri often defy the teachings and methods of others.

In 2010, I started to move toward my Ri. It started with reading a Department of Defense paper on something called "organizational myopia." My eyes were opened to the myopic impacts on an organization, because of silos. This, in itself; however, was not my moment of Ri. When I realized the years of business dogma that I had embraced were wrong – that was my moment of crossing into Ri.

Eventually, this led to my publishing of my first business book, *Overcoming Organizational Myopia: Breaking Through Siloed Organizations*. This was the beginning of a whole new journey of discovery – one based in root cause analysis of the toughest problems in business today.

Achieving Ri should be a primary focus of your journey to becoming unbelievably successful. Those mired in Shu or stuck in Ha might be good at what they do, but they will never achieve the greatest levels of success they are capable of.

Chapter 15 Questions

1. What are the three levels of learning?

2. Why is Ri fundamentally different from Shu and Ha?

3. What martial arts form typically uses Shuhari?

4. Who was the author that made Shuhari popular in the west?

Essay Question

Currently, in your journey of becoming unbelievably successful, where are you in the spectrum of Shuhari and why do you feel this way?

Chapter 15 Notes Page

Use this page to capture notes in each Part and Chapter

Chapter 16
Memory Mastery

Unbelievably successful people have unbelievably good memories. They know all their client's and employee's names. They remember important dates. They remember details about people. But wait! What if you do not have a good memory?

Memory mastery is all about the things you can do to improve your ability to remember important stuff.

The first thing is to determine what is important to remember that helps you become unbelievably successful. Make a list of these things – these become items for your relationship management system for success. A relationship management system is typically a database of all interactions with potential, current, and previous clients or customers. This database tracks when you or your employees talk to them, what was said, what they bought, and key information about them. Marketing and Sales departments in companies use this tool to keep in touch and consistently promote the company and its products and services. Using a spreadsheet or just a simple notebook should also work fine. Create a data collection system for all the information that is important. I use something like this to track networking and mentoring relationships as well as my coaching and consulting engagements.

To improve your memory mastery, the first step is to make sure you get the information right the first time. This requires active listening and active reading. Active means to focus and remove distractions. When reading, we comprehend more when we read aloud. Repeating (or reframing) what was said or written down helps you remember. Refer to the structured approach I shared on reading in Chapter 14.

In Chapter 19, I talk about self-care when it comes to managing stress, but self-care is also important when mastering your memory. Ensure you eat well, get enough sleep, monitor your weight, and exercise regularly. These things stimulate your brain with the continuous flow of fresh oxygen. Like dealing with stress, taking care of yourself allows you to be more focused and mindful in the moment.

There are many ways to train your brain to increase your memory mastery. For instance, Jim Kwik has a book called *Limitless: Upgrade Your Brain, Learn Anything Faster, and Unlock Your Exceptional Life*. In the book, Kwik teaches his secrets of memory and recall. There are multiple memory training programs available – even LinkedIn Learning has online courses on the subject. There are also cell phone applications to help memory that are free. I like Lumosity, Brain Training, and Train Your Brain.

When trying to remember something, there are three techniques I have found that work.

Mnemonics. A mnemonic is a pattern of letters or words that help people remember something. These are like acronyms, but used to remember things, not shorten them. An example is "Roy G. Biv." No, it is not someone's name, it represents the colors of a rainbow: red, orange, yellow, green, blue, indigo, and violet. Mnemonics are popularly used to memorize things in school or in training.

Repeating names. If you struggle with remembering people's names, here is a way to help you remember. When someone tells you their name, repeat their name, in conversation, three times. Use their name at the beginning, middle, and end of a sentence. For example: "John, it's nice to meet you. So, tell me, John, what do you do? It was great meeting you, John." If you do not have the ability to interact with someone, say the name three times to yourself. This helps commit the name to memory.

Visual cues. Some people use visual cues when they meet someone to remember their name or something about them. Things like, "Art is really smart," or "Amber has red hair." Using visual cues is a more practiced approach but can be very effective.

Many of us use some type of system or various systems to help us remember. Taking notes in a notepad is an old-school way, but can be very effective. For years, while in the military, I would carry a small black organizer. On one side of the organizer was a spiral notebook and on the other side there was a small monthly calendar in a plastic sleeve. Every day, I would document the major things that occurred on the calendar. I kept these calendars for years and could always go back to them and they would refresh my memory of what had happened during a particular time. It was similar to how you retrace your steps to find something you misplaced.

Today, with cell phones and tablets, the ability to take quick notes and leave yourself short reminders is very easy. The most important thing is to develop a system to record important information. The more you use it, the easier it is to manage. Create your own memory mastery approach today to propel yourself on your journey to becoming unbelievably successful.

Chapter 16 Questions

1. What are mnemonics?

2. What is the most important thing from this chapter?

3. How many times should you repeat someone's name to ensure you remember it?

4. What is a relationship management system?

Essay Question

How good is your memory mastery and what have you done to improve it?

Chapter 16 Notes Page

Use this page to capture notes in each Part and Chapter

Chapter 17
Interpersonal Relationships

We are constantly influenced in our lives by many different things. Initially, our parents, siblings, and close family start to shape our lives. Then, we start to attend school, which teaches us as much as it molds our lives. Always working to create connections and to fit in, we develop close social groups. As we learn to read, we are further influenced by the words of others. We are additionally influenced in life by things like music, religion, newspapers, magazines, television, and social media. As we go through life, our brains are continually assaulted by information that we must constantly sift through and categorize.

Jim Rohn, motivational speaker, says, "You are the average of the five people you spend the most time with." As I related in Chapter 3, my influential group of five were The Skippers. Although I believe "five" is a rather arbitrary number, I do believe we are definitely influenced by those we spend the most time with. This is especially true in high school – a time where we are most influenced regarding the direction of our lives. I look at the five people who became my lifelong friends: Kevin, Jeff M., Jeff F., Mark, and Greg. As I said earlier, I believe that I was perhaps the worst influence on the group. Why do I say that? All of them knew they were going on to college. Jeff M., in particular, knew what he wanted to be in the future. Kevin went on to become a lawyer – first in New York and then in California. Eventually, he became a Navy Lawyer. Greg worked on the space shuttle and owned several of his own businesses. Mark became a skilled contractor and had his own business. I think about how all their lives might have been different if I had not been such a poor influence.

Now is the time to really examine your interpersonal relationships. Look at your Personal Strategic Plan from Part 2. Think about those you spend time with the most. Think about the lessons in this book. Do those with whom you hang out live these lessons? What would they say if they read this book? What would they say if they were to read your Personal Strategic Plan? You want to surround yourself with people who will support, motivate, and uplift you on your journey to becoming unbelievably successful.

Lorne Michaels once said, "If you're the smartest person in the room, you're in the wrong room." As you journey through your first stages of Shuhari – Shu and Ha – you should strive to expand your knowledge through as many influential people as possible. If you are the smartest person in your circle of influence, you will not learn as much.

Although Rohn promotes that you are a product of your five closest friends, I agree more with David Burkus, from Medium, an open ideas platform. He has studied social networks for years and emphasizes that your circle of influence does not stop anywhere near five people. The bigger your network, the more you can learn.

So, how can you increase and improve your network?

Before we talk about your network, let us discuss Napoleon Hill's concept of a Mastermind. The Mastermind Principle was the second of seventeen principles in *The Law of Success*. Hill defines the mastermind as "Two or more people, who work in perfect harmony, for the attainment of a definite purpose." When I talk about building your network, I want you to focus on filling it with people who help you work towards your purpose in life. Some people want to surround themselves with as many people as possible – you see this on social media a lot. Instead of focusing on quantity, pay attention to the quality of your network. When you surround yourself with the right people, versus just anyone, you can become unbelievably successful much more quickly.

Also, your network has a twofold purpose. First and foremost, is to personally grow and develop the mastermind concept. The second purpose is to be a recognized unbelievable success, which we will cover in Part 8.

I break networks down into four different types: social, business, professional, and social media. In some cases, network types can bleed over onto each other. For instance, I created a social business networking group in San Antonio, called "Whiskey Bid'ness And Cigars." It is a business networking group with people who like to socially meet and connect while enjoying whiskey and cigars, so it is a cross between a social and a business network.

Social networking groups meet around a specific hobby or fun activity. Typically, you will find these on Meetup.com or Facebook. They could be sports related, like running, cycling, etc. They might be a dining out group, or a group that likes to drink beer. I have found that these groups expand your network while you explore an area of interest.

Probably the best-known business networking group is the Chamber of Commerce. Businesses join Chambers, in part, to network with other local businesses. BNI is also a very popular and formalized business networking group. BNI clubs specifically focus on businesses within the club working together and referring work to other businesses in the club. BNI clubs only allow one type of industry in that club at a time. So, there would be only one electrician. This way, you do not have any competition within the club. Aside from professional group websites, Eventbrite.com is a common site to find business networking groups. Some also use Meetup.com or Facebook.

Professional networking groups are like business networking groups, in the way that they support people in their business. They are like social networking groups because they normally center around a topic or interest. When I was in the military, I belonged to professional military associations, like AFSA. When I came close to retirement, I joined professional groups, like ASQ. As I shared, I have been a member of Toastmasters International for many years. To find groups that might interest you, run an internet search and research the websites of any that look interesting.

Probably the most popular way to network today is virtually using social media. The two most popular platforms are Facebook and LinkedIn. Facebook groups provide a powerful way for people to connect around a specific topic. Facebook is always looking for ways to connect people through social topics. LinkedIn is more professionally oriented. Originally, a place to share your professional profile to businesses, it has evolved to become a group that supports more professional teaching and influencing. LinkedIn groups exist but have lost much of their effectiveness. From a business perspective, Facebook is more Business to Customer (B2C) whereas LinkedIn is more Business to Business (B2B).

Leveraging your networks, to develop quality contacts, should be the focus of your networking activities. No matter what type of group you are part of, look for people who are active, interesting, and will help you grow. Social media, more than any other networking group type, can pull you into quantity over quality. If you do that you have defeated the purpose of the mastermind.

Unbelievably successful people are constantly connecting with others who also aim to become unbelievably successful. They are "superconnectors." A superconnector is a person, group, or technology who holds the trust of a large group of people and has a means of reaching out to them directly. They are facilitators of smart connections.

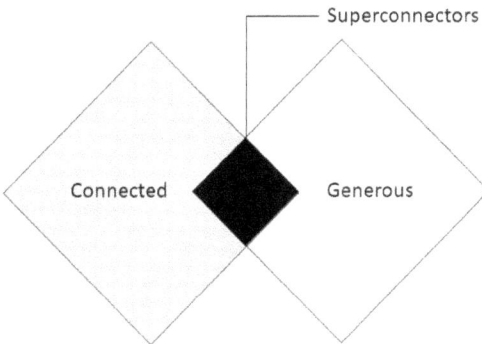

Superconnectors are very connected and equally generous with their information and their connections. Being a superconnector helps you become unbelievably successful.

Chapter 17 Questions

1. You are a product of your closest ____ friends.

2. What are the four types of networks that the author presents in the chapter?

3. What type of networking group would a high school chess team fit into?

4. What is a superconnector?

Essay Question

What is an example of a possible group that spans two or more of the four group types listed?

Chapter 17 Notes Page

Use this page to capture notes in each Part and Chapter

Chapter 18
Agile Perfectionism

Did you know that being the person that strives to be perfect all the time leads to mental illness? There have been many studies that found high levels of perfectionism led to things like depression, anxiety, eating disorders, deliberate self-harm, and obsessive-compulsiveness.

Were, or are you, an A-student in school? Do you struggle to complete work on time because it must be perfect? Do you get distraught if you find an error in your work after you turn it in?

Clearly, when you read my story in Chapter 3, you probably realized that I was not much of a perfectionist as a kid. However, I did know of few in high school. Richard was one of them. Richard was supersmart. He wore Coke-bottle glasses and hearing aids. Yeah, you guessed it, he was picked on a lot.

Richard and I were sort of friends. I do not remember him ever really having any true friends – no one that I noticed. Occasionally, we would have lunch in the cafeteria at school. I remember one day that the rather stoic kid was visibly upset at lunch. As usual, he was all alone, but this day he was crying in the cafeteria. He had received a B+ on a paper. Being a straight A-student, this was totally unacceptable to him.

I remember not knowing what to say, so I just sat there while he sobbed. Life went on and I doubt this transgression in school affected his grades, but this experience stuck with me later in life.

See, as I grew older and started to figure myself out in the military, I started to become a perfectionist myself. I cannot tell you when it happened or what caused it, but I remember listening to Grant Cardone and his new 2011 book, *The 10X Rule: The Only Difference Between Success and Failure*, on Audible. Cardone was talking about taking massive action and going after big goals – specifically not to settle for ordinary. I remember a phrase that I heard many times in the military and later working with Booz | Allen | Hamilton. "Good enough for government work." I also considered Voltaire's famous quote, "The best is the enemy of good." As I listened to Cardone it struck me just how much I had grown to dislike imperfection.

I had quietly become a perfectionist and did not even realize it.

Why had this happened? How had this happened? I was not sure, but it had happened all the same.

I remembered that Cardone's words really hit home with me. It was one of those books that has a profound effect on you, and you do not really understand why.

I had seen this "good enough" syndrome quite a lot by this time. It was very present in the military – especially in headquarters units. I also saw how those who bought into the "good enough" mindset tried to hold others back from success. Even going so far as trying to sabotage the efforts of others.

I think my focus on perfectionism was probably from being in the Air Force Security Police. See, the Security Police had somewhat of an elitist attitude in the Air Force. We prided ourselves on being better than everyone else in the Air Force – or at least we made ourselves believe that. This belief manifested itself in our dress and appearance. Aside from Military Training Instructors and the Air Force Honor Guard, we always exuded the highest standards on base. This was also reflected in our attitude that our job was the best in the Air Force.

Now that I look back on my time as a cop in the Air Force, I realize how the career field was "pulling the wool over my eyes." The career field kind of sucked as compared to most other jobs in the Air Force, and it took me retraining to another career field to realize that. But, if all those in the Security Police (now Security Forces) realized the reality, more probably would have retrained, so we walked around with blinders on, oblivious to reality.

This experience; however, drove a level of perfectionism into my dress and appearance after retraining. I would always wear a tie and my ribbons when wearing blues. I was proud of the uniform and my accomplishments. I remember one day a very young lieutenant came up to me in the office and whispered, "Sergeant Knotts, you need to stop wearing your tie and ribbons, you're making everyone else look bad."

I calmly turned to the lieutenant and replied, "No Lieutenant, you're making yourself look bad."

See, others do not want you to be perfect, because they feel threatened by your perfection. Cardone's message in his book spoke loudly to that, and I really started to realize how I had seen this behavior play out time and time again. Those around you will not want you to be perfect and they will not want you to become unbelievably successful. You will hear things like:

> "Why are you working so hard?"
> "You better watch out or you'll burn yourself out."
> "This sounds too difficult or too risky."
> "You're making us all look bad."

The sad fact is that many people that read this book will not follow its guidance. So, my message is to you – the one in one million that believes in something much bigger and better!

However, the reality does exist. Perfectionism can be unhealthy if you let it. Constantly striving for perfection in what you do, can hurt you personally and professionally.

So, how do you deal with this and still strive for perfection in what you do?

Enter 'Agile Perfectionism'.

The first step is to realize that no one will ever be 100 percent perfect 100 percent of the time. The belief that you have to be will lead you to frustration. You will get a B+ or make some other mistake and that is okay. As long as you accept that you gave it your best shot and you learn from your mistakes.

It is when you accept substandard as the norm that you struggle.

This is why I use the word BHAG's in Chapter 8. Follow Cardone's advice and set your sights way out of reach, but do not get discouraged when you do not reach them right away. Keep on striving and trying. This is being "agile."

Perfection should be a journey, just like becoming unbelievably successful. You should strive "for perfection," not "to be perfect." The difference between these two phrases is so very subtle, but very important. If you always strived to be perfect, then when you are not, you quit and you fail. You beat yourself up about not being perfect and find yourself sobbing uncontrollably in the cafeteria at lunch. You begin to second-guess everything you do in fear of not being perfect. This results in spending too much time trying to be perfect that you never finish.

This book will never be perfect. I have written enough to realize that. But I strive for perfection when writing, editing, and publishing. I am all right with something not perfect because I can learn from it and get better. Being agile is allowing yourself to deliver what is referred to as the Most Viable Product (MVP) but continuing to improve. If we succumb to Voltaire, then we stop at MVP – it is good enough.

This happens with many of the clients I work with. They develop a product or process and leave it at that. When it is good enough, they stop focusing on improving it. They do not look for ways to make it better. The phrase I hear often in process improvement is, "If it ain't broke, don't fix it." This phrase was popularized by Thomas Bertram (Bert) Lance when he was the Director of the Office of Management and Budget under President Jimmy Carter in 1977. Hmmm, a government job!

Other related terms have sprung up that you might have heard, like:

> "Leave well enough alone."
> "Never change a running system."
> "Don't change a winning team."
> "Don't change horses in midstream."

But this mindset is contrary to continuous improvement, and continuous growth. This becomes the enemy of innovation in your life and company. In this recent pandemic, those who were stuck in the way things were, struggled.

It was Einstein that said, doing things the same way and expecting different results was the definition of insanity. However, many of us are stuck doing the same things in our lives and expecting to become unbelievably successful as a result.

To be an Agile Perfectionist and become unbelievably successful

These are the steps to achieve agile perfectionism in your life.

1. As already mentioned, you need to establish the proper mindset (I talked more about mindsets in Chapter 13). The mindset of an Agile Perfectionist strives "for perfection," not "to be perfect." You accept perfection as a scale that can be continuously improved and never fully achieved. And you are at ease with your imperfection along the journey.

2. Always envision the perfect result in every action. Aiming low insures hitting low. Wayne Gretzky said that "You miss 100 percent of the shots you don't take." If you do not envision the perfect result, then you will never be able to achieve it on purpose. As a big golfer, envisioning my perfect shot before I take it is key to my success. Benjamin Franklin said, "By failing to plan, you are planning to fail." I will challenge you that you need to "Plan to Fail!" Wait! What? You may have heard Les Brown say, "Shoot for the moon. Even if you miss, you'll land among the stars." Nope! Aim for those stars! They are so much further away than the moon. If you do not make it – if you fail – you will have gone further than most.

3. With the end in mind (Stephen Covey), you can define the steps to achieve perfection. When a mountain climber decides to climb Mount Everest, they do not simply start their climb. They strive to reach a series of "camps" along their climb to the summit. Even reaching "Base Camp," which is almost 18,000 feet above sea level is an achievement. Along the route to the summit are four more camps. These points along the journey allow the climber to assess the cost of continuing forward. Perfection is the summit of Mount Everest, but it is always about the journey for every climber. If you learned anything from Part 2 of this book, it is that becoming unbelievably successful is a never-ending journey made up of a great deal of steps.

4. The last step is to accept imperfection and keep moving forward. In Chapter 12, I stress the importance of your own self-awareness and self-management. Recognizing your reactions and responses to not being perfect is very important to becoming an Agile Perfectionist. If you are always getting upset and beating yourself up about your imperfection, then you will make yourself sick.

Vince Lombardi was quoted saying, "Perfection is not attainable, but if we chase perfection, we can catch excellence." Being an Agile Perfectionist will suit you well on your journey of becoming unbelievably successful!

Chapter 18 Questions

1. Who wrote, *The 10X Rule*?

2. Who said, "By failing to plan, you are planning to fail?"

3. Should you strive "for perfection," or "to be perfect?"

4. High levels of perfectionism can lead to what things?

Essay Question

How can you strive for Agile Perfectionism in your life?

Chapter 18 Notes Page

Use this page to capture notes in each Part and Chapter

Part 3 Questions

1. What concept is made up of three concentric circles of learning?

2. Why are interpersonal relationships important?

3. What is the first quadrant of Emotional Intelligence?

4. What are the three components that make up structured lifelong learning?

Essay Question

Of the topics presented in this Part, which do you feel will be the most influential to your success and why?

Part 3 Notes Page

Use this page to capture notes in each Part and Chapter

Part 4
Stress Management and its Importance in Unbelievable Success

"Change is inevitable. Growth is optional.
~ John Maxwell

Chapter 19
Self-Care

Stress is a response to changes (real or perceived) that impact our lives every day. Living a journey of becoming unbelievably successful will undoubtedly prove more stressful than a normal life. Thus, it is important to understand stress and learn realistic ways to deal with that stress.

There are two different types of stress: eustress and distress. Most people believe that all stress is bad, but that is not true. Eustress is considered a form of beneficial stress. Eustress helps us stay motivated, work towards our goals, and live a full life. Distress, on the other hand, causes anxiety, creates concern, and generates an unpleasant experience. COVID placed a lot of long-term distress on people, but during this crisis, positive stressors could occur as well (e.g., starting a new job, moving, having a child, etc.). Working towards and receiving your goals in your Personal Strategic Plan will create a great deal of eustress.

Do you know how to purposefully create stress that motivates you to greater success?

I recently shared a great poll on LinkedIn to discuss how stressed people are and how they deal with their stress. Over 18,000 people viewed the poll and 550 people responded -- great response rate! Close to 80 percent are dealing with some sort of stress right now (Slightly to Seriously Stressed).

Are you a stressed out professional?
You can see how people vote. Learn more

Highly Stressed	35%
Slightly Stressed	43%
No Stress	22%

556 votes • Poll closed

What is great is that several people shared how they deal with their stress, and I hope that helps others.

My question today -- I always have a question -- is do you purposefully create stress in your life? I do!

As mentioned above, there are two kinds of stress, distress (bad) and eustress (good).

Stress is basically energy. When things happen, we experience this chemical reaction in our body, and we often see it as uncomfortable. For instance, when you are getting ready to speak in front of a crowd, you call it butterflies.

In our equitherapy program, we teach participants to embrace this energy and harness it towards positive action. When you are faced with a problem (a negative thing) you experience energy and feel like the victim – this causes distress. Look at the problem as an opportunity and step into the creator role, harnessing the energy in a positive way, as described in Chapter 11.

This part of the book is focused on managing stress in your life, so you do not become overwhelmed and non-functioning. Too much of any stress, but specifically distress, can cause physical and mental issues.

Self-care is about initiating regular activities that promote positive mental, emotional, and physical health. The following chapters on health and fitness, financial management, and spirituality, are within the realm of self-care, but we will cover them separately.

The number one excuse for not committing to self-care activities is "not enough time." Look, I get it! When you embark on the road to becoming unbelievably successful, your life will become very busy. As you live day-by-day according to your Personal Strategic Plan, you will find your days filled with things that need to be done. These things may leave little time for doing other stuff that does not appear directly correlated to your strategy. In fact, Chapter 24 focuses specifically on ways to manage your time more effectively. Be sure to remember that your Personal Strategic Plan includes self-care. You need to take steps to take care of yourself, otherwise you may never witness your ultimate vision of unbelievable success.

There are six categories of self-care – they are as follows:

- Emotional self-care
- Mental self-care
- Social self-care
- Physical self-care (covered in Chapter 20)
- Practical self-care (partially covered here and in Chapter 20)
- Spiritual self-care (covered in Chapter 22)

In order way to make self-care a priority you must incorporate self-care activities into your Personal Strategic Planning Process. In this chapter, I will provide the six recommended self-care activities that should find their way into your daily life.

Get a hobby. Most of us have things we like to do – fish, garden, scrapbook, golf, etc. Find something – preferably something that you can do with others – that you truly enjoy. If possible, make your hobby a priority in your life every week. Sometimes, a hobby, which is an emotional self-care activity, can also be a physical and social self-care activity. For instance, clearly, I like golf – it is part of my Personal Strategic Plan. I belonged to a large golfing group that played every Saturday morning at a different golf course around town. When I played, I would always walk and carry my golf bag – even on the hottest of Texas days. This fulfilled emotional, physical, and social self-care activities for me.

Relaxation. Regarding mental self-care, I have three suggested activities – two can be combined. The first is to establish a routine of daily relaxation. This can be something more in-depth, like meditation or yoga, but it can be a simple daily breathing exercise as well. Find a quiet and comfortable place and conduct the 4-7-8 Relaxation Breathing Exercise for at least one minute. The simple steps are as follows:

- Inhale slowly to the count of four
- Hold your breath to the count of seven
- Exhale completely, with a whooshing sound, to the count of eight
- Repeat three cycles once or twice a day

I personally like to do my daily breathing exercises early in the morning, generally with my dog resting on my lap. This incorporates a little social self-care activity as well.

Journaling. The next two mental self-care activities can be combined into one overarching activity. We have already talked about journaling several times throughout this book. Journaling is a mental self-care activity. Many people also incorporate some type of gratitude statements in their daily journaling. I have found that writing down things for which you are grateful really expands how you look at the things that have occurred – even negative things. So, keep a journal and make sure you show gratitude for things that happen in your life.

Social self-care is about spending fun and relaxing time with others. When I say others, this can include family, friends, and even your pets. Go to dinner with friends and family, have a weekly movie night with your spouse, or take your dog for a walk every day. These are social activities that should become habit-forming in your life. As you know, my wife and I own a horse farm. Simply put, we are animal people. Of the 40 horses we have on our property, about a quarter of them belong to us and the farm. We personally own two dogs and there are about 15 cats currently on the property. Regularly, I go out and groom and spend time with my horse – Legend. He is a huge lovable guy who enjoys my company.

5S. The last two self-care activities include practical application of organization and routine. Have you ever moved into a new home? Well, if you have not, take it from me, it can be a stressful time – both eustress as well as distress. I know – I have moved 15 times in my life. Every time you move, you have to pack and then unpack. When your home is full of boxes, how does that make you feel? Stressed, right? Clutter creates stress – the more clutter, the more stress. Even after you have moved in, open your junk drawer (we all have one) and tell me how you feel when you see it. In Lean – a process improvement methodology – the first step to improving anything is to organize it. Specifically, the approach used is called 5S (more in Chapter 23). However, the simple solution is as follows:

1. Clean everything up and keep it clean.
2. Get rid of stuff you do not need or use.
3. Create a place for everything you keep.
4. Put everything in its place.
5. When you use something, put it away when you are done with it.

This is also true with your digital stuff. What does the file structure of your computer look like? How about your computer's desktop? You can apply the same techniques to your digital life as you do to your physical life.

Routine. The last practical self-care activity that I will talk about in this chapter is routine. Routine is a form of organization. You already started this self-care routine by implementing your Personal Strategic Planning Process. This is about establishing a daily routine, specifically when you wake up and before you go to bed. You may have seen the commencement speech, on YouTube, from Admiral William McRaven. It is called, *Make Your Bed*. It is like the concept of micro habits – small daily changes that can improve your life. If you start your day with a series of simple, yet effective activities, this sets up your entire day for successful task accomplishment. The same can be said for ending your day with a routine. This allows you to prepare for a good night's sleep, which we will discuss briefly in the next chapter.

Good financial management is another practical self-care activity. It is basically organizing your finances. We will discuss that more in-depth in Chapter 21.

These six simple activities of self-care can easily be incorporated into your daily life without taking up a great deal of personal time. In fact, making these routine in your life will probably help you find even more available time to tackle your Personal Strategic Plan. Use these tactics to combat the distress in your life and focus on enjoying the eustress of becoming unbelievably successful.

Chapter 19 Questions

1. What are the two types of stress in our lives?

2. What are the self-care activities listed in this chapter?

3. What way did the author combine three self-care activities into one?

4. What document should you highlight your self-care activities in to make them a part of your daily life?

Essay Question

What is one emotional self-care activity that you do now, or you can start today?

Chapter 19 Notes Page

Use this page to capture notes in each Part and Chapter

Chapter 20
Health and Fitness

This chapter is not designed to turn you into a gym-rat or the next Olympian. If that is your goal, you probably do not need to read this chapter. However, if you are at all like me, this chapter will help you understand the specific importance of physical self-care. I break it down into two very simple items.

1. Eat well.
2. Engage in physical activity.

You cannot spell "Diet," without spelling "Die!" Every day, I talk to someone or hear someone talk about the current diet they are on. But this is not surprising, because there are well over 100 different diets in the world today. Did you know there is actually a "Werewolf Diet?" No kidding! We are so obsessed with losing weight that new diets seem to appear every month!

Diet. Well, "Diet" is not such a bad word when it is used as a noun and not a verb. A diet (noun) is the sum of food and drink that a person habitually consumes. Stop "dieting" and start "eating a good diet." A good habitual diet includes sufficient hydration and healthy eating. Unbelievably successful people take care of themselves by controlling their diet. Keep it simple. Drink about half of your weight in ounces of water every day. If you weigh 200 pounds that would be 100 ounces of water every day – about 6 typical 16.9 fl. oz. bottles of water. Eat leaner cuts of meat and vegetables – remember the food pyramid. Keep portion sizes reasonable and keep those sweets and saturated fats to a minimum. The reason diets do not work is because you deprive your body (and mind) of things it craves. Dieting might work for a while, but eventually you will revert and binge on the potato chips and pizza you missed so much.

Activity. The second item is engaging in physical activity. I am not stressing that you need to run out and get a gym membership or buy a Peloton bike – although, if they want to pay me a referral bonus ... just kidding. Live a more active lifestyle. Take walks with family and pets; park farther from entrances of stores, work, or school; take the stairs; and find a physical hobby that you enjoy. We do not all need to look like Arnold Schwarzenegger or Lance Armstrong. Just get out there and become more active.

Why are these important?

Eating well and staying active will make your heart healthier, improve your cholesterol, help you get better sleep, boost your immune system, and resist the effects of aging. Most importantly, the improvements to your overall health will help you respond better in stressful situations. If you are out of shape and overweight, a stressful situation could impact you exponentially.

Measurement is key. To ensure you are living a healthier lifestyle, fit for someone unbelievably successful, you need to measure your progress. Of course, weight is a typical and easy measure that can let you know how you are doing. Simple things, like counting calories and steps can help you see your activity as it occurs. When calories go up and steps go down, the natural expectation would be an increase in weight.

Thinking Strategically About Your Health and Fitness

Why do health and fitness activities and goals fail? I believe that they are not strategic in nature. In Chapter 33, I will talk about why many goals fail. I believe that this is one of the biggest goals that people fail at in the world – getting healthy! The Health and Fitness Industry is reported to be at $22 billion. Let us face it, does the medical world really want us to be healthy? If we were all healthy and did not need to see doctors and take medicine all the time, there would be a lot of people out of a job.

Thus, it is incumbent on you to take charge of your own health and fitness. Just prior to the release of this book, my wife and I sat down and planned out our seventh goal area for my Personal Strategic Plan. This was specifically focused on our self-care. A large part of it involved health and fitness, but the goal area encompassed much of the teachings in this part.

The difference between a goal and a goal area is that all the objectives are related to my vision. My original Personal Strategic Plan was developed in 2000 and I have followed it religiously since then. My plan is to live happily into the next 30 plus years to continue to grow into my vision and to enjoy it. This new goal area was designed to make this a reality.

Again, this chapter was not about becoming the poster child for public health. If that is your vision (or at least one of your goal areas, like me), then more power to you. But unbelievably successful people take care of their health and their fitness, so they live happier, longer, and stress-free lives.

Chapter 20 Questions

1. What is the self-care activity shared in this chapter?

2. What are the two self-care approaches that are described in this chapter?

3. How should you focus on the word, "Diet?"

4. What is key to the success of this self-care activity?

Essay Question

How does this self-care activity manifest itself in your life?

Chapter 20 Notes Page

Use this page to capture notes in each Part and Chapter

Chapter 21
Financial Management

In 2018, MarketWatch shared that money was our biggest source of stress. The American Psychological Association (APA) reported that 72 percent of adults feel stressed about money. If you are stressed about money, how can you ever expect to become unbelievably successful?

This section is not designed to teach you about investing or how to become wealthy. It is about managing your stress through the effective management of your money. Money stress occurs from not having the money to buy the things we need and want (more need than want) and from having too much debt. Consistently ensuring that you do not deal with a lack of money and controlling your debt will help you significantly lower your money stress. This may seem simple, but when 72 percent of adults feel stressed out about money, I suspect that this is important to share.

Not having enough money.

Not having enough money for what you need and want is what creates debt in the first place. We start spending money we do not have by racking up credit card and loan debts. When you get too deep in debt, you do not have enough money to keep up. Having with enough money is your first concern. If you do not have enough money to buy food, pay for housing, or get around, you find yourself at the lowest tiers of Maslow's Hierarchy of Needs (see Chapter 5). You need to fix that first and keep it fixed.

Your first step is to create and maintain a monthly budget. Determine how much money is coming in every month and where it is coming from. Then, determine how much goes out every month and where it goes. The simple activity of creating and maintaining a budget tends to solve many people's money stress. This is because you immediately see ways to decrease the money going out each month to offset spending more money than you have coming in.

The next step is to reduce unnecessary expenses and increase your income. You must balance your budget otherwise you will always be underwater. Get rid of expenses that you can live without (mainly entertainment, travel, and dining out). Look for new ways to save money on things you spend money on today (buy cheaper brands; get used items versus new; and find sales, coupons, or discounts). Then look for ways to make more money. Look at picking up another job, see if there is a way to take on more responsibility at work to get paid more, or simply look for a higher paying job. This is all about managing to your budget to get things under control.

After you have created a manageable budget and adjusted your income to expenses ratio, you start creating an emergency fund. The rule of thumb is to have at least three months' worth of expenses in savings. If something unexpected happens, you can pay for it without taking on more debt. If you lose your job, this gives you some time to replace the lost income. Living paycheck to paycheck must stop – close to 50% of all people live this way!

Getting out of debt.

Once you make enough money and you have an emergency fund, eliminate your debt – especially revolving debt, such as credit cards. The first way to remove debt is to stop adding to the debt. So, you must stop using credit cards and start paying them off every month. Dave Ramsey would tell you to only use cash, but that might be extreme. If you are going to use a credit card for daily purchases, pay off what you put on the card every month – do not build more and more debt.

After you stopped increasing your debt, start to pay off one debt at a time. You can do this in different ways, based on interest rates and your personal opinion, but let me share my recommendation. Take your smallest debt and use any extra money you have to pay towards that monthly bill. All other monthly bills get their minimum payment. Once you pay off your smallest debt, move to the next smallest debt. Every time you pay off a debt, you will build your confidence and reduce your stress – I have done this.

Living debt free.

Imagine your life completely debt free! Look at your budget and add up how much money you spend on debt-based bills. Removing all your debt is like giving yourself a huge pay raise without doing any more work!

When you are debt free, learn how to make your money work for you. Robert Kiyosaki explains this concept in *Rich Dad Poor Dad*. Use excess cash to invest your money in something that builds your wealth. In Chapter 13, I talked about the importance of having an abundance mindset. Having an abundance mindset will help you.

I know that this advice seems simple, but the time it takes can be long. However, removing your money stress will be a huge weight off your shoulders. Getting good at managing your money and staying out of debt is the only way to do this. And, trust me, you can do it. Read Dave Ramsey's, *The Total Money Makeover*, and see how he has helped thousands of people live a new life.

Chapter 21 Questions

1. In financial self-care, what must stop?

2. What are the three steps to financial self-care?

3. Who would tell you to always use cash?

4. When should you pay off what you put on a credit card?

Essay Question

Why is financial self-care so important to stress management?

Chapter 21 Notes Page

Use this page to capture notes in each Part and Chapter

Chapter 22
Spirituality

Spirituality means being connected spiritually (through the spirit and soul) to something bigger than yourself. It is a broad concept that might include a relationship with organized religion or something more esoteric. Typically, spirituality brings about a feeling of peace, increases meaning and purpose, and helps you increase your perspective. These feelings help you reduce your personal stress.

Learning about spirituality is the first step to creating and increasing spirituality and, thereby, controlling your stress. Taking the time to research religions and beliefs puts you in control of determining the path of your own spirituality. Conforming to a religion or a set of beliefs because it is expected of you, could add to your distress. Take charge and make decisions about your spirituality with your eyes wide open.

Spiritual connection or religious practice is typically performed through prayer, meditation, relaxation, or by inner reflection. Attending a religious service on a regular basis not only connects you to your beliefs, but to others who share your beliefs. Learning more about your chosen path of spirituality will deepen your connection.

Finding spirituality is an extremely personal decision and is different for everyone. It involves the recognition of a feeling or belief that there is something greater than yourself, something more to being human than the sensory experience, and that the greater whole of which you are part is cosmic or divine in nature. Just an acceptance that the universal laws (Chapter 6) exist is a step toward spirituality.

Now, I am not a very religious person. In fact, I consider myself as agnostic – a person who believes that nothing is known or can be known of the existence or nature of God or of anything beyond material phenomena; a person who claims neither faith nor disbelief in God. However, that is not entirely how I might describe myself. Since I have a very internal locus of control (Chapter 10), I do not put my "faith" in anyone but myself. However, I have seen things that lend credence some higher power, and I do recognize the comfort others derive in their beliefs. Moreover, I mostly do not subscribe to "organized religion."

My parents were Protestant, but growing up, we never went to church. Surprise … I turned out pretty well, all things considered! When I went to college – the one I failed out of (Chapter 3) – the friends I hung out with were pretty diverse. Diversity was not a "thing" back then, but I figured it out. One of the diverse things about everyone was that everyone came from different religious backgrounds. So, we decided to take each Sunday to attend each person's church services, so we could see what they were like.

Not being religious, I did not even know what being Protestant meant. When the group asked what religion I was, I blurted out, without thinking about it, "I'm a Druid … I worship nature." They shrugged and were like, "Okay, let's go sit around a tree." We did!

What I realized over the years is that spirituality should be about finding peace and relaxation in something bigger than yourself. By finding this peace and relaxation, you reduce your stress levels. Being less stressed helps you become unbelievably successful.

Chapter 22 Questions

1. What are the benefits of spiritual self-care?

2. What is the first step in spiritual self-care?

3. What could add to your distress with respect to spirituality?

4. How do you "connect" through spirituality?

Essay Question

Why do you feel spirituality is so important to managing your stress?

Chapter 22 Notes Page

Use this page to capture notes in each Part and Chapter

Chapter 23
5S Your Life

Since the pandemic, many spent most of their life stuck in their homes, working virtually, and only going out for essential needs. Tables, normally used for dining, now double as desktops. Dishes are piling up in the sink. Tons of to-go containers everywhere. And the trash always seems to need to go out!

The crossover of our business and our personal lives, during this pandemic, has caused more than the normal amount of clutter in our homes.

However, what is all this doing to our minds?

Our brains prefer order and structure. These constant visual reminders of disorganization and mess are causing our stress levels to rise, which is affecting our physical and mental health.

According to the Mayo Clinic, some of the warning signs that stress might be affecting us include the following:

- Headaches
- Muscle tension or pain
- Fatigue
- Upset stomach
- Sleep problems

With the pandemic, politics, riots, recessions, and the holidays, we have enough to worry about. It is time to do something about your life – the part we have ultimate control over.

5S is a Lean workplace organization method that follows five Japanese steps: seiri (整理) "to Sort," seiton (整頓) "to Set in Order," seisō (清掃) "to Shine," seiketsu (清潔) "to Standardize," and shitsuke (躾) "to Sustain." This Lean methodology helps companies organize for better efficiency and effectiveness and can be used in your life as well.

How to apply 5S to your life

<u>Sort</u>
Dedicate some time to sorting through everything in your house and doing what they call "red tagging." You do not have to use the physical tags, but the concept is the same. Dedicate a day for each cluttered room in your house. Review every item in that room (whether in drawers, cabinets, closets, or desks) and make a red tag determination:

- Leave the item where it is
- Relocate the item to where it belongs
- Dispose of the item, by throwing it out
- Recycle the item, and either make money from it or give it away

If you are not sure what to do with the item, you can put it in a holding area. An offsite storage place is good for this. Once you have completed the sorting of your entire house, go back to your holding area, and make a final red tag determination on each item.

Set in Order
Now that you have gone through everything in your house, it is time to ensure that all items left are organized and each item has a designated place. Organize all the items left in each room in a logical way so they make it easier for you to access and use the items.

Here are some examples:

- In the kitchen, make it easy to access your typically used spices
- In your closet, place commonly used clothes near the door
- In your bathroom, strategically place regularly used items easily within reach

The key quote, typically related to 5S, actually came from Benjamin Franklin and was, "A place for everything, and everything in its place."

Shine
Now that you have sorted and set everything in order, it is time to clean everything and then set a routine in place to keep everything clean. This involves the routine tasks such as vacuuming, mopping, dusting, etc. However, it also involves recurring maintenance activities such as changing out batteries on things like smoke alarms and remotes, updating clocks on appliances, and replacing furnace filters.

Standardize
Now that you have everything uncluttered and clean, establish a documented routine to keep it that way. If you have kids, take a picture of their room, closets, cabinets, and drawers, and put them in a small book. You can do the same for the other rooms in your house. Set a schedule of shine activities and routine 5S reviews – once a quarter is usually good enough. Make sure you inspect rooms using the standards you set.

Sustain
Sustaining over time is probably the hardest task with 5S. But recognizing your continued success and making a game or competition out of it helps. Give extra allowances to your kids or buy them small gifts if rooms are kept clean and organized. Go out somewhere nice to eat as a celebration if the whole house is kept up to standard.

Perfection seldom happens, but every quarter should be easier and easier to keep everything in line.

With just a little dedicated effort, you can declutter your life and reduce a lot of unwanted stress on your whole family. Follow these proven Lean steps to a brighter future on your journey of becoming unbelievably successful!

Chapter 23 Questions

1. Who said, "A place for everything, and everything in its place?"

2. What is 5S?

3. How many steps are in 5S?

4. Which step in 5S is the hardest?

Essay Question

Where in your life today could you use or apply 5S?

Chapter 23 Notes Page

Use this page to capture notes in each Part and Chapter

Part 4 Questions

1. What is positive stress?

2. What are the different types of self-care?

3. Working out in the gym is what type of self-care?

4. Being connected to something bigger than yourself is what type of self-care?

Essay Question

What do you feel is the most important self-care activity and why?

Part 4 Notes Page

Use this page to capture notes in each Part and Chapter

Part 5
Business Transferable Skills of Unbelievably Successful People

"People with highly transferable skills may be specialists in certain areas, but they are also incredible generalists – something businesses that want to grow need."
~ Leah Busque

Chapter 24
Time Management

Do you agree that the business world changes superfast these days? Outsourcing, automation, technology, disruption – these are just some of the external drivers of this business change.

When you perform a job, you learn how to do the job and the tasks associated with it. Over time, you get good at the job – remember the 10,000-Hour Rule from Chapter 6? But what happens when your job is no longer required or is under threat of elimination? Suddenly, you fall to the second lowest tier of Maslow's Hierarchy of Needs (Chapter 5) and your hope of self-actualization quickly fades.

If you are too focused on saving or rebuilding a career, how can you ever hope to become unbelievably successful?

Since your career is so vital to you, you will perceive any chance of it changing or going away as a threat. This will make you incredibly resistant to any change that might impact your job. How do you build your own confidence to not only embrace, but to lead change?

I personally have studied change – specifically business change – for over 14 years. In fact, I first discovered the concept of change management in 1999. I dedicated a chapter in this part of the book to change management, and specifically change readiness. However, this entire part (Part 5) of this book is how you embrace and lead change in your career. Two foundational books to read on this subject are *Who Moved My Cheese*, by Spencer Johnson, and *Our Iceberg is Melting*, by John Kotter.

What I propose, with these next eight chapters, is a concept called "Business Transferable Skills." Jeff Hiatt, with a company called Prosci, created a model for change called "ADKAR." Each letter in ADKAR stands for something key to successful change.

- A – Awareness
- D – Desire
- K – Knowledge
- A – Ability
- R – Reinforcement

When change occurs – which happens all the time these days – people can successfully navigate the change if: they are aware of the change before it happens, they understand why the change is happening; they have the desire to change; and they know how to change – they are trained.

What if your whole job was changing? You know, that thing you are really good at doing? Suddenly, your ability to demonstrate the skills and behaviors expected in the change come into play. What if you do not have them? If you possess business transferable skills, you can transition to anything in business easier. Sure, you will have to learn a new job or new ways to do your old job, but that is the easy part, because it is just a series of recurring steps and activities. It is the softer skills that make the transition easy.

There are eight business transferrable skills. The beauty is that you do not need to become a master of these eight skills – they are not your full-time job. You just need to know enough to be able to be confident during change. Once you have a strong understanding of these transferrable skills, you can confidently look for opportunities to change, which can lead to improvements in your business, and make yourself a very valuable asset to any company.

Time management

I used to work closely with a First Sergeant in the Air Force, who always had a saying, "I don't manage time, time manages me." Business change is always hectic. In the midst of making the changes required, you are also learning how to successfully adopt the change and operate effectively. With everything else going on in your life, time can overwhelm you. I remember this First Sergeant returning from a weeklong vacation. He had over 1,000 unread emails waiting for him. He highlighted all 1,000 emails and hit the delete button. I asked him if he was crazy. He simply replied, "If it's important, they'll email me again."

This is not time management!

Good time management allows you to accomplish more in a shorter period of time. More specifically, great time management lets you accomplish more of what is most important! A focus on time management also lets you take advantage of growth opportunities, such as reading, learning, and self-care. People with great time management skills become unbelievably successful.

Develop a strong business transferable skill in time management by doing the following three things:

1. Time Study.
2. Prioritization.
3. Technology.

Time Study. Earlier in this book, I shared the importance of measuring things that you hope to change. Chapter 31 will explore the concepts of measurement more in-depth. But, before you embark on an effort to improve your time management skills, start by understanding how you currently manage (or do not manage) time right now.

Get a pad of paper or notebook. We are going to use it to conduct a two-week time study of your life. First, you must record your activities throughout the day for two weeks. Do not be tempted to do this at the end of the day (it will not be accurate). Second, make sure you conduct this study over a normal two-week period. Do not conduct the study when something out of the ordinary is happening, like going on vacation. You will be tempted to start to change things in your life while conducting this study – do not do this! Get an accurate two-week picture and you can change away after that.

From the moment you wake up to the moment you go to bed (to sleep), record everything that you do. Your study log should look something like this:

Date	Start Time	Stop Time	Total Time (min)	Activity

This will be a detailed and tedious exercise, but everyone that I have ever done this with has benefited tremendously. Make sure to include enough detail about each activity to be able to know what it was two weeks later. Do not combine activities – for instance, split "cooking," "eating," and "cleaning up," versus just writing "dinner." Make sure your time study also records the amount of time you sleep each night. When calculating your total time, do so in minutes for easy computation later.

Your study will be filled with all types of activities. Once you have completed it, it is time to analyze the data. I recommend waiting until the end of the two weeks before you begin your analysis, so you are not tempted to make changes as patterns appear. To start the analysis, transfer your study onto a spreadsheet on your computer. This will make analysis much easier. Create a column for the activities. To the right of the activity's column, add a column called "Type." For each activity, annotate in the Type column if it was "productive," "nonproductive," "nonproductive, yet valuable," or "nonproductive, yet required." You can use these abbreviations:

- P – Productive
- NP – Nonproductive
- NPV – Nonproductive yet Valuable
- NPR – Nonproductive yet Required

Date	Start Time	Stop Time	Total Time (min)	Activity	Type

So, what do these four things mean?

<u>Productive time.</u> This is time that you spent doing something that specifically aligned to one of your strategic goal areas in your Personal Strategic Plan. Obviously, time spent working and earning a paycheck would probably be considered productive. Going to

school to earn a degree, training and testing for certification, and writing a book are all productive for me because they align with my goal areas. The next three categories will help you further define what productive is and what is not.

Nonproductive time. This is a broad category. Make sure you understand the differences between nonproductive valuable time and required time (below) to really understand where your activity fits. Nonproductive means just that – it is not productive. Cooking dinner, sleeping, reading a book for pleasure, and watching television are all considered nonproductive activities. However, the activities that get just an "NP" next to them can be further classified as valuable or required (see below).

Nonproductive yet Valuable time. Perhaps you are watching a documentary on the history of World War II. Unless one of your goal areas includes learning this type of history, that would be considered nonproductive time. However, it still creates a value by teaching you something. Basically, this type of time gives you value, but not in support of your goals. There is a fine line between nonproductive and nonproductive yet Valuable, but you make the determination.

Nonproductive yet Required time. Sleeping and eating are definitely in this category. If you do not do either of these, you will die. Driving to work is also nonproductive yet required, unless you fill the travel time with an audiobook – then it could convert to valuable or even productive time (if it supports your goals). Basically, these are things that you have to do to survive and live your life.

A point on work. What if your day-to-day job is not helpful in meeting your strategic goals? It is nonproductive. If it is giving you valuable knowledge, skills, and abilities, mark it as nonproductive yet valuable. If it is just because you need the money, list it as nonproductive yet required.

Once you have annotated each activity type, add up the total time involved in each of them. This may be a little eye-opening. In 2 weeks (14 days), we have a total of 336 hours (20,160 minutes) available to us. If you get 8 hours of sleep every night, you consume 112 hours (33 percent) of your available time in those 2 weeks. Typically, we work 8 hours a day, 5 days a week, which is 80 hours over 2 weeks. Add in an hour every day to commute. This is what the average person spends commuting prior to COVID. That leaves 134 hours in a 2-week period available. Conservatively, we easily spend five hours a day on things like cooking, eating, cleaning, doing laundry, taking showers, and using the bathroom. That is another 70 hours gone, which leaves us with about 64 hours or less to do what we want. The question is, what do you fill this remaining time with?

So, what can we do now that we know how we spend our time each week? Let us first look at your job or school (if you are a full-time student) – this consumes nearly a quarter of your life or maybe more. Is this productive or nonproductive time? If it is nonproductive, you should think seriously about getting a new job – you are spending

25 percent of your life going nowhere towards success. Until I was 35 years old, I was working, but not toward a goal other than money and security.

Look at your strictly nonproductive time. Things like watching television, reading fiction, playing video games, hanging out drinking and dancing with friends, etc. Before you simply cut these things out of your life, look at ways that you can move them to another category. I love hanging out with people, having drinks, and enjoying life. So, I go to a lot of business networking events in the evening. Networking is specifically a goal area of mine, so I moved some of my "going out with friends" from strictly nonproductive to productive time. That way, I am doing something I enjoy and getting strategic value out of it.

Let us talk about social media for a moment. Estimates average that people spend over two hours a day on social media – I am sure these numbers were higher during the pandemic. However, mindlessly surfing social media is as bad as watching television as a diversion or playing a mindless video game. Consider how you can turn your time on social media to a more productive use. For me, social media is a brand-development and professional-marketing tool.

The idea is to get away from nonproductive time as much as possible and spend most of your day in productive time. When you think about nonproductive yet required time, I have some thoughts.

Get a good night's sleep. I recommend that you try to get seven to eight hours of sleep, but what works for you is what you should follow. Elon Musk reportedly sleeps six hours a night. Richard Branson clocks in at about the same. Steve Jobs typically was a seven-hours-a-night guy. Too much or too little sleep increases your risk for a whole host of physical problems. It is believed that poor sleep puts you at greater risk for coronary heart disease, stroke, and diabetes. Find your optimum sleep program.

Consider outsourcing mundane, everyday activities such as cooking, cleaning, laundry, and lawn maintenance. These required items can really add up. What if you could outsource these items? Figure out what an hour of your time is worth, based upon what you get paid at work. Then, figure out how much it would cost to hire a maid, cook, or landscaper. For several years, I lived alone in a large house. I found someone to live in a spare bedroom and she kept the house clean, did laundry, and mowed the lawn. I enjoy cooking and I had an odd schedule, so aside from an occasional meal, I did all my own cooking. Man, what a timesaver this was, and I knew because I fully understood my time.

A subsection of this time study can also look specifically at what you do during your work hours. How truly productive is your workday? You might be surprised at the results.

Now that you know how to quantify your time (P, NP, NPV, NPR), it will be much easier for you to determine productivity in the moment. When I start to binge-watch Netflix for a weekend, I quickly calculate time lost to this nonproductive activity.

Armed with this data, you can look for ways to combine activities to make them more productive. I already mentioned the "Auto University," where you listen to audiobooks or podcasts on your commute. You can network over meals and coffee breaks. Look for ways to make nonproductive time less nonproductive.

Prioritization. We are already looking at prioritizing your time, by moving more of it into the productive category. Now, we need to look for a way to prioritize the productive time. Remember when we built your Personal Strategic Plan in Part 2? When we talked about implementing the plan, we created a weekly to-do list. As much of your time as is possible should be productive. By using this weekly to-do approach, you ensure you are getting the right things done every week. By getting rid of nonproductive activities and being very productive (goal-oriented) with your available time, you will become unbelievably successful even faster. Regardless of whether you use the specific tools presented in Part 2, make sure you are prioritizing your daily, weekly, monthly, quarterly, and annual to-do lists.

When I identify nonproductive or routine productive tasks, I consider looking at ways to DEAL with them. DEAL stands for Delegate, Eliminate, Automate, and Leverage.

<u>Delegate.</u> If you are doing something that is nonproductive yet required, look for ways to delegate (or outsource) these tasks. For instance, I have a pool that must be cleaned and maintained on a regular basis. This can take time and probably does not fall in my area of expertise. Instead of spending my time on this nonproductive task, I found someone to do it for me – especially someone that really knows how to do it.

<u>Eliminate.</u> Truly nonproductive tasks that are not valuable or required should be considered for elimination. These nonproductive tasks waste your productive time.

<u>Automate.</u> If you notice that you have repeated productive activities in your time study, you obviously do not want to eliminate them, but you could want to minimize their impact on your time. I like to think about handling repetitive processes with an intelligent process automation approach. Typically, businesses jump right into an automated solution when it comes to repetitive tasks – normally this starts with robotic process automation but could also fall into machine learning or artificial intelligence. I touch upon this briefly in Chapter 30. However, I do not recommend jumping straight to the shiny automation object.

The intelligent process automation approach, which I discuss in my upcoming book, *Breaking Your Intelligent Process Automation Paradigms*, starts with standardizing and measuring recurring processes. This includes writing down the steps so that it can be repeatable (meaning you do it the same every time) and reproducible (meaning someone else can do it the same way you do it every time). Lately, I have seen a push to over-automate and people start to lose sight of their processes. Not paying attention to what has been automated will mean that mistakes could happen which will impact your brand. Your brand reflects how others perceive and remember you.

<u>Leverage.</u> The last step in DEAL is to leverage others who are much better at doing something on your productive list. I can build a website. I know HTML and can create a site on pretty much any system. However, I am not great at it because it is not what I do all the time. Hence, it is in my best interest to hire someone to design and build my website. When doing this; however, you tend to put yourself into a situation where you cannot change or update what has been done. So, you need to really consider what you are leveraging and why.

Technology. I cannot emphasize enough how today's technology can help you with your time management. First, ensure that you have systems and processes that help you operate efficiently. Do not be like the First Sergeant and delete 1,000 emails! Figure out how to set up your email system so it is easy to manage. Learn shortcuts and special keystrokes for productivity software. Create shortcuts on your computer and organize your files so they are easy to find – see Chapter 23. Learn how to fully leverage the tools you have first.

Look for ways to adopt technology to fill the gaps. There are many different phone apps that track activities, appointments and help you manage tasks. Find tools that help you. Consider finding a project management tool to keep track of your activities and to keep you on track. Two great books to read that will help you with time management and task completion are *Getting Things Done*, by David Allen, and *Execution*, by Lawrence Bossidy and Ram Charan.

My last point on technology is using your calendar to perform time blocking. Time blocking is a time management method of breaking up your day into blocks of time. Establish these time blocks on your calendar to work on specific activities. These activities might be productive, like schoolwork or writing, or other activities like lunch (NPR) or fitness (NPV). By blocking time in advance, you are making a conscious effort to focus your time. Plus, using your calendar this way protects your time from being usurped by others.

Unbelievably successful people are very good at managing their time. You marvel at how much and how easily they effortlessly get things done. And most of what they do is productive – focused on meeting their goals. In fact, when things do not support their goals, they often abandon them. Get good at time management – manage time before it manages you!

Chapter 24 Questions

1. What was the bad example of time management the author described in this chapter?

2. What is the difference between good and great time management?

3. What are the three things used to create a business transferable skill of time management?

4. How long should you conduct a time study for?

Essay Question

Why do you feel it is important to fully understand how you currently manage your time?

Chapter 24 Notes Page

Use this page to capture notes in each Part and Chapter

Chapter 25
Strategy and Culture

One of the most powerful transferable skills in business and in life is understanding strategy and culture. In fact, this book was built on the foundational concepts of strategy and culture. You may have heard Peter Drucker's famous quote, "Culture eats strategy for breakfast." But your strategy and how it is implemented should define your culture – without strategy, culture will create itself. If your strategy has not foundationally establishing what your culture should look like, then your strategy will never be effective.

Strategy – more specifically, strategic planning and implementation – is the most important skill I have. It is often the most unused or misused skill in the world! Understanding what strategy is, what it impacts, how to create it, and how to implement it, will make you super valuable anywhere. In my book, *Overcoming Organizational Myopia*, I discuss the importance of good strategy and culture when breaking through siloed organizations. A future book, *Think Big Take Small Steps*, will address the five reasons all strategies fail to achieve defined goals.

In Part 2, you learned hands-on application of good strategy development and implementation. A great strategy is made up of four things: mission/purpose, vision, values/principles, and goals. Too often, when an organization creates its strategy, it is just words, created in a boardroom and plastered on the organization's walls. They mean nothing and they drive nothing. Startups and small businesses often build a business plan because someone told them to build one. They download a template from the Internet and struggle to fill it out. These "plans" are never looked at again – mainly because they were worthless to begin with! Knowing the true basics of creating and implementing a strategic plan will propel you head and shoulders above everyone around you. Just remember. You need to create one properly. Anyone who has ever participated in strategic planning thinks they are an expert – not true.

I first learned about strategic planning in 1998. My mentor, Master Sergeant Jerry Peña, involved me in an effort to create the Air Force's 11-step Strategic Planning Model. It was a very detailed approach with many more sub steps than the high-level 11, but it was a very thorough approach. I eventually taught others how to facilitate strategic planning, using that model. We even used this approach to assist the Belgian Air Force in creating its first successful strategic plan.

A few years later, I worked with the Air Force to create a simpler approach to planning – the Air Force Performance Planning Approach. This was in response to Congressional direction called the Government Performance Results Act (GPRA). This Act directed all government agencies to create performance-based strategies that demonstrated measurable results. This was about the same time that I started building my own Personal Strategic Plan.

Three years later, I found myself back at the design table working with the Air Force on its Capability Planning Approach. The military had gone through several theater and minor conflicts and was being stretched very thin. They needed a way to continue to meet GPRA requirements, and to be able to respond to everything going on in the world. Also, by now, I had over seven years of experience as a military war planner.

Until I went to work for Booz | Allen | Hamilton, I would not say I was very good at strategic planning. I thought I was, but I was wrong. I was in my Ha period of Shuhari (see Chapter 15), and I was learning from many different sources. This is also when I discovered the five reasons all strategies fail, and embarked on my Ri journey with strategic planning.

This chapter will provide you with my many years of knowledge in an abbreviated version, so that you can be well-versed in strategy development and implementation.

Mission. Your mission is what you do, and your purpose is why you do it. Too often, people want to list how they do something in their mission. The best mission does not describe how the job gets done, just what the job is. Your purpose is *why* you do it, written from the customer's point of view. If you make head coverings (hats, caps, headscarves, beanies, etc.) then your purposes are to cover the head, protect the scalp, and make people look good. Your stated purpose should never be "to make money," or "to be the best." A mission and purpose should intrinsically motivate you and all who support or interact with that statement. When combined, (mission and purpose) this becomes your mission statement.

Vision. Too often, vision statements either sound just like the mission (just reworded some), or they lack any way to measure success. I often see things like this:

> *Mission: We make hats and caps to protect your head.*

> *Vision: Make world-class hats and caps.*

This does little to motivate anyone and provides little measurable direction. Here is another way to make mission and vision statements that might excite people a little bit more:

> *Mission: We protect your most valuable asset – your brain – and make you look good doing it.*

> *Vision: The brains of the world protected by the best-looking head coverings available.*

I know, this hat company may not be your style, but you get the concept. People want to get together behind something bigger than themselves. These statements leave a great deal of freedom for the how – headscarves to military helmets. The vision pushes for global domination (brains of the world) and beautiful design, all while protecting someone's noggin.

Values. Every company should have defined values or principles. In chapter 12, I described how you can create your own personal belief system. Companies should establish a set of guidelines as well. These simple words should drive expected behaviors in an organization. Usually, the value or principle is kept short, but it is fully explained in a separate document that outlines each value or principle. In 1997, during the Air Force's quality movement, it published *The Little Blue Book*. This was a small core values handbook that explained the values of Integrity First, Service Before Self, and Excellence in All We Do. These three simple values have lasted with the Air Force for 25 years now.

Values are created to embody the desired behaviors of a company and dissuade the undesirable. For my coaching and consulting practice, my core principles are Trusted Advisor and Solution Provider. Embedded within these two statements are nine key values. These define how my company operates and what my clients can expect.

Goals. The last key component of a strategic plan are the goals of the plan. Each goal is actually a broad area of objectives, initiatives, and actions that move the company closer to its vision. This is why your vision must be measurable. Just like we did in Part 2, goals are created to close the gaps between where your company is today and where it desires to be in the future. A strategy without goals is not a plan. All too often, goals are created by going around a conference room table and having each executive list the most important project they are working on. Where is the strategy in that? Goals are long-term in nature (three to five years) and, as I said above, broken down into objectives, initiatives, and actions.

Once you have these four elements established, you have a great strategic plan ready to implement.

Culture is a product of two things – your strategy and what you allow to happen. Your mission, purpose, vision, values, and principles all define what your organization should look like and how it should operate. However, what happens, or is allowed to happen, is what truly becomes your company's reality. This is culture.

I worked with a company that had a well-defined set of values. These values were embedded throughout the organization, and you could see evidence of them at work everywhere.

However, it also had an unspoken culture, based on things that were allowed. Leaders of the company were constantly coming up with new ideas. The problem was that before an idea had been fully formalized, the company and the leaders were on to the next new idea. Thus, there were years of unfinished projects in the company, and what ideas it did keep had very little rigor.

Because of this, employees across the company saw everything as something new, and that people would just move on quickly. Thus, the employees never replied to requests to do things because no one ever followed up. Essentially, everyone in the company simply focused on their business-as-usual work and ignored new projects because they knew the leaders would soon lose interest and focus on another pet project. The company had great values, but its behavior had also created poor cultural norms.

To establish a culture, start with the strategy. Do people know it? Do the company and its employees follow it? Once you have identified what the company's culture is, look for the way things get done or do not get done in the company. Some poor cultural norms I have seen in the past are as follows:

<u>Socializing Risk.</u> New activities, projects, or endeavors are approved by committee, so no one can be held accountable. No one person takes initiative or the lead. Ideas take forever to get approved. The company is extremely risk-averse and has low innovation.

<u>Meetings equal Productivity.</u> The belief that attending meetings means that you are getting things done. The day is filled with meetings. There are no minutes or action items from the meetings. Multiple meetings tend to be about the same thing.

<u>Need to Add Value.</u> All too often, senior executives feel that they need to always be adding value to work products. They change words in papers and presentations that never affect the meaning. Employees end up turning in sloppy, unfinished work because they know their boss will change their work no matter how good it is.

<u>You Are Making Us Look Bad.</u> As a process improvement professional, I see this all the time. When someone works hard or tries to improve themselves or the job, those around them try to stop them. Everyone is happy to live and operate in a substandard life. When someone steps forward, everyone beats them down because they see that person who is trying to improve as making them look bad.

You do not have to be an expert at creating a strategic plan, implementing strategies, or building a culture. However, being knowledgeable in these things will help you become unbelievably successful.

Chapter 25 Questions

1. Who said, "Culture eats strategy for breakfast?"

2. When it came to strategic planning, in what stage of Shuhari was the author while working at Booz | Allen | Hamilton?

3. What was the government act that directed strategic planning in the military?

4. What two elements does a mission statement include?

Essay Question

Why do you feel that knowing about strategic planning is important to anyone?

Chapter 25 Notes Page

Use this page to capture notes in each Part and Chapter

Chapter 26
Leadership and Management

I always believed that you cannot be a great leader without being a great manager. Conversely, you cannot be a great manager without being a great leader. This concept is what I refer to as "Leaderment." I originally created this term in 2004, while attending the Air Force Noncommissioned Officer Academy at Lackland Air Force Base, Texas. I later defined this term in a 2014 blog.

Most people realize that leadership and management are two different things. Some people see them as just roles in an organization, but leaders and managers have different perspectives on the business.

Management is a process of controlling programs and projects or people to achieve a desired outcome or goal. The five basic functions of management are: planning, organizing, staffing, leading, and controlling. You might note that "leading" is considered one of the five basic functions. But a manager is not a leader? Or is it?

If management, according to the American Management Association (AMA), is the art of getting things done through others, and having them do it willingly, how is this different from leadership? Leadership is the art of influencing others to do things they normally would not do on their own. In essence, managers and leaders want the same thing – people doing things and accomplishing objectives. Management; however, is a "controlling function," where leadership is an "influencing" function." Leaders motivate people in a direction through vision setting and inspiration. The question is, would a good manager be better if they could influence as well as control? Would a good leader be better if they knew how to effectively control as well as influence? The answer is, they would be great! The best managers and leaders easily transition in and out of the appropriate roles of leader or manager, as appropriate for any given situation.

Those who have mastered Leaderment, engage their entire organization (employees, partners, and customers) to willingly participate in the continual improvement and growth of the company. What does this engagement look like? Great leaders and managers (masters of Leaderment) create an environment that fosters, promotes, and supports constant and consistent engagement. This is performed by focusing on four key organizational elements. They are as follows:

1. Direction.
2. Communication.
3. Development.
4. Quality.

Let us refer to our employees, partners, and customers as "stakeholders." The employees work for the company. Employees range from the highest-ranking leader to the front-line contractor. Your partners are those who support your company through services and support. Your customers drive your company through the purchase of your products and services. Today, many companies still only attempt to focus on engaged employees. This chapter is designed to educate you on how to employ Leaderment for full stakeholder engagement. Therefore, when discussing engagement, we will use the term stakeholders to include all groups described above.

Direction. The first role in Leaderment is to establish strategy and culture (see Chapter 25). Regardless of your level or role in a company, you can establish these things. If you are the senior leader (owner, president, managing director, or CEO), you obviously set the direction for the entire organization. Everyone below that level learns, understands, aligns, and promotes the direction. Stakeholders engage more when an organization has an inspiring direction that is bigger than itself.

I have always liked the full stakeholder engagement examples of companies like Apple, TOMS Shoes, Disney, and Harley Davidson. These companies created inspiring directions that their stakeholders flocked to. Look at those who demand that their Apple i-whatever is the best thing ever, people running around with mouse ears on, or Harley owners – bet you cannot pick them out of a crowd! This is full stakeholder engagement, starting with direction at its finest.

Leaderment creates, promotes, and lives an inspired direction. This is why your direction – your mission and vision – in your Personal Strategic Plan is so important to get right first. I spent 21 years in the Air Force. I started out making $16,000 a year (less than $8 an hour) and I was entrusted with the protection of multimillion-dollar aircraft and munitions. Munitions that could devastate a population! Thousands of Americans enlist in the military every year – over 150,000 to be exact. Most enlist for some tangible benefit (e.g., money, security, education, etc.). However, these men and women of the Armed Forces willingly put their lives on the line every day of their enlistment. For what? For a concept called "Freedom." They, like teachers, doctors, nurses, police, fire, volunteers, and many others, do what they do because of the direction even though many get paid very little or nothing for their tremendous sacrifices.

Communication. In Chapter 28, we will discuss personal and professional communication as a business transferable skill. Communication, in the context of full stakeholder engagement and Leaderment is more organizationally led. And organizational communication is perhaps the most difficult thing for businesses to master. Hence, communication is typically one of the top problems I see when coaching and consulting.

How does Leaderment solve and overcome the communication conundrum? What can you do to improve communication and master Leaderment? Excellent communication, which engages stakeholders, exhibits seven factors. They are as follows:

1. Strategic.
2. Constant.

3. Consistent.
4. Multimodal.
5. Transparent.
6. Honest.
7. All-directional.

Strategic communication is communication with purpose. Poor communication is haphazard and without direction or stated expectation. Leaderment always communicates with purpose. That purpose might be for awareness, understanding, acceptance, or advocacy, but all communication is well-thought-out and specifically tailored to the audience with measured expectations.

When communication is consistent, it aligns with a strategic purpose as well as with past communications. Have you ever seen someone talk out both sides of their mouth? Ever had someone tell you something, but tell someone else something different? Ever witness someone tell you to do something, but not do it themselves? These represent inconsistent communication and poor Leaderment.

I was working with a client who said no one was following the company policy. I asked if the employees were aware of the policy. She ensured me that they were aware – she had sent it out in an email to everyone … Once! This is a typical problem with communication – the fire and forget mentality. Constant communication continuously transmits a consistent and strategic message and ensures that it has been heard, understood, and acknowledged. This is why soldiers in the Army use the phrase "Hooah," also spelled "HUA." Military members respond to verbal direction with this motivated response to emphasize that the message got through to them. Leaderment relies on consistent and strategic messages presented in a constant manner to drive a heard, understood, and acknowledged (HUA) mentality in stakeholders.

Constantly communicating a consistent and strategic message over a single channel of communication means that it will still only reach a limited audience. Multimodal communication means that the organization employs every possible and probable mode (or channel) of communication. Key messages might be communicated via face-to-face, one-on-one, email, print, television, radio, social media, etc. Good communication is replicated across many different modes of communication.

Transparent communication can be very hard for people – especially leaders and managers. Transparent means to openly communicate all that you know, all the time. Those who have not mastered Leaderment hold back information for various reasons – sometimes it is due to greedy control and other times due to protection. Bad communicators hide behind all manner of excuses to prevent the open sharing of information. I shared my experience previously of being laid off as the COO of a company. I was the second in command of that company – the right hand to the CEO. However, the week prior to my layoff, the CEO stopped communicating with me – he shut off transparency.

Imagine if he were to ask me to rejoin the company after COVID. What might I say? How engaged would I be, always wondering if he was keeping important details from me that might impact my very existence?

Along with transparency comes honesty. Tell your stakeholders the truth. If you do not know the truth, tell them you do not know. A lack of transparency and honesty destroys trust, and trust is the most important thing you must have to build full stakeholder engagement.

The last factor important to communication is all-directional. Your communication must encourage more than simple downward- or outward-directed approaches. All-directional communication allows stakeholders to communicate openly with you and with each other. The leader or manager who restricts communication, restricts engagement. Making everyone go through you and not directly to others, or making people go through others to communicate with you, is not all-directional.

Development. The leader and manager who continually develops their stakeholders also practices the Law of Compensation from Chapter 6. In Simon Sinek's book, *Leaders Eat Last*, Sinek shares that the most important thing you can give people is your time. However, I believe freely giving one's time to help others grow is perhaps the most selfless of acts. I have always loved this anonymous quote, "You are never taller than when you stoop to help a child." This embodies the essence of developing others to encourage engagement. Development can take many forms when working with your stakeholders. Helping employees with direction, by creating a development plan, provides a clear and unambiguous roadmap to growth. Supporting someone's goals is part of development, as is teaching and imparting knowledge and wisdom. This book is a tool designed for your ultimate development to become unbelievably successful.

Quality. Stakeholders can recognize an emphasis on quality when they see it. When Leaderment measures performance and results, and holds people accountable to these measures, quality happens. Do those you work with all do the same job differently? If they do, then quality is not predictable. Does your company deliver its products and services and hope that nothing goes wrong? Are there people around you who do not carry their own weight? These are all signs of poor quality. Building quality is actually very easy. In fact, Chapters 30 and 31 help you understand the transferable skills necessary to build quality in any organization. Leaders and managers set expectations, measure performance and results, and hold people accountable. When your engagement is high, stakeholders will always look for ways to make your products and services better – they will feel empowered to improve.

Leaderment is a state of great leadership and management that anyone can achieve. You do not need to hold a position of power to practice Leaderment. Those who do practice Leaderment focus on driving the highest levels of full stakeholder engagement by focusing on direction, communication, development, and quality.

Collaboration and Teamwork

Collaboration and teamwork are key capabilities for anyone in leadership and management to have. This means being able to accept that you do not have all the answers. It is generating diversity of thought. Are you able to negotiate many ideas – some passionate? Do you make everyone feel as if they were part of the decision? This is powerful.

However, I believe there is a difference between being collaborative and then making a decision, and what I refer to as "socializing risk."

I have worked with two large Fortune 500 companies where they use the guise of collaboration to socialize risk. When the decision itself is collaborative, then you have a problem.

This is not true collaboration. Typically, the people who want something done will hold pre-meetings to get everyone on their side. They are collaborative one-on-one, but they have an agenda. They just want everyone to collaboratively agree on the decision so there is no one person to be held accountable.

This is not true collaboration that leads to teamwork, and it displays poor leadership and management traits. Consider this on your journey to becoming unbelievably successful.

Chapter 26 Questions

1. What are the four organizational elements of full stakeholder engagement?

2. What is Leaderment?

3. What is one example company from the chapter with a strong direction?

4. What is one of the top problems the author often sees when coaching and consulting?

Essay Question

Describe when great leadership and management (Leaderment) would be important outside of a business environment.

Chapter 26 Notes Page

Use this page to capture notes in each Part and Chapter

Chapter 27
Change Management and Change Readiness

Previously, in multiple chapters, I talked about change. In fact, this has been one of my most studied subjects. In 2019, I even built a workshop for future leaders on leading change. Your ability to manage change as it occurs will define your ability to become unbelievably successful.

This part of the book, as highlighted in the beginning of Chapter 24, is all about preparing you for change which is inevitable. As a result of this book, I expect you to become a change zealot! To become unbelievably successful, you must constantly seek change. This is what your Personal Strategic Plan is designed to do – change you.

So, this chapter is designed to provide you with a basic understanding of change.

When I discuss change and change management, Kurt Lewin's model for change is always where I start. Take a block of ice that you want to turn into a beautiful ice sculpture. You might have seen some people hack away at the ice with chisels, axes, and saws to create a sculpture. In fact, this is how many people manage change. They use brute force to shape the frozen block into what they desire, hoping not to make a mistake and ruin the sculpture. But there is a better way.

Take the time to define what your sculpture will look like. Build a mold of the sculpture. Melt the ice into water. Pour it into the mold. And then refreeze the water into the desired shape and structure, using the mold.

This is how you effectively manage change. The thing you want to change is like the frozen block of ice. You can go to work chipping, sawing, and chopping at it to turn it into something only you can see. Or you can build a mold and let everyone see what the ice will look like when you are done. Which is better? Providing a vision of what the change will look like, in your head and for others to see, is the first step in change. Otherwise, everyone around you will wonder what it will look like when you are done. This creates fear and concern, which drives resistance. The better you can picture the end result of change and the benefits from the change, the easier the process of change will be accepted by you and those with whom you work.

Consider the aggressive cutting and shaping of the ice block. How efficient is this process? Is it easily replicated? What is the chance that something will go wrong? What would you have to do if you made a major mistake? Now, consider the process of using a mold to make the sculpture. How easy would it be to make this sculpture over-and-over again? If you made a major mistake, how hard would it be to correct it? Establishing an efficient, effective, and repeatable approach to change helps you make changes much easier and quicker. Think about your Personal Strategic Planning Process. This process produces constant changes in you – moving you ever closer to your goals. The more you employ this process, the faster you change. Look for ways to manage all change efficiently and effectively in your life.

When you complete a change, recognize the accomplishment, and learn from any mistakes you made along the way. In the military, after most projects, everyone comes together to conduct an after-action review. They discuss what worked, what did not work, and what they will do differently next time. This behavior creates an ever-growing and evolving capability. It allows one to expertly and efficiently face an ever-changing volatile, uncertain, complex, and ambiguous (VUCA) world.

If you wish to manage change in an unbelievably successful manner, you must create a clear vision of the change; find ways to make the change efficiently and effectively; and take time to recognize and reflect on the change itself. This is simply all there is to change management.

When you are competent at managing change, it is easy to embrace change. You begin to look for opportunities to make things better through change. You become a change zealot. Those who embrace and seek out change opportunities also practice change readiness.

Being change ready is crucial to becoming unbelievably successful.

In the business world today, most companies are "managing" change. This means they are dealing with change as it occurs, and they are trying to make sure that the changes that are occurring will enhance some or all the organization. However, because change in business is happening almost-constantly, simply managing change as it occurs will leave the business behind the power curve. By preparing your organization and its stakeholders for constant change, you create change readiness which makes you more effective in the business environment.

Today, I love change. This was not always the case. As it is for many others, change represented the unknown and I was afraid of it. I talk more about overcoming fear to increase your personal motivation in Chapter 35. Typically, anyone who fears change, will resist change. And it follows that when we are resistant to change, we look for ways to avoid change as a way of protecting ourselves. We expend energy, and hence waste it on activities that are focused on *not* changing. When I started to simply accept and, as a result, adopt change, I was able to move on and move forward. That is the benefit of becoming very good at embracing and managing change.

Chapter 27 Questions

1. What happens when we resist change?

2. What are the three steps to change, based on Lewin's model?

3. Using a mold for change creates what kind of approach?

4. What workshop did the author create that was related to change?

Essay Question

How do you feel about change in your life and how does it affect you?

Chapter 27 Notes Page

Use this page to capture notes in each Part and Chapter

Chapter 28
Personal and Professional Communication

In my story in Chapter 3, and in relating my Personal Strategic Plan in Part 2, I talked about becoming a recognized speaker. You might be thinking that I had always been someone that liked to get up in front of an audience.

Not so!

In senior high school, I was required to take my first speech class. I think most of us are required to take Speech in school at some point. Well, I was terrified of speaking in front of people. I was so terrified that I would cry and become speechless.

Did you know that over 80 percent of the world's population is afraid to speak in front of a group? Did you also know that the fear of public speaking (glossophobia) is the number one fear in the world – ranking higher than the fear of death? If you fear the podium and speaking before a crowd, you now know you are not alone.

Communication is not all about standing in front of thousands of people and sharing a message. That is just one of the scarier parts of communication. Communication has multiple meanings and definitions. However, at its basic root, communication is simply the transference of information.

Everyone should master writing, speaking, and listening as business transferable communication skills. Imagine if this book were full of errors and did not make any sense. You certainly would not have made it to this chapter. You probably would have put the book down a long time ago. Becoming an effective writer is one step to mastering communication. You must take the time to organize your thoughts; express them in a logical and understandable order; and eliminate spelling, punctuation, formatting, and grammatical errors. I am constantly amazed by how sloppy some are in their published writing.

Obviously, there is a difference in personal and professional writing, as much as there is a difference in written versus spoken communication. You may have noticed that I have not used any contractions in this book, unless "they're in quotes" and represent something someone actually said. Using contractions can be considered a form of informal (or personal) writing. Professional writing is detailed and technical in nature, with main points repeated for emphasis. For instance, I emphasized how each subject in this book is related to your Personal Strategic Plan, which is designed to help you become unbelievably successful. Depending on your audience, your professional writing may need to be concise and without repetition but, in general, professional writing should have a more formal style than your personal writing, which is probably informal and may even be somewhat humorous.

Always remember to edit! Regardless of whether your written document is personal or professional, edit your writing before sending it. I was recently reviewing someone's published book on their personal development journey. It was so poorly written and full of so many errors I found it almost impossible to read. I suggest you employ the following editing methods. In personal writing, whether it is a simple text message, email to a friend, or an online post, set it aside for a few minutes (at a minimum), then give it a second look. You will be amazed at how many small errors you will find that you did not notice making when you composed the communication. If the work is professional, but not crucial, use the same method. If your important professional work will be seen by several people, it is always helpful to have a second set of eyes review the document before you send it out. If your work will be seen by many and will be lasting, get several people to review it. Why leave a sloppy or unprofessional impression when you have the ability to avoid doing so? Once you have delivered a product with errors, the damage is done.

When speaking, regardless of whether you are doing so on a personal or professional level, focus on three things: clear, concise, and effective. Speaking clearly means you can be heard and understood. Speaking with a serious accent, mumbling when you speak, or speaking far too softly, are examples of barriers to effective communication. If you struggle with these things, work to fix them.

Unlike some types of writing, speaking needs to be to the point. If someone is rambling in a book or a paper, it may be distracting, but you can just jump ahead. If someone is rambling while speaking, you are forced to listen to everything (or totally zone out). If you cannot be concise and to the point, most people will zone out and stop listening.

Effective speakers eliminate distractors from their presentation. Verbal pauses, like "um," "uh," and "ah," become annoying after a while. Overusing filler words such as "like," "you know," "literally," and "basically," detracts from your message and makes your message less concise. We use these verbal pauses and filler words because we do not like silence – it is uncomfortable. So, we put noises and words in between our thoughts. This makes our message difficult to understand and even annoying. It is ok to pause while you are organizing your thoughts, just do not do it verbally.

So, how did I change from being deathly terrified, as I mentioned at the beginning of this Chapter, to wanting to become an expert presenter?

I took college speech classes, joined Toastmasters International, I studied, and I practiced. I faced my fears of public speaking a couple of years in the Air Force, by taking two speech classes in college at the same time. One class was personal and the other was professional communication. Over time, I became more comfortable and confident in public speaking. I joined Toastmasters International about 10 years after I completed those 2 speech classes. I wish I had joined Toastmasters so much earlier! I recommend everyone join Toastmasters to become better speakers. Toastmasters teaches about speaking, listening, and evaluating, which are valuable for becoming unbelievably successful. Additionally, they have one of the best business leadership development approaches I have ever seen.

The last skill to master is listening. Toastmasters, again, is very helpful in teaching you to listen – specifically because you are often listening to evaluate. Two things unbelievably successful people are really good at are actively listening and listening to understand.

Active listening requires the listener to fully concentrate on, respond to, and remember what was said. Active listeners remove all distractions when someone is talking to them, so they can focus on what is being said. They repeat, reflect, and reframe messages and take notes where required. They also document important conversations quickly after the conversation is over.

All too often, we listen so that we can respond rather than understand. When we listen to respond, instead of actively listening, we start formulating our response while someone is still talking. And, accordingly, lose much of the message. In addition to learning to become an active listener, here are three things that you can do to improve your listening and, therefore, your understanding:

1. Do not interrupt.
2. Be empathetic.
3. Ask open-ended questions.

"We were given one mouth and two ears, so we should listen twice as much as we speak," Epictetus. But we do not do this. Why? My wife and I often accuse each other of interrupting while the other are talking. It has such an impression on me, that I try to consciously not interrupt in all conversations, not just those with my wife. As humans, we tend to naturally want to respond to someone speaking to us, even when we have not heard everything they said. Try this and you will realize how often you unknowingly interrupt others. Pick one person with whom you have a lot of interaction and consciously refrain from interrupting them when they are talking – focus on listening instead. This may help you to become aware of your listening habits and form new ones.

When someone is speaking, more is being said than the words coming out of their mouth. We communicate both verbally and nonverbally. Verbally, aside from the actual message, the words used to convey that message are also important. People who are upset or being forceful will use more directive and demanding words such as "must," "will," "should," and "shall." When upset, they might also use profanity. The speaker's tone of voice and rate of speech can also say a lot about their mood. Nonverbally, watch their facial expressions and body language. Many times, someone's verbal message does not match their non-verbal signals. By paying greater attention to verbal and nonverbal communication cues, you can become more empathetic to the speaker's message.

Another method to become an active listener and understand more is to ask open-ended questions. Instead of simply responding, or just nodding, respond with the purpose of understanding. Asking open-ended questions, those that cannot be answered with a simple "yes" or "no" response, will help you to become a more active listener. These questions require the speaker to elaborate on key points of their message which helps the listener better understand the speaker's message.

More and more, computer programmers are perfecting predictive text algorithms. These provide simple and quick responses on social media, text messages, and I have even started seeing them in email software. What I have noticed; however, is the responses seem very close-ended, basically shutting down further conversation. "I am driving. I am in a meeting. I'm occupied," etc. I have stopped using predictive text to respond to messages because of their close-ended nature.

Exceptional communicators write, speak, and listen very well. Developing these skills will help you in every facet of your personal and professional life and will propel you along your journey of becoming unbelievably successful.

Chapter 28 Questions

1. What communication skills should you master?

2. What three things do you focus on when speaking?

3. What is glossophobia?

4. Why do we use verbal pauses when we speak?

Essay Question

How can you improve your listening skills?

Chapter 28 Notes Page

Use this page to capture notes in each Part and Chapter

Chapter 29
Program and Project Management

These next three chapters will discuss more technical business transferable skills. Although the five previously discussed business transferable skills are taught in school, only these last two have a formalized body of knowledge around them. Program and project management is perhaps the most quantifiably transferrable of these eight transferable skills. The Project Management Institute (PMI) has professionalized these skills by creating course and certification work that leads to one of the most recognized professional certifications in business today – Project Management Professional (PMP).

This chapter is not a certification primer. It is not designed to make you a program and project manager. However, whether you realize it or not, everything in the world happens through programs and projects, so this is a very important business transferable skill to learn. Think about it. Even when you decide to take a vacation, what do you do? You plan it. The vacation is a project!

A project is an individual or group undertaking that is carefully planned and designed to achieve a particular result which is usually to create, change, or remove something. Projects have a defined beginning and end, with a limited duration. Programs, on the other hand, are a planned series of future events designed to achieve a particular result. These long-running activities employ projects to create, change, or remove things within the program. However, not all projects are part of a larger program.

I want you to think about each goal area in your Personal Strategic Plan as a program. Every objective within your goal area operates like a project. For me, becoming a proven expert was one of my six goal areas, thus, one of my six programs. It was an ongoing, long-term activity to professionalize myself through training and certification. When this goal area was created, I knew very little about certifications or how to obtain them. One of the first projects I embarked on was to research and find business certifications and training activities that would further my credibility in the business world and move me towards my vision.

Projects should have a definite start and stop. In the formal world of project management, the official start of a project is normally signified with a written contract – often called, "The Charter." This document outlines the expectations of the project, or its success criteria. Once the criteria are met, the project is complete. My first project in my proven expert goal area was to identify appropriate certifications and determine their requirements. The next step was to develop a plan and a time frame in which to obtain them.

Sometimes, a completed project will result in a repeatable process embedded in a program. These repeatable activities keep programs operational over time. My first project – to identify certification and training activities – resulted in an initial list. However, over time, the certifications and activities changed, and new ones were created so I am continually adjusting my list. Twenty years ago, Six Sigma Green and Black Belts were becoming available certifications and the PMP certification was gaining popularity. The combination of Lean and Six Sigma was just a concept back then. The only company focusing on change management certifications was Prosci, and I did not even learn about that certification until 2008. Certifications in Agile project management have only been around for about ten years.

My initial project to research certification and training became a repeatable process. Every year, I reevaluate current certifications, log any training I have completed, and evaluate future opportunities. One rule I instituted at the outset of my journey was that I would never get a certification that required me to spend money to recertify every few years. Can you imagine if I had over ten certifications, each requiring annual recertification activities and costs? I would end up spending most of my time maintaining expensive recertifications rather than focusing on continually growing with my Personal Strategic Plan.

Now that you understand what programs and projects are and how integral they are in our lives and your Personal Strategic Plan, let us focus on the basics of project management.

When you decide to undertake a project (or someone asks or tells you to), the first step is to clearly define expectations. What do you intend to accomplish with this project? Too often, we, as humans, simply start working on something without really understanding what is expected or what is to be accomplished. I refer to this phenomenon as "Jumping To Do!" We excitedly rush in to work on the project without mapping out a project plan. We then find ourselves well into the project, or even done with it, only to find out that we went in the wrong direction. So, your first step is to understand the expectations (or success criteria) for completion of the project.

After writing down the expectations for the project, consider how you will measure them to ensure they have been obtained. These measures can be milestone-based, qualitative, or quantitative. You may determine that you currently do not have a way to measure completion of an expectation. If this is the case, you will need to create a way to measure as part of your project. Often, you will want to collect a baseline metric prior to doing anything on the project. Baselines provide a starting point for your effort. I will discuss this more in Chapter 29.

Knowing the expectations for the project, and how to measure the achievement of those expectations will help tremendously towards a successful project. Once I have my expectations and measures, I like to define planning specifics. These are things like who will oversee the effort, who is sponsoring the project, and whether a team is required. Importantly, you will need to determine whether you will need a budget for the project, whether the project has already been budgeted and approved and, if so, whether the money is available. Do some research to see if something like this has been done before.

Someone may have made a similar effort in the past – and it might have failed. Find out what happened and what lessons can be incorporated into your effort. Determine whether you need additional information or details to be successful. If so, research those before doing too much on the project.

Armed with all this information, lay out the high-level steps and milestones that you think will be required to implement this project. Do not forget that part of the project must include the steps to be taken to make the changes from your project stick, such as communication, documentation, training, and measurement. When your project is backed by clear, measurable expectations, it will be much more successful.

This approach to planning will be fully described in my upcoming book called, *Stop Jumping to Do*. I created this simple approach to project management working with a client's strategic implementation plan 14 years ago. The Air Force Civil Engineer had a strategic plan (not created by me). One of the strategic objectives was to create new Fire Department training. The Fire Department was managed by Civil Engineering in the Air Force. The Colonel in charge of the objective – a project – went about creating and implementing new training as required in the strategic plan. I remember the meeting well. When the officer presented the objective as "Completed" in a strategic planning update meeting, the Civil Engineer asked if fire awareness and preparedness had increased, and false alarms decreased. He also rattled off some other questions – expectations. The Colonel, a bit surprised, replied that he was unaware that these were expectations of the objective.

Every day, people start work on projects without fully understanding why they are doing them, or what is truly expected. I am adamant that your Personal Strategic Plan be very clear to avoid landing in that trap. Practice asking these questions before you begin any endeavor, because, to become unbelievably successful, you need to get very good at implementing successful projects (for yourself and others) quickly and effectively.

Chapter 29 Questions

1. What is a project?

2. What is a program?

3. What is the most recognized professional project management certification in business today?

4. Are your objectives in your Personal Strategic Plan considered programs or projects?

Essay Question

Provide and describe an example of a program and project from your own personal life.

Chapter 29 Notes Page

Use this page to capture notes in each Part and Chapter

Chapter 30
Process Management and Process Improvement

If everything is a program or a project, as highlighted in Chapter 29, then you can think of process management as a program, and process improvement as discrete projects within that program. My journey of improving businesses started when I learned about process improvement in the early 90s. At that time, I learned about the Air Force's Seven-step Continuous Improvement Process. The concepts of Lean and Six Sigma were still growing in popularity and would not be combined into one approach until much later. Since the early 90s, I have continued to learn about process improvement and the various methodologies that exist to provide myself with the best knowledge and tools available – all aligned to my Personal Strategic Plan.

The various methodologies aside, process management and improvement are easy to understand as business transferable skills. If everything we do is a project within a series of programs, then how we do everything is a process within process management. This is how everything in the world works, including in business. Some things might not feel like they are a program, project, or process, but that is simply because they lack visible rigor and standardization.

When you get up in the morning, you enact a series of processes – from feeding your pets, to making coffee, to getting dressed. Everything – simply everything – we do, every day, is done via a series of steps with a start and finish. Once you recognize this, your life will forever change.

This chapter is designed to make you dangerous with a new business transferable skill. Experts in the field of process improvement certainly exist in the world today. They are typically identified by a certain color "belt," or they are called "sensei." Recently, I was sitting with a new client, and we were discussing her restaurant operation. I was highlighting some of her typical processes– serving customers, making food, pouring drinks, etc. She had never considered any of these as a process. "How do you know all of this stuff?" She asked. I told her I had many years' experience in process improvement and was a Lean Six Sigma Master Black Belt. Like many people, she thought I was talking about a "belt" in martial arts. In similar fashion to martial arts, colored belt designations are awarded to individuals as they progress through the various levels of Lean Six Sigma.

In the military, we used to use a phrase called, "Just Educated Enough to Pass" (JEEP). You were called a JEEP when you were new at anything in the military. This entire part of the book, on business transferable skills, is designed to turn you into a JEEP. So, let us discuss process management and process improvement at the "JEEP-level."

Process management – more commonly known as business process management – is basically taking a program-based view of continuous process improvement in an organization. Too often, process improvement occurs in companies in an unregulated and haphazard manner, which is what happens when things are done without a plan and a rigorous approach. Process management organizes process improvement so that it is managed and controlled to align with the company's strategic direction. Improvement, in a process management framework, does not happen in a vacuum, or as a one-off activity. Typically, a company's process management function is overseen by someone very experienced in process improvement. The program should establish standards for how process improvement projects are run, as well as professionalizing the process mindset across the organization.

As you might have noticed by now, all of the chapters in this part of the book work in concert with one another – together, they form the foundations of true operational excellence.

As a JEEP in process management, understand that process improvement is not nearly as effective on its own as it is when accompanied by strategy and direction. Improving processes without considering upstream and downstream impacts is called sub-optimization. Improving a part of your operation might make things worse for the whole of the operation.

Process improvement, on the other hand, is a very tactical response to dealing with problems in your organization. This is a project-based activity designed to fix issues and exceptions (known as "defects" in the process world) or reduce time or costs – allowing the company to do more with less. Essentially, process improvement is focused on making things better, faster, and cheaper.

You do not need to be an expert at process improvement to be good at managing and improving processes. Expertise is required to run large management or process improvement efforts, and to mentor, coach, and teach people in an organization. Here, you will learn a simple approach to process management.

A simple approach to process management

Process management, as a business transferable skill, starts with accepting ownership of the processes under your jurisdiction, and understanding how they fit into the flow of the rest of the operation. What does process ownership mean?

- Knowing the processes that you control
- Knowing the upstream and downstream processes that turn raw material into a finished product or service
- Knowing who the end customer is, what they expect, and how your processes impact this expectation
- Knowing how well your processes operate, how fast your processes operate, and how much they cost to operate

- Assigning sub-process ownership (sub-processes make up the major processes that you own)
- Ensuring sub-process owners know the sub-processes they own as well as you know the major (your) processes
- Ensuring sub-process owners know the necessary steps to complete their sub-processes

If every organization possessed this approach to process ownership, the need for external professional process expertise would be very small. However, many companies do not operate this way. Learn and practice this skill and you will be head and shoulders above your fellow peers.

When process owners "see" the defects in their processes, the speed (or lack of speed) of their processes, and the costs of their processes, they see that it is much easier to simply fix what is wrong and then, later, improve what is right. This is what should drive process improvement. However, it is often driven on gut feelings and knee-jerk reactions by those who do not know what is really happening or even what to look for. Do you see how valuable process management can be?

When the process owner asks for and obtains information (defects, speed, and cost) about their processes, they are using data to observe and manage their processes. In Chapter 31, I will discuss this topic in depth. For now, know that what all process owners really need to know are four simple data collection and visualization tools. They are the Check Sheet, Flowchart, Pareto Chart, and Control Chart. I will cover the two latter charts in the next chapter, but we will discuss the check sheet and flowchart here. These tools are the simplest for collection and visualization but are still extremely powerful.

Check Sheet. A check sheet is a data collection methodology used to collect real-time data for future use and analysis. At its basic form, it is a log used to count how often something occurs and, possibly, when or where it occurs. The check sheet can be modified to track any type of information on a real-time basis. This modified approach goes beyond simply counting because it records the details of the activity. Have you ever walked into an office and had to sign in and out? That type of check sheet typically collects data for who signed in; the time they signed in and possibly the time they signed out; and the purpose of the visit which might include who they were there to see. Remember in Chapter 24, I had you do a time study? The log you used was essentially a modified check sheet.

Check sheets allow you to record how often things occur, when they occur, and some detail around why they occurred. Structure your check sheet to easily collect information that is important to your process. Here are some examples of data to collect:

- How often and when does the process occur? Measure the frequency of the process by date and time.
- When does the process (or specific process steps) start and stop? Measure the process cycle time.
- Who was involved with the process? Capture all those in the process stream (i.e., customers, process operators, or others).
- How and when do defects occur?

Check sheets can be deceptively simple, but they require a level of rigor and accountability. As a process owner, if you make use of check sheets, your job will be to ensure that they are used correctly. Otherwise, any decisions made from the data could be flawed. Also, make sure that you are only collecting the data that you really need to understand and improve your process, and that the process operators understand the importance of accurate completion of the check sheets.

Flowcharts. Flowcharts – also called process maps, lean value streams, process charts, and flow diagrams – are used to design and document processes in a visual manner. Flowcharts can have many different looks and serve many purposes. Their main use is to show what is happening in a process (at a high level) and where potential problems might exist. All sub-process owners should have current individual flowcharts for each of their processes. The process owner should have a macro flowchart of the entire process with a breakout of all the sub-processes under their control.

Flowcharts do not need to be incredibly detailed. They can be as simple as a set of step-by-step work instructions for operators performing the work. Work instructions and flowcharts should be updated as process and procedure changes are made and reviewed at least once a year.

Without visibility into how everything operates, process owners are flying blind. Once the owner has full visibility, with check sheets, flowcharts, Pareto charts, and control charts, they can effectively and efficiently evaluate, modify, and operate. They can see what needs to be fixed or can be improved, where the improvement should occur, and why. Armed with this data, process owners can affect process improvement.

Process improvement efforts vary in size and complexity. However, typical continuous improvement processes are normally small and easy. Owners and operators should be able to make small improvements that make a significant impact. When projects involve multiple processes, especially under multiple process owners, or, if you are fixing a major problem, you should engage an expert in process improvement.

I was working with a document processing client who had a team that printed and mailed checks and associated letters to customers. This team had eight separate processes. After we mapped their processes, we identified eight potential defects. We used check sheets, Pareto charts, and control charts to track the defects for three months. After three months, I analyzed the data and found that several of their defect counts had significantly dropped after the first month. I thought they had possibly stopped using the check sheet correctly. No! They fixed the problems that were causing the defects!!! Just like that, with zero training on process improvement, they identified and fixed the problems!

A simple approach to process improvement

Any process owner must clearly understand and see what is happening in their process. Good process ownership that drives good process management will enable the process owner to identify and fix problems. If you know about the problem, you know what you expect the process improvement effort to fix. Be very clear about what is affected, what is occurring, how often it occurs, what it impacts, and what improvements you expect from the process. Albert Einstein said, "If I had an hour to solve a problem, I would spend 55 minutes understanding the problem and 5 minutes fixing it." I think that makes a lot of sense.

Remember the project management approach we discussed in Chapter 29? Use your project management skills for process improvement efforts.

I have found, through my many years of experience, that problem identification makes or breaks good process improvement. As we previously discussed, most process owners are not aware of or do not really understand component parts of the process they own. So, problems are often incorrectly or ambiguously defined and overblown or under appreciated. When the problem is not well defined, those tasked with correcting it spend a great deal of time determining if the problem even exists or end up solving the wrong problem. Thus, time and money are spent but nothing happens that has any positive impact.

Never lead with symptoms or solutions. As an owner, you can see when something is not working right just by looking at your tools. However, these tools only show you that you have a problem, not why. Once you have identified the problem, determine why it occurs. This is identification of the root cause of the issue.

First, analyze the data to look for trends. You cannot fix everything at once. Instead of working on everything, using your data analysis, identify and then focus on the biggest problem areas. Once you have targeted a specific area, use the 5 Whys analysis tool. Simply put, like a little kid, keep asking, "Why," until you have run out of answers. You know you have dug deeply enough, when the answer is, "It just is ... Okay!"

There are various tools that can be used for root cause analysis. Statistical analysis, cause-and-effect diagramming, and failure modes and effects analysis are all effective. You will be dealing with simpler issues that do not require a massive effort with deep experience, or complex issues requiring expert root cause analysis. Keep your root cause analysis simple. If the problem is extremely complex, retain an expert.

Once you have an idea why your process is not performing well, you can brainstorm potential solutions. Sometimes, the solution is obvious, while other times, you might identify several potential solutions. If you have more than one potential solution, prioritize the with respect to the order in which you want to test and evaluate by rank ordering across four things:

- Likelihood of solving the problem
- Level of effort to implement
- Amount of time to implement
- Cost to implement

Once each solution is ordered by rank, you can make an informed decision as to which to try first. When I say, "try," I really mean try. Do not go out and fully implement the top ranked change. Start with a controlled test or pilot project and see if the change you have chosen makes things operate better. If it is effective, fully implement.

Once you have improved your process, follow the guidance in Chapter 27 regarding change. Get rid of the old process; document the new process; train everyone affected, make sure they can perform the new process; and communicate the changes across the organization, as appropriate. Validate that your process improvement actions achieved your initial expectations. If so, close the effort. If not, look to other possible solutions to get you where you expected to be.

Intelligent Process Automation

The business world is changing very fast. Three types of process automation are impacting businesses everywhere, every day: Robotic process automation; Machine learning; and Artificial intelligence. From a business transferable skill perspective, these three skills are important because they are driving a lot of change in how work will be done in the future. In my upcoming book, *Breaking Your Intelligent Process Automation Paradigms*, I discuss running a process automation program effectively and efficiently.

Good process ownership, as described in this chapter, makes the transition to process automation much simpler. As with a standard non-automated process, check sheets, flowcharts, work instructions, and data provide the basic foundation for the intelligent process automation journey. Often, a strong process owner can quickly and painlessly adopt automation to drastically improve process quality, reduce costs, and eliminate risk. As you learn more about process management and process improvement, keep your eye on automation as well.

As you can see, a strong, but basic, understanding of this subject can be very beneficial in today's business world. This will become foundational in your journey of becoming unbelievably successful.

Chapter 30 Questions

1. What are the four data collection and visualization tools all process owners should know?

2. What does a modified check sheet do for you?

3. When do you use experts for process improvement?

4. How does the 5 Whys analysis tool work?

Essay Question

Describe a process that you perform on a regular basis.

Chapter 30 Notes Page

Use this page to capture notes in each Part and Chapter

Chapter 31
Business Insights

Although this is the last business transferable skill in this part of the book, it most certainly is not the least important. This skill is used everywhere in life, but many do not know how to use it effectively. In fact, it is really three interrelated skills: 1) Researching, 2) Collecting data, and 3) Analyzing the data collected.

When you make any decision, in business or otherwise, how do you make it? Do you rely on your gut or intuition? Do you shoot from the hip? Do you engage in fact finding? Maybe you have never really thought about it. The business transferable skill of business insight is, essentially, looking before you take the leap.

Throughout my life, insight was critical in forming **some** of my decisions. When I researched my desired career as a big rig driver, I learned that was not what I wanted to do with my life. After struggling with dead-end jobs, my research led me to make the decision to enter the Air Force. For my first 10 years in the Air Force, I was a cop. During a period of early separations in the Air Force, I saw my fellow enlisted members struggle to find jobs, and they ended up working as either a state trooper or prison guard. Deciding that was not the direction I wanted when I got out, I eventually retrained within the Air Force into Manpower and Quality.

However, I have made many other decisions in my life without thinking. Sometimes, they have worked out well and other times, they have not. Business insight helps you make well-thought-out, data-driven decisions in your life as well as in business.

Business insights start with curiosity. I considered creating a separate chapter on curiosity in Part 3 of this book, but decided that, without curiosity, there is no business insight. So, let us take a moment to talk about curiosity before we discuss researching, collecting data, and analyzing data.

When you are curious, you have a strong desire to know why. Curiosity creates the desire to become a lifelong learner, as we discussed in Chapter 14. The truly curious constantly seek new challenges and experiences to broaden their opportunities and their horizons.

Those who are curious by nature tend to create grander versions of the visions we discussed in Part 2 of this book and develop bigger kinds of the purposes we discussed in Chapter 4. As you can imagine by now, curiosity is a key component to becoming unbelievably successful.

In a survey, conducted by Curio Collection, only 20 percent of people said they had the "wanderlust gene." However, 91 percent considered themselves to be curious. It seems to me that more curious people could also have wanderlust. I think we all want to see ourselves as naturally curious, but in my experience, most people do not live a very curious life.

There are many ways to feed your curiosity – some outlined in this book. Chapters 11, 14, 17, and 36 all speak to ways you can become more curious in life. If you want to further increase your curiosity, a great book to read is called, "Curious," written by Ian Leslie.

Not too long ago, I was working with a CEO of a small business. We were discussing what we thought were desirable employee traits and which ones we felt were the most important in business, especially for executives. We settled on "being curious." Why? Because, when you are not curious, you mindlessly respond to what is happening or what you are told. Business seldom grows when that is what the employees do. Also, the employees do not grow on either a personal or professional level.

Here are three ways to improve your curiosity that have not already been covered in this book.

1. Be a kid again.
2. Take an "Innovation Holiday."
3. Drop the planning – for a moment.

1. **Be a kid again.**
   Allow yourself time to explore your inner child and just have fun. Think about some of the fun and inventive things you did as a kid and relive those experiences. When I lived in Berkley, Michigan, I had a close friend I hung out with. We would build plastic models of cars, trucks, and tanks. Then, we would take them to the park and blow them up with firecrackers. We would gather up all the pieces and rebuild Frankenstein-versions of new vehicles. We had a great time doing this.

   I am not recommending playing with firecrackers as a kid (I told you I made some bad decisions in life), but you could buy four different models of vehicles, pour all the parts into one box, and make one vehicle out of the four. Whatever you do, make it fun and inventive and tap into your inner child.

2. **Take an "Innovation Holiday."**
   In business today, this is referred to as a "hackathon." Hackathons are structured curiosity events that organizations run to find creative solutions to a problem or to come up with new product ideas. I have been part of many very fun and exciting hackathon-like events. A hackathon is an event where people engage in rapid and collaborative problem solving over a relatively short period of time.

To do this on your own, schedule a day once a quarter to dedicate as your Innovation Holiday. Each quarter, pick a problem. It can be a problem you are facing or that society is facing – it does not matter. Spend the day researching (see more on that in this chapter), brainstorming, and hypothesizing a solution. Whether the solution is actually viable does not really matter, as what you want to achieve is the act of being actively curious about the problem.

3. **Drop the planning.**
Yes, you read that right. This idea flies in the face of everything I have said in this book. However, it cannot hurt to step away from planning, at least in small spurts, once in a while. When I was stationed in Germany, I would, on occasion, simply get in my car and take off on a drive of the back roads. Every intersection had signs that directed me to the next town. If the town name sounded interesting or fun, I went in that direction – it was completely random. I might spend several hours driving around the German countryside without an actual destination in mind. The thing was, I could not get lost because eventually I would run into on autobahn (highway in Germany). Once I had my fill of exploring the German towns, I would take the autobahn back home. They did not have global positioning satellite (GPS) navigation back then, but today you could always use GPS to find your way home if you decide to go for a drive without a planned destination.

These are just some ways to continually stimulate the curiosity muscle in your brain. Trying them is worth the effort. Without a strong emphasis on curiosity, you will be much less inclined to seek or develop business insights. The combination of these three ways to improve your curiosity makes you unbelievably successful with everything you do.

Research

Although I had been data-driven before I entered into my doctoral studies, they taught me the full importance of research. Research, according to the Organization for Economic Co-operation and Development (OECD), is considered "creative and systematic work undertaken to increase the stock of knowledge." Research involves unbiased collection, organization, and analysis of information to increase one's full understanding of a topic or issue. Research does not take something at its face value, it validates the information.

Have you ever had someone ask you a question but you knew the answer was very easy to find? So easy, in fact, that all they had to do was a little research that would probably take them the same amount of time as finding you and asking you the question. Annoying, right? Your ability to perform effective and efficient research makes you incredibly powerful and much less annoying.

Four years ago, my wife and I bought our horse farm. We purchased a Ford F350 diesel dually truck via auction. When we started using the truck, the engine was not running right. Our property manager, Dustin, started his research. He determined that at least one injector had gone bad in the diesel engine. He borrowed a friend's tester and figured out that, in fact, two were bad. Using YouTube, he watched videos on how to tear down the engine and replace the injectors. That night, he worked all evening on the truck. The next morning, the truck was running like a champ. We still have that truck today and use it regularly to haul horses and do other farm-related work. Dustin's ability to research and find a solution kept the truck useful.

Today, answers to questions are a Google search away, including on mobile phones to which most everyone seems to be constantly connected. So, I am still amazed when someone asks me a question that they could have easily researched for themselves. Take the time to research. You might even find out more interesting facts than you were initially looking for.

Define your topic or question. When you start to research, your question might be very broad, but with some simple Internet searches, you should be able to quickly narrow the parameters of your search. Cultivating your curiosity is helpful to the initiation of research. I often ponder why or what something is. Then, I research it. For instance, consider how I researched for this book. I asked, "What is the origin of the word, success?" What an interesting question! The word success, like many words we use today, was derived from the Latin word, "succedere." The Latin meaning was "come close after." From there, the word evolved to "successus," meaning "advance, a good result, and a happy outcome." I constantly feed my curiosity with questions like this and look for answers to hone my research skills.

With a solid topic in hand, you can start your research. We are not writing a doctoral research paper, so do not go too overboard. When I research, I follow few simple research tactics that can help you:

<u>Google.</u> I like to start with a simple Google search. I am always amazed at the sheer magnitude of information available via this simple search tool. This step also helps you refine your research question.

<u>Wikipedia.</u> Education zealots hate Wikipedia, but I love it. I do not always trust it, but the articles often have great references. When you research something via Wikipedia, scroll to the bottom of the page and follow the links to sources that were used to create the article.

<u>YouTube and Amazon.</u> I like to go to YouTube and enter my research topic to see what videos might be out there on the subject. Then, I search Amazon for potential books. Amazon is usually my last step, because it could result in a purchase, while the other research is typically free.

Google Scholar. Sometimes, I go to Google Scholar. This specialized Google search engine performs a broad search across scholarly literature. Often, you can find PDF copies of papers and documents that help with, or are otherwise related to your research.

Google Books, Four Minute Books and the Library. If you are interested in a book, but do not want to invest in it for a single topic, Google Books might help. Sometimes, the book is available on Google Books for free. Also, Four Minute Books has a lot of great summaries of many business books. And of course, there is always the public library.

When you start your research, you will have either a broad or specific research topic. If the topic is specific, your research should quickly identify that the topic is part of a broader subject. If your research is broad, you will probably narrow in on specific topics. Either way, you will find information on both the narrow topic and its broader subject matter. The first universal law (see Chapter 6) I learned about was the Law of Attraction. This is not surprising, since it is probably the most popular of all the laws. I decided to research the Law of Attraction. As I started my research of this Law, I learned it was part of a series of Universal Laws. Researching all the Universal Laws at once was a big endeavor. However, learning a little about the existence of the Universal Laws, of which the Law of Attraction is a part, was helpful. Once I completed my research on the Law of Attraction, I further narrowed in my research on each specific law. While researching them, I found how they interact as well as other related universal-type laws and the names for those laws. A good researcher expands and contracts their research to fully understand the subject.

Data Collection

Data collection is important for business insights. It takes time and effort, so many people skip this critical avenue of insight. They make decisions based on opinion, instinct, gut reaction, or just plain luck. If they make a good decision (i.e., they were lucky), they chalk it up to an effective decision-making system and they keep making decisions the same way. The more decisions they make based on luck that turn out well, the more they rely on their flawed system of decision-making.

To make effective business decisions, data should be collected and analyzed. Effective data collection rests on the answering of five key questions:

1. What questions are you trying to answer?
2. What data exists today and what data does not already exist?
3. How will you collect, manage, store, and present the data?
4. Do you have a baseline for your data?
5. How long will you need to collect the data in order to be able to effectively analyze it?

Questions to answer. The important first step in data collection is to clearly understand what questions you are trying to answer. I often see people grab data that was previously collected and try to generate answers using that data to a different or newer question than that for which the data was collected. Or I see people furiously collecting data without any question in mind to answer with that data. By framing the initial question and asking follow-up and clarifying questions, you can define the type of data you need to collect and how you will present the data in order to answer the question or questions. The biggest mistake people make is not determining what questions they want to answer with data before collecting data.

Data exists or does not exist. In today's information technology-ridden world, we have a ton of data available to us. The problem is, we often do not know that we even have the data or have access to it. Data can often be locked in a software system, and we do not know how to access it, or that it even exists. A good process owner (see Chapter 30) should fully understand the technology systems that support their processes and what data is or could be available from those systems. When you do not know what you have available, you often end up creating one-off, ad hoc data collection solutions. I was working within a large human resources function at a major company. They had recently transitioned from one human resource information system to another. The company had an entire data, analytics, and reporting team that supported the entire company. In two years, that group had amassed over 4,000 one-off reports, many times these discrete reports answered the exact same question. This occurred because they never recognized what they had done in the past, or what reports they already had.

Using the data. Good data collection starts with a plan. Unfortunately, people often start without thinking – they Jump to Do (see Chapter 29). Determine, before you start, how you will collect the data in the most reliable and efficient manner possible. Who will have access to the data? How will it be protected? Data can be valuable to competitors and could be damaging if inadvertently released. Personal, financial, and medical data should always be protected and controlled. Based on the level of protection required, identify the type of storage required. Simple work counts are entirely different than customer financial records and require different types of storage and security. Answering the questions that lead to the collection of the data will guide how you present it. Some data can be presented in table format to adequately answer the questions posed, but you will usually need more visual manipulation into charts and graphs to show trends and answer questions.

Baseline. We either collect data to tell us something about our operations, or to fix and improve operations. The latter may come as a result of the former. So, once you have answered questions 1 through 3, take a snapshot of the data you currently have. If you do not already have any data, collect enough to determine what the operation looks like today before you go any further. Baseline data helps you judge how things change over time. If you do anything to your processes (Chapter 30), you want to be able to gauge your impact – that is what a baseline, and baseline data, is for.

Collection timeframe. You must have a certain amount of data collected before it can be used for insightful analysis. Generally, you need a minimum of six points of data to be able to create useful analysis. I like to think about how often the data occurs to determine how much of it I will need before I begin my analysis. If you have an operation that occurs multiple times a day, I suggest obtaining two weeks of typical operations data. You will want to compare different days of the week and times of the day over that two weeks of the operation. If an operation only happens once a year, decisions based on one years' worth of the data will probably be flawed but might be necessary if you have to make a decision before you have six years' of data. Make sure to also collect and examine data from a typical timeframe. Do not rely on data from a busy season to evaluate how to proceed during a slow season.

Analysis

Armed with data collected over time you can begin your analysis. There are a ton of business intelligence platforms and tools available today. These tools, such as SAP, Power BI, and Tableau, are extremely powerful and some are easier to use than others. There is one tool, however, that everyone should be good at – the common spreadsheet. From a business transferable skill perspective, knowing how to use popular spreadsheet software like Excel, Smartsheets, Google Sheets, Numbers, etc., can help you on your path to becoming unbelievably successful.

Typical analysis tools should become second nature to you. An unbelievably successful person should be able to turn a spreadsheet of data into one or more of the following:

- Pie chart
- Bar chart
- Line chart
- Histogram
- Pareto chart
- Control chart

A pie chart is nothing but a simple presentation of one hundred percent of a group of data. It is typically presented in a circular pie.

The line chart presents information plotted over a series of dots that are connected by a line showing the continuous nature of the data. An example of this would be monthly sales for the year.

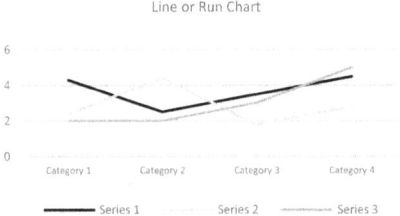

A bar or column chart is used to show amounts in relation to each other. These can be horizontal or vertical. Vertical bar charts are the more common presentation approach. These charts compare different areas or time frames with counts for each category and make it easy for the viewer to understand what is going on.

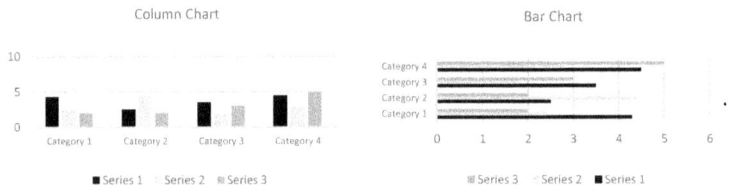

In many cases, bar and line charts can be used interchangeably and tend to present the same data just in a different view. Understanding these basic charts will help you to better present your data and understand other types of charts used to present more in-depth data for specific analysis.

A histogram uses a bar chart format to look at values, or groups of values, over their distribution. With a histogram chart, you can look for the predictability of data in the process (shown in Figure 5). For instance, you can plot hourly volume for a process over an entire day if you look at it in groups. A histogram examines the distribution of the data examined.

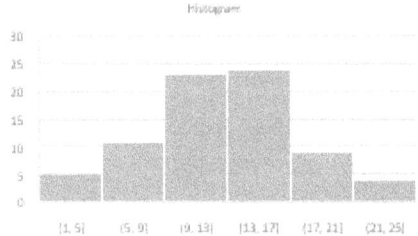

Combining column and line charts in a skewed histogram view helps employees understand and use a Pareto analysis. Setting control and specification limits to line charts creates Control Charts. As stated in the beginning, these chapters are not designed to make you an expert. Here, I present the concepts of things you should delve deeper into over time.

Knowing how to create and read charts is crucial to data analysis. However, analysis does not stop with this. Interpreting and presenting data is only the first step. You should also look for trends that drive you to dissect the data into groupings to better understand what is happening and why. Many data collectors will give you the data you asked for in tables, and some will put it into a presentation format for analytical consumption. Very few will provide it in a manner that truly answers your questions. Get good at collecting and analyzing data and you will become unbelievably successful.

Chapter 31 Questions

1. What are the three interrelated skills of business insights?

2. How can you cultivate your curiosity?

3. What is the first step in data collection?

4. What comes after creating a chart from data?

Essay Question

Describe a typical data presentation tool that you use all the time.

Chapter 31 Notes Page

Use this page to capture notes in each Part and Chapter

Part 5 Questions

1. What does ADKAR stand for?

2. What are the four ways to quantify and identify your time in a time study?

3. What is Leaderment?

4. What is a process?

Essay Question

Discuss how the eight business transferable skills interrelate and work together toward operational excellence.

Part 5 Notes Page

Use this page to capture notes in each Part and Chapter

JOHN KNOTTS

Part 6
Personal Motivation to Unbelievable Success

"People often say that motivation doesn't last. Well, neither does bathing – that's why we recommend it daily."
~ Zig Ziglar

Chapter 32
Understanding Motivation

When your motivation and drive are at their lowest levels, you just want to crawl back into bed and ignore the rest of the world. When you embark on the journey of becoming unbelievably successful, your personal motivation will become the most important aspect of your journey!

Increased motivation helps us change our behaviors, develop ourselves, and live better lives. The term "motivation" is often used to describe how driven and happy employees are in a company. In business, a motivated team is more productive and innovative, has less absenteeism and turnover, and often has a great reputation, which leads to a greater ability to recruit others to the team. Everybody wants to be part of a great team.

Personal motivation, in the context of this book, is about your own motivation every day. To be unbelievably successful, you need to be self-motivated. We are not specifically talking about someone external to you motivating you. Rather, you need to find a way to motivate yourself.

I have known about extrinsic and intrinsic motivation for a long time. Recently, however, I learned about the concepts of identified and introjected motivation. This part of the book talks about what motivation is, how to feed your personal motivation, and how to overcome motivation derailers.

	Action	Non-Action
External	Extrinsic	Identified
Internal	Intrinsic	Introjected

Daniel Pink, in his groundbreaking book, *Drive: The Surprising Truth About What Motivates Us*, explores extrinsic versus intrinsic motivation in depth.

Extrinsic motivation comes from the world around us and is typically tangible in nature. Extrinsic motivation means behavior is driven by rewards or incentives. These rewards and incentives include things like praise, fame, awards, or money. Here are some examples of extrinsic-driven behaviors:

- Working because we earn money from work
- Studying in school because we want a good grade
- Helping someone and expecting a thanks in return
- Volunteering because we can get out of work if we do it
- Participating in a sport in order to win an award

Normally, extrinsic motivators only produce short-term results. In the Kano Model, Professor Nariaki Kano determined there were two primary factors to customer satisfaction. They are delighters and basic expectations. A delighter is something special that you give a customer to excite them to buy your product – an extrinsic motivator. Basic expectations are the things that a customer expects from the product – also an extrinsic motivator. If the basic expectations are not met, the chances of the customer buying or using your product are greatly reduced. Over time, most extrinsic motivators become basic expectations – essentially entitlements. They hold less value and meaning to truly motivate individuals. And, over time, they fail to be effective.

Intrinsic motivation, on the other hand, comes from inside us and is much less tangible in nature. Intrinsically-motivated behaviors occur without any obvious external rewards. Some examples of intrinsic-driven behaviors are as follows:

- Working because it makes you feel good
- Studying in school because you want to learn and grow
- Helping someone in order to see them successful
- Volunteering because you learn valuable life lessons
- Participating in a sport because it is fun

Intrinsic motivation drives us to do things that are personally rewarding and fulfill our beliefs and expectations. We are intrinsically motivated by inspiring people and when we feel that we are part of something greater than ourselves.

Identified and interjected motivation are considered nonaction motivators.

Identified motivation is when you know you need to do something, but you have not done it yet, or decided to do anything about it. If you know that you need to build a Personal Strategic Plan, but you have not done it yet, then you are dealing with identified motivation.

Introjected motivation is similar to intrinsic motivation in that it is internalized. It is also similar to identified motivation, as it is something that you know needs to be done, but you have not done it yet. The distinctive aspect of this type of motivation is that you feel the tension of guilt for not doing what you know needs to be done.

Motivation is often seen as something that someone can influence through rewards or through punishment (i.e., the carrot and stick approach). The "carrot" represents a reward in a way of motivating others to do what someone wants. The "stick" represents a punishment, encouraging people to do something or not do something. Both of these are extrinsic in nature.

In the military, when I was in a poor work environment, invariably I would hear (or use) the saying, "Beatings will continue until morale improves." This was always a joke, of course, but it demonstrates the use of negative motivators often at work by poor leaders and managers.

Intrinsic motivation is always considered more powerful than extrinsic.

We have discussed the four types of motivation (extrinsic, intrinsic, identified, and interjected). Now, let us look at the specific six motivators that exist. Some of these are extrinsic in nature and others are intrinsic in nature.

Motivators	
Extrinsic Motivators	Intrinsic Motivators
Rewards	Avoidance
Power	Achievement
Fame	Growth

Extrinsic Motivators

Rewards. This is the most well-known of extrinsic motivators. Typically, this is represented by monetary wealth and materialistic things. Most, starting out, will tell you that they would be happy with one million dollars of wealth and assets. However, this really is a product of the Law of Relativity (Chapter 6). For many, one million seems like a great deal of money. But, when you have one million in accumulated wealth and assets, people often find that it is not really that much at all. In fact, the number that really seems to be the target these days is 10 million.

Power. Being a powerful person in personal life and/or business is a strong motivator. Look at some examples in history of those who sought power – Attila the Hun, Genghis Khan, Joseph Stalin, and Adolf Hitler. The power does not have to be bad. Mahatma Gandhi and Mother Teresa were powerful people in history. Power often represents control and being able to manipulate people for good or bad.

<u>Fame.</u> This is often related to an overactive need to belong (Chapter 5) on the Hierarchy of Needs pyramid. This is often referred to as the "social factors" motivator. Ever know someone who was considered "popular" in school or someone who valued their self-worth by how many connections in followers they had on social media? These are probably people motivated by fame.

Intrinsic Motivators

<u>Avoidance.</u> This is also called the "fear of consequences" motivator. People are motivated to action to avoid something painful or unpleasant. Someone might have grown up poor and they were motivated to never be poor again, so they surrounded themselves with wealth and material things that represent not being poor. Some people say that "freedom" is a motivator, but, in reality, it is simply an avoidance of things that make them feel like they are imprisoned. This is why avoidance is intrinsic in nature because it is measured mentally, not tangibly.

<u>Achievement.</u> Also known as "mastery," those who seek achievement, seek to be the best they can be at what they do. My Personal Strategic Plan is a byproduct of my desire for achievement over the other five motivators. Michael Jordan and Tiger Woods are very poignant examples of people driven by the achievement motivator. In Tom Rath's book, *Strengths Finder 2.0*, my number one strength is Strategic. My number two strength is Achiever. This points to my number one personal motivator.

<u>Growth.</u> Growth is not in the nature of rewards, power, fame, or achievement, specifically. The growth motivator is an innate desire to always want to feel as if you are growing in a specific area. Thus, there really is no measurable amount that someone focused on growth will strive for – they just always want more of it. They need to feel as if they are constantly moving forward and progressing.

"Becoming Unbelievably Successful" is specifically centered around the growth motivator, because success is a never-ending journey towards the things that motivate you the most.

We are all motivated by at least one of the six motivators and we could be motivated by all six. For all of us, we have a primary motivator and the rest take a second seat. As I said, I feel that achievement is my strongest motivator, followed closely by growth. I personally recognize how the other four motivators drive me as well (or do not). None of the motivators are either bad or good in nature. I know you have heard that "Money is the root of all evil" and "Power corrupts, and absolute power corrupts absolutely." However, it is the person and how they seek and use their motivators. Some of the richest people in the world are absolute saints and some of the most powerful, like Gandhi, never harmed a soul. What you do with your success, in achieving what motivates you, defines you – not the motivator itself.

The rest of this part of the book is dedicated to specific ways to increase your personal motivation (crushing goals, building confidence, overcoming fears, being creative, and overcoming complacency). However, I want to share three simple habits that you can easily adopt every day that have been scientifically proven to increase your personal motivation. They are as follows:

- Power poses
- Chocolate
- Seeing green

Power poses. Amy Cuddy, a social scientist and professor at the Harvard School of Business, gave a TED Talk in 2012 about using body language to change your life. From this talk came the "Power Pose Movement." Researchers have found that holding a power pose for at least two minutes will increase your testosterone levels (increasing confidence) and reduce your cortisol levels (decreasing stress).

The Habit: Every morning, after you wake up, strike a power pose for at least two minutes to kick off your day. There are many different power poses that will make you feel powerful. Try them in front of the mirror and settle on one. Here is my recommended pose – The Superhero. Stand straight, feet spread a shoulder width a part. Puff up your chest, raise your chin like you are looking up to the horizon, and ball your fists and place them on your hips. Imagine yourself standing there like a traditional superhero with your cape flowing in the wind.

Chocolate. If you are allergic to, or do not like chocolate, you can change this out for any other reward-like item. If you like chocolate, get yourself a bag of small dark chocolates. One small piece of chocolate (or similar reward) can increase serotonin and release dopamine into your system.

The Habit: Every morning, as part of your daily habit, reward yourself with one (only one) small piece of dark chocolate. Savor the reward, do not just cram it into your mouth. Let yourself really enjoy the daily treat.

Seeing Green. The color green is considered to provide the biggest boost to personal energy and motivation of any color in the spectrum. And, it does not have to take a lot either!

The Habit: Find some way to start your day with something green. This can be simply having a green cloth hanging in the bathroom, to taking a stroll outside (if your yard has green grass, bushes, and trees). Find a way to incorporate at least 10 minutes of green into your every morning.

These three low-cost/no-tech habits, applied every morning, will help you boost your personal motivation every day.

To become unbelievably successful, you will need to maintain high levels of personal motivation at all times. This will not be easy, because it means that you will always be working on it. Like stress, discussed in Part 4, unbelievably successful people need more emphasis on motivation than anyone else.

Chapter 32 Questions

1. What is extrinsic motivation?

2. What is intrinsic motivation?

3. How do identified and interjected motivation differ?

4. What happens to extrinsic motivators over time?

Essay Question

What is one way that you can intrinsically motivate yourself to accomplish a task?

Chapter 32 Notes Page

Use this page to capture notes in each Part and Chapter

Chapter 33
Personal Goal Setting

Nothing is more intrinsically motivating than setting and meeting goals every day. Navy Admiral, William McRaven's famous commencement speech, *"If you wanna to change the world, start off by making your bed,"* emphasizes this point. When we achieve little things every day, they build to successful big things. The same concept is elaborated in James Clear's *Atomic Habits* book.

When you set objectives in front of you, and then achieve them, this feeds your personal motivation. This starts with establishing a big vision; breaking that vision down into specific goal areas; establishing steps or objectives to meet your goals; and then accomplishing things every day that get you closer and closer to achieving your vision.

Sound familiar?

It should – this is Part 2 of this book! By creating your purpose (ikigai), your vision, and your Personal Strategic Plan, you set yourself on a path. Implementing and successfully completing things in line with your plan will feed your motivation. This is why that part of the book is so important.

When setting goals, you should keep two things in mind. First is that your goals should always be SMART. Second, your goals should always be written down.

What are SMART goals? SMART stands for Specific, Measurable, Attainable, Relevant, and Time-bound.

Specific goals mean that they are clear and well defined. A vague or generalized goal, like, "Get Healthy," is hard to achieve. Remember, we talked about setting expectations in Chapter 29 and creating a clear problem statement in Chapter 30. Be specific when setting a goal, so you are clear when you have achieved it.

Measurable goals provide a clear gauge that you can judge progress against. Without anything to measure, you have no way to know if you are getting close to completion, or if you actually completed the goal. Therefore, measurement (see Chapter 29) is so important.

Attainable goals mean that you can reasonably achieve the goals you set in front of yourself. There is something to be said for the statement, "Aim low, hit low." Setting goals that are too easy to attain does little to make someone unbelievably successful. But setting an unachievable goal could demoralize you. Break those BHAGs from your Personal Strategic Plan down into easier-to-achieve goals (or objectives).

Relevant goals speak volumes to the whole purpose of this book! As I often ask my business clients, "If you are working on something that doesn't support your strategy, why are you working on it?" Relevant means that your goals will move you in the direction of your vision, as outlined in your Personal Strategic Plan.

Time-bound goals are structured with an expectation of when they should be completed. Remember Chapter 7, when we were creating your Personal Strategic Plan? We identified the gaps in your goal areas and then set some time limits for them. My whole plan was time-bound by the amount of time I expected to complete getting my PhD – 20 years. When you set your goals, make sure they have a designated time window, or they might go on forever.

As I wrote this book, I was getting close to 10,000 followers on LinkedIn. As you remember, part of my Personal Strategic Plan was to increase my social media network. In 2020, I decided that I would reach 10,000 followers on LinkedIn. Every quarter, month, and week, I had a specific number that I worked to obtain. This is an example of a SMART goal. It is specific, measurable, attainable, relevant, and time-bound.

The second important tip, when it comes to goalsetting, is to always write your SMART goal down. Do not keep it in your head. You will either forget the goal entirely, or it will change over time. When I created my Personal Strategic Plan, it took me two years to finally write it all down. Over the years, I have rewritten my plan and adjusted my goals, but they have always been written down. By following the planning process, outlined in Chapter 8, you will get good at documenting and tracking your goal progress.

I must admit, I was never a fan of SMART goal setting. Do not get me wrong, I love methodologies and systems. And I am a strong believer in having goals on writing and annual planning, both personal and professional. However, I never felt that the SMART concept was good enough. It is a great acronym but, content-wise, it is kind of repetitive. For example, how could an objective be specific without being measurable?

I was listening to the training course, *Success Habits*, by Chris Croft (a MUST DO training and an amazing teacher) … and eureka!!! Chris had already broken that mold with his SPVEM framework. And it makes so much sense. So, what is SPVEM?

Scary: As Chris says, "Your goals should be ambitious to the point that they make you a little bit anxious. This is the feeling of your subconscious coming out of the comfort zone and starting to believe that it can achieve more than it previously believed." Am I the only one who gets excited by this description?

Positive: Chris explains, "In order to work, goals have to be framed in the positive so we can work towards them. Our minds cannot visualize the absence of a negative thing. So, we need to visualize the existence of a positive new one." Brilliant! If you have an objective, such as "stop doing x", we should instead reframe it and replace it by something like "start doing y" … makes perfect sense.

Visual: "The clearer the picture in your mind, the better," describes Chris. He recommends taking pictures and visualizing how our objective will look like if we achieve it. And that is so true ... when you want something so badly that you can see all the details of it, chances are that you will get it.

Exciting: As Chris explains, "Your goals should excite you. They should stir your emotions because that is the fuel to overcome your actions. To overcome your natural fears and laziness (see Chapter 37). To make things happen." Can we all agree to that?

Measurable: Well, this is the same as in SMART and the one that is was always easiest for me to understand and follow...

I started to use this framework in 2020 and I just love it.

Visualization

The last point I will make about goal setting is to always visualize your SMART goals once they have been written down. As I have said, I love golf. Before every single shot in golf, professionals visualize their shot and commit it to memory. How the ball will fly, where it will bounce, and how much it will roll. Every time you set your SMART goal, visualize what the end result looks, smells, tastes, and feels like.

There is a Japanese proverb that says, "Vision without action is a daydream. Action without vision is a nightmare." With a vision, you can effectively set SMART (or SPVEM) goals, and with these goals you can become unbelievably successful.

Chapter 33 Questions

1. What is the title of James Clear's book that talks about setting and achieving small habits every day?

2. What does SMART stand for?

3. Why should you always write your goals down?

4. Before each shot in golf, or starting any goal, what should you do?

Essay Question

Share an example of a SMART goal, associated with your Personal Strategic Plan, and describe your visualization of that goal.

Chapter 33 Notes Page

Use this page to capture notes in each Part and Chapter

Chapter 34
Confidence

Confidence, self-esteem (Chapter 5), self-efficacy (Chapter 10), etc. are all important to your personal motivation. If you lack confidence, you often lack the will to even try. If you do not try something, you will never achieve it – "We miss all the shots we do not take." Wayne Gretzky. Without confidence, you cannot become unbelievably successful.

Confidence starts with honesty. Many people who lack confidence fool themselves into believing they are confident when they are not! The first step to becoming confident is to be honest with yourself. As I wrote this book, I constantly questioned my writing. "Will anyone read this?" "Is this really worth writing?" "Do I even know what I'm talking about?" This is often called the "Imposter Syndrome." We believe we are not as good as we really are. On your journey, you will face this challenge – probably more than once. It is important to recognize it and get past it quickly.

The most impactful action you can take to increase your confidence is to set goals and accomplish them, as highlighted in Chapter 33. This is because people really enjoy checking things off of their to-do lists. Some, like me, even add items to their list, just so they can check them off. What frustrates people and challenges their confidence is not getting things done. This can happen when you have a large thing you are trying to accomplish, but is not getting done. Therefore, it is important to break big things down into small steps – things you can accomplish quickly. If you owe a lot of money on credit cards (see Chapter 21), then focus on paying off the lowest card first. The confidence that you can be debt-free grows with every credit card you pay off.

Confidence grows when you grow. When you learn something new, lose weight, get in shape, and meet new people, you grow. Growing intellectually, physically, and emotionally continually increases your own confidence. Ways to do these things have been shared throughout this book and they all bring other benefits as well.

I have talked about journaling several times in this book. Your journal is a good place to write down positive affirmations. However, affirmations can be written on notes anywhere (e.g., mirrors, refrigerator, monitors, etc.). Also, some people find saying affirmations to themselves in front of a mirror helpful. Positive affirmations that come from your friends and family are even more important. Therefore, who you spend most of your time with is extremely important (see Chapter 17).

Helping other people, through work or volunteering, has a positive impact on your confidence. My whole purpose is to be a Success Incubator – the success of people I work with is my success. This is why the quote, "You are never taller, than when you stoop to help a child," resonates so much with me.

In Chapter 46, I discuss the importance of awards and recognition when it comes to being a recognized success. However, these things can have a positive impact on your confidence as well.

A lot of times, our confidence is held in check because we hold ourselves back. The thing we fear is rejection. I will talk specifically about overcoming fear in the next chapter but let us focus specifically on rejection due to its implicit impact on our confidence. Jia Jiang made rejection notable with his infamous *100 Days of Rejection* effort. Jiang pretty much turned rejection into a game. Every day, for 100 days, he asked for something ludicrous, knowing he would be told, "No." Jiang found that every day asking for something crazy was personally empowering. This led him to create a whole program designed to help others get over their rejection.

A word on overconfidence. My wife always gives me a hard time, because I believe I can do anything I put my mind to. This level of confidence was instilled in me by my mother when I was a kid. I think believing in yourself like this is not a bad thing. But I also recognize that this is me being a bit overconfident. When you become "blindly" overconfident; this is when the problems start. This often leads to making poor life choices. A lot of times overconfidence comes from something else, like power, fame, or money. These things blind you to your true capabilities because you get away with things – look at some of the disasters of many entertainers, sports figures, and politicians. When you are overconfident and you let everyone know it, you are seen as arrogant. This also can be true when you are simply confident, and you want everyone to know it. Do not let your confidence go to your head.

Confidence breeds success and feeds your motivation. The more confident you become the more these things increase. Much of this book discusses ways to improve your success in specific ways, but all has an impact on your confidence.

Chapter 34 Questions

1. What happens when you are overconfident, and you let everyone know about it?

2. What is the Imposter Syndrome?

3. What are positive affirmations?

4. Who created the *100 Days of Rejection* effort?

Essay Question

What is one area that you lack confidence in, and what is one way that you think you can improve that area?

Chapter 34 Notes Page

Use this page to capture notes in each Part and Chapter

Chapter 35
Overcoming Fear

There are two types of fear. Fear of the known and fear of the unknown. Fear protects us. I am afraid that, if I jump off a 30-story building, I will die. However, I am not afraid of heights – I am just afraid of doing something stupid like that! Though I am sure you have seen many thrill seekers who defy fear in crazy ways. I will not touch a hot stove because I am afraid of getting burned, yet many people walk across hot coals every year. Firewalking has been part of Tony Robbins' coaching program for over 40 years.

Fear is what keeps you safe. It is what protects you from anything you perceive that could hurt you. Fear can also demotivate you and destroy your confidence (Chapter 34). Fear; however, is just an emotion – it is our personal risk management system. Our mind perceives something as a risk, and then physically encourages us to avoid that risk as a mitigation tactic. Fear manifests itself in many ways: sweaty hands, upset stomach, crying, even complete withdrawal due to panic.

The problem is when fear is of an imagined danger. When we buy into false evidence appearing real (F.E.A.R.), then we lose our motivation. Overcoming fear from imagined dangers – especially those who hold you back – is critical to becoming unbelievably successful.

The Zone of Fear is what keeps us from moving out of our Comfort Zone and into the Zones of Learning and Growth (See Chapter 1). However, this Zone of Fear is manifested in our own limiting beliefs. We create this Zone in our own minds.

Courage and fear are like bedfellows. The Wizard gave the Cowardly Lion a medal in the classic 1939 movie, *The Wizard of Oz*. But it takes more than a medal to build courage. Ways to increase your courage and deal with your fears are as follows:

- Understand that fear is just an emotion and the fear itself cannot hurt you
- Name and then face your fear
- When you start to feel afraid, stop and breathe – relax your body

Getting good at overcoming fear. You may have heard people say, "Do something every day that scares you." Well, there is validity in that statement. The best way to overcome fear is to repeatedly face it in small doses. The first step is to recognize what you are afraid of and how it is impacting you. Understand what your fears are preventing you from doing. I was afraid of public speaking, and I was afraid of water (specifically swimming). Both of those fears have been overcome. I beat them back by facing them – confronting them – little-by-little. When you recognize your fear, then you can work to overcome it. The most powerful weapon in your fear-fighting arsenal is your mind. You need to overcome your fear by telling yourself that you are not afraid of your fear.

I think that many people believe that overcoming fear means that the fear is gone. I do not think so. I am still afraid of public speaking. I still get butterflies in my stomach before I speak. However, I recognize that public speaking will not hurt me. Then, I focus on the nervous energy that fear causes and turn that into positive energy on stage. I use that fear to make me a better speaker. As I like to tell people, "I get my butterflies to fly in formation."

What fears are holding you back? What are your fears preventing you from accomplishing? Confront and overcome fears that attack your confidence and motivation. Otherwise, your fears will prevent you from becoming unbelievably successful.

Chapter 35 Questions

1. What does the acronym, "F.E.A.R.," stand for?

2. What did the Wizard give the Cowardly Lion to help him overcome his fear and build his confidence?

3. What are the two types of fear?

4. What were the author's two fears that he overcame?

Essay Question

What fear is holding you back, and what is something small that you can start doing today to overcome that fear?

Chapter 35 Notes Page

Use this page to capture notes in each Part and Chapter

Chapter 36
Creativity

Motivation and creativity each have a positive and negative effect on each other. Being unmotivated creates a "why bother" mentality and saps a person's creativity. Feeling uncreative can demotivate you and everyone around you. We have talked about several ways to increase your motivation. So, let us discuss ways to increase your creativity.

Studies have shown that when children express creativity early in their life, they are more successful later in their life. Creativity also feeds your innovation and allows you to lead a more successful life. Here are some ways to increase your creativity.

Immerse yourself in creativity. When you surround yourself with creative stimulus, it inspires your own creativity. Reading, listening to music, visiting an art gallery, even enjoying nature, are ways to immerse yourself in creativity and stimulate your creative mind. When I write, I like to listen to New Age music. While writing this book, I read *The Motive*, by Patrick Lencioni (my favorite author). I actually read that book in a day! But reading his book sparked all kinds of creative ideas about business. When I am struggling to come up with a daily post on social media, I will read and comment on other posts first. This tends to feed my creativity and I normally come up with an idea.

Adopt creative hobbies. Singing, playing a musical instrument, dancing, painting, sculpture, drawing, and even writing are all examples of creative hobbies. When you release your mind to a creative diversion, your mind tends to open and other creative ideas flow. My wife – a professional lawyer – doodles on her papers while in meetings. This stimulates her mind as she listens to what is transpiring in the meeting. I worked with a guy that brought his guitar to the office and would occasionally pick it up and play a song when he was mentally stuck. Photography is big for me. I am a pareidolia – someone who sees objects and patterns in seemingly random objects. So, I often see things through the frame of a camera that other people miss. When I look at a picture in color, I often imagine what it might look like in black and white.

Surround yourself with toys. Imagine yourself working in a toy store, where you could play with anything your store sells. I think this is why movies like *Big*, *Mr. Magorium's Wonder Emporium*, and *Willy Wonka and the Chocolate Factory* do so well. As I wrote this book, I was playing with a fidget spinner. In my office, I have several small toys that occasionally distract me, but also feed my creativity. At USAA, I often had different magic tricks I would share around the office, or to kick off a meeting.

Keep a creativity journal. When does creativity hit you? In the shower? While you are sleeping? As you are driving to work? Creativity is elusive – it tends to sneak up on you when your mind is at rest. Keep something handy – physical or technological – to record your creative thoughts as soon as possible. Why? Because, as I said, creativity is elusive! If you do not write it down quickly, the idea might be gone in a minute. Do not let your creativity get away. If creativity tends to strike when your mind is at rest, and you are working on improving your creativity, find ways to put your mind at rest. Take a walk, sit quietly in a room, or meditate. Find a way to simply relax and not think about anything. But make sure you have that journal nearby!

Force creativity. When you attend a class or a workshop, how do you take notes? If you are like most people, you highlight workbooks, write down key concepts, and generally record what is being said. We do the same thing in meetings, conferences, etc. Next time you take a class or sit in a meeting, bring a pen and a blank sheet of paper. As people teach and talk, instead of taking notes, draw pictures that represent ideas that are being conveyed to you. When the event is over, look over your page, full of pictures, and let it remind you what you learned. Do this enough times and you will get very good at remembering everything important taught or said.

Build creativity through collaboration. Two heads are better than one. This can be true for creative thought. I find that when I am looking for ideas, or just thinking through something, bouncing ideas off someone else helps. This is where "back-of-the-napkin" ideas come from. Two or more people at the bar talking about something and a good idea just hits you. My Whiskey Bid'ness "And Cigars" social business networking program is good at generating these back-of-the-napkin moments. One event resulted in a group of people coming up with an idea for a podcast. Not being an extremely spiritual person, I sought thoughts from others who were. This helped me expand on my thought with Chapter 22 on spirituality.

Creativity comes from many different sources. Mostly, these sources vary from person to person. Being creative – coming up with creative ideas – increases your motivation. The more creative you are the more creative your purpose and vision in Part 2 will become. Creativity is a necessary element in becoming unbelievably successful.

Chapter 36 Questions

1. What is a necessary element in becoming unbelievably successful as highlighted in this chapter?

2. What type of impact do motivation and creativity have on each other?

3. What are some hobbies listed that might help you increase your creativity?

4. What type of creativity results in back-of-the-napkin moments?

Essay Questions

Describe one way that you can improve your creativity.

Chapter 36 Notes Page

Use this page to capture notes in each Part and Chapter

Chapter 37
Persistence

Persistence in the face of success. "Success breeds complacency. Complacency breeds failure. Only the paranoid survive." Andy Grove.

In many ways, complacency and boredom will become your biggest challenges along your journey to becoming unbelievably successful.

For 10 years in the Air Force, I was a Security Police Officer. Our role in the Air Force was to protect the expensive and dangerous assets owned and employed by the military. We used to have a saying in the Security Police, "The job was 99 percent sheer boredom and 1 percent sheer panic."

My last assignment as a Security Police Officer, was working with the USAFE Elite Guard. This was a handpicked, elite team of very successful Air Force enlisted. We were a ceremonial unit, but we were also responsible for protecting the headquarters and staff. In the military, complacency kills! In 1981, before I even entered the Air Force, a terrorist drove into the USAFE compound and was allowed through the entrance by an inattentive (complacent) security guard. The driver parked under the overhang in front of the headquarters building and he ran from the vehicle. When the car exploded, it injured 14 people. Of course, several security changes were implemented. However, the incident all came down to security becoming complacent when it came to protecting the USAFE Headquarters.

So, what does complacency and boredom have to do with success? Unfortunately, everything!

As Grove highlighted, in his famous quote above, when we are successful, we tend to "rest on our laurels." When becoming unbelievably successful, this behavior will be very derailing. Success causes one to feel accomplished. It gives us confidence (see Chapter 34) and makes us feel powerful. You may have heard of the phrase, "getting a big head." Success, especially several successes back-to-back, can cause you to stop working toward the next success.

This is when you become bored with your success. Honestly, when success becomes an everyday occurrence, it can be very easy to simply decide to step back and relax. Some people even start to think that success "comes naturally" and they do not have to work at it anymore – they become lazy about achieving success.

The problem is that it can be very easy to ride out past successes for a long time without working on it. When I was stationed at Vandenberg AFB, we had a young, enlisted member that saved the lives of a camera crew caught in a wildfire. His story of uncommon heroism was amazing, and it earned him the Airman's Medal – an award for being distinguished by a heroic act. For close to a year, this person was put up for, and received, all sorts of awards and recognitions. However, his fame faded fast, and he did little to keep the successes coming. A year later, his achievement was "old news," and seen as nothing more than a "flash in the pan."

Your journey will be marked with great and wondrous achievements. These will be the kind of achievements where you can sit back to relax and enjoy them. However, becoming bored with constant success will derail your journey. This is when you become complacent.

How do you know if you have become complacent with your success? What signs might warn you that you are on the slippery slope of becoming lazy?

Are you taking too many risks or too big of risks? Many of my clients start seeing massive successes soon after implementing their Personal Strategic Plan. Becoming unbelievably successful can lead one to an attitude of ignoring risk. They get a feeling of being bulletproof and they do not take the time to really analyze what they are trying to accomplish. This level of complacent attitude can result in ignoring warning signs and overextending yourself.

Complacent behavior slows and even stops learning. Many business executives suffer from this issue. You achieve a certain degree, certification, or job level, and simply quit learning. As discussed in Chapter 14, lifelong learners become unbelievably successful. When you stop learning, you stop growing – when you stop growing, you start dying! Just because you have achieved something, this is now the time to set the next goal in a line of goals. For me, one of my initial goals was to become a published author. Officially, I did this in 2012, when I published *One Dead Marine*. In 2019, when I published *Overcoming Organizational Myopia*, I could have called it quits. However, I witnessed this behavior with others like me. In a few years, their material became stale and used up. It can take years to get back on track and some never do.

If you are getting a feeling of being stuck or becoming stagnant, chances are that you have become complacent with your journey of becoming unbelievably successful. People who experience this find that they are not really challenging themselves anymore. They are taking the easy option or route to getting things done. Easy typically provides short-lived success and is hardly ever effective in the long term.

If you feel as if your life has become routine, then you know you need to shake things up. Typically, you are feeling stuck because you are avoiding or rejecting change. You have probably become stuck in your comfort zone and do not want to try anything new in your life.

Breaking out of complacency

The first thing is to double down on your Personal Strategic Plan. Have you stopped using your weekly to-do list? Are you planning every quarter and annually, like you should? When a major change occurs, it can derail your planning efforts. This happens to us all. When my wife and I decided to open Fine Print Farms, this was not on my plan. It derailed everything and I let it. Almost to the point of saying, "Why bother?" Working at USAA, I became caught up in office politics and moved away from my plans. These things slowed my goal attainment. However, when I blew the dust off my plan and went back to it, things just "clicked" into place. Even this book took a back seat to other activities and delayed planned publication for over a year!

With a plan, you can recover!

Set goals and stick to them when it comes to your lifelong learning. If you continue to follow the guidance in Chapter 14, you will continue to develop and grow. Making the decision to become a lifelong learner is very easy. However, sticking with this decision can be very hard. We become overcome by events or worse, bored and complacent with learning altogether.

I remember when we were reengineering the entire process improvement program for USAA. We knew that we needed to teach the executives about leading through process excellence. However, the executive, who was over the effort, pointed out that executives were "too high level" to be taught anything. He shared with us, as an executive, that they did not need to be taught anything – only reminded.

Bull!

"When we stop learning, we stop growing," Loyal Jack Hewman. Anyone who has achieved a position where they feel they do not need to learn anymore, has sealed their fate. In your Personal Strategic Plan, weave in personal and professional development goals that continually support your goal progression. By setting lifelong learning objectives, you will continue to focus on your personal development.

Taking the easy option to making decisions in your life, every day, will drive you to complacency. From the moment you wake up, to the moment you go to sleep, you are faced with hundreds, if not thousands, of decisions throughout the day. Each and every decision has one of three options: Easy, Normal, and Hard (see Chapter 13). Your alarm goes off at 5 am. Do you turn off your alarm and go back to sleep (easy option); hit the snooze a couple of times (normal option); or get up and start your day (hard option)?

These questions or decisions seem so simple, do they not? If you take the easy route, this results in immediate gratification – you get to sleep as long as you want. If you take the hard route, you might be tired, but you will have much more day available to you and you will not feel rushed in the morning. The options we choose, when faced with decisions throughout the day, define how we end up living our lives. Imagine the decisions you face every day and consider what options you normally choose.

Living a life of predominantly taking the hard option, keeps complacency at bay. By analyzing your life on a regular basis, you can recognize and adjust your behavior (Chapter 12). When you always get up at 5 am when your alarm goes off, you form the habit of getting up at 5 am. Soon, your body clock takes over and you simply wake up at 5 am without an alarm. I am not saying that you need to wake up at 5 am every day. What I am saying is that this is an example decision, just like setting the alarm in the first place. If you want to avoid complacency on your journey to becoming unbelievably successful, then focus on the hard options whenever possible.

Have you ever got your vehicle stuck in the mud? It happens a lot when you live on a horse farm. Quite soon after we bought our farm, we got our truck stuck in the field during a rainstorm. In life, we often "get stuck," and cannot seem to go anywhere.

What options were we faced with, with our truck stuck in the pouring rain? We could keep spinning our tires, getting more and more stuck in the process. After all, it was Einstein who said that the definition of Insanity was, "Doing the same thing over and over again and expecting different results." Too often, we get stuck in life and stop moving forward, but keep doing the same thing that once worked in the past. That does not work – obviously.

We could have waited until the rain stopped, the sun to come out, and the ground to dry up. That would have work. However, it rained the entire first month we bought our farm. That truck would have been stuck in the field for a long time. But we often give up when we have an obstacle in life. We simply throw our hands up and walk away – so dramatic! This behavior, although personally gratifying (trust me), does not work either.

When faced with getting stuck in the mud the most effective way to get unstuck is to change the situation. You put cardboard under the tires for traction, you throw on chains to add grip, or you get help. The most effective is to get help – in fact, we waited for the rain to slow, we walked up to the front of the property, we got the tractor, and we used it to pull the vehicle free. Getting help, when you are stuck, is the best way to get unstuck. However, it just might cost you something.

Now our tractor never gets stuck in the mud. It is the only vehicle, in over seven years, that has never become stuck on the property. This speaks to the importance of having the right tools for the job at the start and staying clear of things that will get you stuck in life. The most important of these is having an accountability partner that you can turn to when you think you might get stuck or are stuck. Many times, this is a paid coach. A coach will do everything in their power to keep you from getting stuck in your life and might immediately step in to help you if you do become stuck.

The best way to continue to become unbelievably successful, is to avoid complacency all together. However, it has an insidious way of sneaking up on you when you least expect it – especially when you drop your guard. Know the warning signs and what to watch for. When you recognize it, deal with it immediately.

Passion then Obsession

Are you passionate about what you do, or are you obsessed with what you do?

Mary Henderson, a close business friend of mine, from Australia, and I had a very interesting discourse regarding whether someone is 'passionate' or 'obsessed' with what they do. Fantastic conversation! Really got me thinking.

Here is an interesting quote to ruminate on:

"Passion is a strong and barely controllable emotion, while Obsession is an idea or thought that continually preoccupies or intrudes on a person's mind." Mary Henderson.

We often talk about the importance of being passionate about something to be good at it – "Entrepreneurs need Passion." But, as Mary pointed out, to Become Unbelievably Successful, you need to turn your passion into an obsession.

So, how do you build obsession – how do you become obsessed with something?

1. Put pictures of it everywhere: office, bathroom, refrigerator door, cell phone screen – everywhere.
2. Align what you watch, listen to, and read to that subject – eliminate all else.
3. Adjust your social circle and activities to focus on that thing – make it your life.

What are your thoughts? Are you obsessed and if so, how do you do it? What could you do to become more obsessed?

Chapter 37 Questions

1. Who said, "Success breeds complacency?"

2. What happens when you become bored with your success?

3. What can complacency do to learning and development?

4. What is the best way to get unstuck?

Essay Question

Predominantly, do you take the easy, normal, or hard option and why?

Chapter 37 Notes Page

Use this page to capture notes in each Part and Chapter

Part 6 Questions

1. What are the three options you can choose based on decisions in your life?

2. What are the four types of motivation?

3. Is overconfidence bad?

4. What is one way to immerse yourself in creativity to increase your personal creativity?

Essay Question

What do you believe is the most effective way to increase your personal motivation and why?

Part 6 Notes Page

Use this page to capture notes in each Part and Chapter

Part 7
Volunteerism Leads to Unbelievable Success

"The best way to find yourself is to lose yourself in the service of others."
~ Mahatma Gandhi

Chapter 38
Volunteering and Self-Actualizing

It was in 1992 that I first got involved with volunteer organizations. I learned more about being successful, as a volunteer, than I ever did in a real job. It was also in the early 90s that I learned about Maslow's Hierarchy of Needs (discussed in depth in Chapter 5).

Between 1993 and 1995, I was on the board of a local Make-A-Wish charity. If you do not know what they do, they grant wishes to children with terminal illnesses. What an incredibly rewarding program! When we would bring everything together – money, travel, family, dreams, etc. – into a successful wish, the feeling was incredible! Since 1992, I have experienced that feeling of ultimate success (self-actualization) many times.

A few years ago, I was sitting on the front porch of the clubhouse at our horse farm. Next to me was a woman that had participated in our veteran's equitherapy program for several months. We were watching her daughter ride a horse. She turned to me and said, "The week before I came out here, I was contemplating suicide. You saved my life." I had my high points at work, winning awards; being recognized for good work; etc., but little compares to the feeling of success with my nonprofit involvement. What I realized is this is what self-actualization really feels like.

Since then, I discovered that feeling in many ways. The first time I learned how to hit an actual draw with my golf club. Breaking 90 in a golf game (I have not broken 80 yet). Riding across the Top of the World Highway. Sailing through the Panama Canal. Getting that perfect photograph. Seeing the Colosseum in Rome, Italy. Self-actualization can happen anywhere if you let it.

Therefore, I think it is appropriate to address volunteering in this book. First and foremost, you learn the experience of self-actualization very quickly. That is … when you volunteer for the right reasons.

In Part 6 of this book, we learned about the difference between extrinsic and intrinsic benefits when it comes to motivation. These concepts spill over into volunteering. However, I refer to the terms as "perceived" and "earned" benefits. When I was in the military, we reviewed performance and recognized people on the "whole person concept." Whole person meant that they were impactful in their job; they were constantly learning and growing; and they were engaged in the community.

I witnessed some poor behaviors because of perceived benefits when it came to volunteering. First, some people would only volunteer for things during work hours. They knew that it was important to the military that they volunteer, and that the military would let them have free time off to participate. So, they used these activities to get out of work. The second was worse. If being involved in the community was recognized, then being a community leader was the pinnacle. Because of this belief, many people would run for a leadership position in an organization without ever being involved in that organization before. To make matters worse, once in their position, they did little to nothing required of the job. These types of behaviors occur everywhere. A fellow homeowner ran for president of our homeowner's association (HOA) after I had stepped down. He did it because six months later he was running for city council and wanted the votes from everyone in the community. I was part of an effort (as a board member) in catching the executive director using a nonprofit organization's resources for her husband's personal business. When you focus on the perceived benefits of volunteering – the tangible things you can get out of it – then you do not learn why volunteering is important.

Earned benefits occur when you get behind the reason the volunteer organization or activity exists in the first place. Every nonprofit has a bigger than life purpose – when you get involved because of that purpose and not because of some perceived benefit, something incredible happens. You start to undergo experiences and feelings that you never realized were possible. The highest earned benefit of volunteering is obviously self-actualization. But not just any self-actualization. The amazing feelings that you will experience will probably be more intense and exhilarating than anything else.

Chapter 38 Questions

1. When did the author first get involved in volunteering?

2. What did the lady say to the author on the porch of the clubhouse?

3. What highway was the author traveling on when he experienced self-actualization?

4. What are the reasons you should volunteer?

Essay Question

Describe a volunteer experience that you have had and how it made you feel.

Chapter 38 Notes Page

Use this page to capture notes in each Part and Chapter

Chapter 39
Acceptable Environment to Fail Forward

My good friend, Mary Henderson, says "Failure is Feedback." John Maxwell is often quoted saying, "Fail early, fail often, but always fail forward."

This might, on the surface, sound like sound advice to become unbelievably successful. But let us be honest with each other. How often is your boss going to accept you failing? Not too often, I would imagine. In fact, failures in business can be very disastrous to the bottom line and your career longevity!

So, how do we follow this sage advice without losing our jobs?

The answer – volunteering.

When I went to my first AFSA meeting, I was immediately appointed to their AAC (refer to Chapter 5). That first year, I totally failed in that job! Its impact on my career – zero!!!

It was not as if I did not try. My problem was that I did not know what I was doing. Since the position was brand-new for AFSA, no one in the chapter knew either. However, no one got angry with me or complained about my lack of progress.

See, unlike anywhere else in life, failing as a volunteer will probably never negatively impact you!

In fact, most volunteer organizations are just happy that you showed up and stepped up. In a membership-based organization, it has been my experience that about ten percent of the membership is at all active and less than one percent of the membership actually steps up to a leadership role. So, when you are willing to step up, few people find fault in those not getting everything right.

The question is, what did I learn from that failure? I learned a great deal – in fact, I eventually went on to lead the largest division in AFSA, with over 18,000 members. As I started to lead AFSA chapters and divisions, I was able to recruit and mentor my own AACs and we created some of the greatest programs in the organization. So much so, that AFSA International finally adopted my AAC model and created their first international ACC position, under my guidance.

None of this would have been possible in a for-profit company. If I had been hired into a newly-created position and spent the year doing nothing, I would be unceremoniously fired without a thought. In fact, I probably would not of made it past 90 days!

But this is the power of volunteering. You can confidently take on greater and greater challenges and responsibilities and learn into the roles, even if failing. The experiences that I enjoyed since 1992 have far outweighed most anything that I experienced in the corporate world.

Final Thought on Volunteering

What was your biggest achievement this past year? Mine, for 2022, was also book related.

On November 1st, 2022, EBR held its annual Author's Night and released, *Lessons in Life Long Learning*.

Now this was not my book and Author's Night was not my program, but I led both of these activities. Both were designed to raise money for the EBR, but, more importantly, to support Robyn's N.E.S.T., which goes into the inner-city of San Antonio and teaches underprivileged kids to read.

In 2021, we raised about $5K for Robyn's N.E.S.T. and I was planning to double that this year. In fact, we raised an amazing $43K for the nonprofit program, which will significantly help their mission!

Why was this so important?

Because I did not benefit from these actions in any way!

Now, that is self-actualization!!!

The volunteer environment is a lot more accepting of people trying and failing. This makes it a great learning environment for people who want to become unbelievably successful.

Chapter 39 Questions

1. Who said to "Fail early and fail often?"

2. Why is the volunteer environment a safe place to fail and learn?

3. What was the role that the author failed at when volunteering?

4. What model did AFSA International eventually adopt?

Essay Question

Why do you feel that failure in a nonprofit and volunteer role is more accepted than anywhere else?

Chapter 39 Notes Page

Use this page to capture notes in each Part and Chapter

Chapter 40
Being Active versus Being Present

This chapter and the next further expand on the overall earned versus perceived benefits concept of volunteering. Simply belonging to a volunteer effort does very little to help you become unbelievably successful. You need to be active.

AFSA had about 125,000 members when I retired from the Air Force. For the most part, maybe five percent of those members were active within the organization in any given year. Many would join because they thought it looked good on their performance reviews. Most members barely even attended meetings. Since AFSA lobbied for Air Force enlisted benefits on Capitol Hill, membership numbers were very important. However, membership participation was much more valuable.

As a longtime Toastmaster, I saw many people in and out of the military join Toastmasters so they could list it on their resume. However, many never came to the meetings, never participated in the clubs, and hardly ever gave any speeches. Toastmasters International is a great learning laboratory for public speaking and communication. But not if you pay and do not participate. You cannot simply get better at communication by paying for an annual membership!

The same goes for the earned benefits from volunteering. Simply belonging to something might help the overall organization because of dues paid and membership strength. But it does you little good in the direction of becoming unbelievably successful.

Now, I am a lifetime member of AFSA. And, I have not participated much in the organization for the last 14 years. But I know that my membership carries weight – lobbying strength – on Capitol Hill. However, I still actively volunteer through organizations of my own design these days. Through leading my own nonprofits, I continue to grow and move forward in the completion of my goal areas.

The thing is, if you do not do anything with volunteer organizations that you belong to, then they will be of little value to you. You will never self-actualize if you do not get involved. You will never learn through failure if you do not get involved. Being a member on the roles might be okay for the organization but getting active is where it is at. Depending on the organization, there are many ways to get active. Below are some ideas:

- If they have regular meetings, attend them when possible
- Participate in the philanthropic activities and social events
- Assist with programs, like recruiting other members or writing for their newsletter
- Help the organization with fundraising or running annual programs

- Step up into a leadership role (see next chapter)

I am not saying to run out and get involved in every volunteer organization you can. But, if you do, getting true value from the experience means getting involved versus just belonging.

Chapter 40 Questions

1. List two ways that you can get active in a volunteer organization.

2. How can simply being a member help an organization?

3. How does simply being a member help you?

4. What organization is a great learning laboratory?

Essay Question

Describe a way that you can get more involved in a nonprofit, volunteer organization.

Chapter 40 Notes Page

Use this page to capture notes in each Part and Chapter

Chapter 41
Leading versus Participating

In Chapter 39, I talked about how volunteer organizations allow you to fail forward. In fact, volunteer organizations offer one of the most important opportunities of all. They let you fail as a leader without repercussion.

As I said in Chapter 40, you should consider being active versus just being present in a volunteer organization. Just belonging does not do anything for your growth. But consider taking things to the next level – become a leader in a volunteer organization.

Over the past 30 years, I have been an active volunteer in over 15 different volunteer organizations, with countless clubs and chapters. Over these past years, I was always in some leadership role with one or more of the organizations I belonged to. Consider this; when I first got involved in AFSA, I had been in the Air Force for about three years. I think I was a newly promoted Senior Airmen – I might have still been an Airman First Class. Regardless, I did not have any opportunity to lead and supervise in the Air Force at that rank. In fact, I did not become a noncommissioned officer until 1995, which was three years later. However, over those three years, I managed hundreds of people and led several major programs and projects. As a Staff Sergeant (the lowest noncommissioned officer rank in the Air Force), I led the largest AFSA chapter in all of Europe. In fact, we were awarded the highest recognition ever presented in AFSA – the Lee R. Thompson Award of Excellence. I went on, as a Technical Sergeant, to run the entire European division in AFSA with chapters in multiple countries. This experience, coupled with many other leadership roles, taught me way more about Leaderment (Chapter 26) than I could ever have learned in the jobs I was paid to hold.

There are many ways that you can lead in a volunteer setting. Most, if not all, volunteer organizations have several events throughout the year. These might be designed to raise money, recruit new members, recognize people, or otherwise support the organization. In Make-A-Wish, I worked as a Wish Giver who would work with the family and the organization to discover a child's wish and then make it happen. There are many easy ways to just help a little more by taking a leading role in one of the projects.

Often, a volunteer organization has ongoing or recurring types of programs. These could be as simple as running a monthly meeting to something elaborate like monthly comedy nights or an annual haunted house (both of which I have done). These major programs, just like the supporting projects, need a good leader who wants to help and learn.

When people talk about leadership in a nonprofit, they often picture sitting on the board of directors and running the affairs of the organization. However, there are typically way more options that are less engaged, but still worthwhile. The typical leadership positions in all nonprofits are president, vice president, secretary, and treasurer. These positions (or ones like them) are normally required. Additionally, a board of directors will normally include additional director positions. They often have some associated role, like membership, finance, programs, ways and means, etc. Together, these positions guide the organization. In larger organizations, you normally have local clubs or chapters, with some type of divisional leadership and a national or international leadership body. There are usually nonvoting leadership positions as well, which oversee ongoing programs and activities of the organization.

Most importantly, do not try to jump to the front of the line in a leadership role. Learn your way into a volunteer organization. Start out volunteering. Then, take on some projects or a program. Run for a low-level position and work your way up. You will be amazed at what you will learn as you climb the ladder in a nonprofit.

Becoming an active leader of a volunteer organization, focused on their mission and purpose, will provide you with the most earned benefits you can possibly enjoy from an experience. This experience will propel you forward in your journey to becoming unbelievably successful.

Chapter 41 Questions

1. What award did the author's AFSA chapter win?

2. How many different volunteer organizations has the author been involved with?

3. What is the lowest level of leadership in a volunteer organization?

4. What are the four positions found in most volunteer organizations?

Essay Question

Describe a volunteer organization and leadership path that might support your Personal Strategic Plan.

Chapter 41 Notes Page

Use this page to capture notes in each Part and Chapter

Part 7 Questions

1. What was Gandhi's quote at the start of this part of the book?

2. What could be synonymous with "that feeling of ultimate success?"

3. If you fail in a company, what will most likely happen?

4. What is potentially the highest level of volunteer leadership, according to this book?

Essay Question

Explain the value of volunteering when it comes to becoming unbelievably successful.

Part 7 Notes Page

Use this page to capture notes in each Part and Chapter

Part 8
Becoming a Recognized Unbelievable Success

"Don't worry when you're not recognized. But strive to be worthy of recognition."
~ Abraham Lincoln

Chapter 42
Social Networks

Becoming an unbelievable success is not always the end of the journey. Many might also desire to be recognized as unbelievably successful. You probably have heard the phrase, "If a tree falls in the forest and no one is around to hear it, does it make a sound?" This concept highlights a notion of perceived and unperceived existence. Can something exist without being perceived by consciousness? The question is quite metaphysical in nature, but it definitely bears some truth in real life.

I was working with an executive on the development of their strategy. The leadership team was looking for ways to describe the company. They threw out words like honest, innovative, progressive, inclusive, and collaborative. The executive questioned all these words. "How can we call ourselves any of these things? These are the words we would want our customers to use to describe us." We went on to create programs that demonstrated these words that we ascribed to be seen as (our brand). When a customer said, "You are like no other company we have worked with. You remind us of Google and Apple," we knew we were getting somewhere. Proverb 17:28, King James Version of the Bible, says, "Even a fool is thought wise if he keeps silent, and discerning if he holds his tongue." The more common quote we are familiar with goes, "Better to remain silent and be thought a fool than to speak and to remove all doubt."

What this all speaks to is that you can believe you are unbelievably successful, but you may only be fooling yourself. How you are, and what you are, requires external validation. This part of the book explores some of those ways.

The first avenue of validation is free, yet time-consuming. This avenue is through your social networks. Social networks include social media, but also mean family, friends, coworkers, and other groups of people. As you know, possessing a strong network was one of my six major goal areas (see Part 2). Thus, I have spent considerable time over the years cultivating this subject. For the most part, your social network is your validation point of your true success. I consider social networks in three ways as follows:

- Personal
- Professional
- Social Media (which can be either personal or professional)

Personal social network. This network starts with your family and friends. These people are usually the closest to you and are often the most honest (and sometimes critical) with you. Listen to what they say about you. Are they proud? Do they wonder how you get so much done? Although, this network can have a dark side too. It might be protective in nature, or it could be just plain old jealousy rearing its ugly head. What might happen is that those closest to you could become your biggest critics. They start saying things like, "Why do you work so hard?" "You better not do so much, you might fail." "You're going to burn yourself out." I am not always sure where this negativity comes from, but as you progress along your journey of becoming unbelievably successful, you will probably experience this.

The other personal social network is with groups where you share a common interest and hang out together. Usually, these social groups revolve around some type of hobby or sport. Perhaps you are part of a bowling team or play basketball with a group. It could be a dinner group or a fun group of wine tasters. Sometimes these people bleed over into friends and family, but most of the time it is just a group of people with a similar social interest. Often, these people are very interested in what others in the group do, and they like being connected to successful people. Some jealousy could form, but usually it is to a minimum.

Professional social network. The most typical of these groups are those people who you work with, if you work for a company. This network is a total mixed bag. Some people will totally get behind your successes, and many people might openly ask if you can mentor them – this is a great sign. A few people – especially those above you – might feel very threatened by you. Pay attention to this as it could cause work-related problems. When at work, pay attention to how you are introduced, especially by those with power. This tells you a lot about what people in this network think about you or want others to think about you.

The second most common professional social network exists with professional associations. I do not know of any type of work that does not have at least one professional association that supports it. These associations allow people with like interests to meet and get to know one another. Many of these associations provide some type of educational sources, like magazines, conferences, training, and even certification programs. Typically, these associations build grassroots activity through local chapters, clubs, and offices. Most of these associations are nonprofit in nature and membership based.

The last professional social networking avenue is through the concept of business networking. In every major city, you will have several types of business networking organizations. Probably the best-known business networking-type organization is a Chamber of Commerce. Less well-known, but often aligned to chambers, are Economic Development Foundations. These entities serve a twofold mission. First, they help the community they support by bringing in and growing local businesses. Second, they provide support and services to local businesses to assist them. There are many service-related professional clubs that you can engage with. Some of the more popular ones are Rotary International, Kiwanis, and Lion's Club. Typically, these organizations are made up of professionals that believe in a specific cause, but also like to interact and network with other professionals with similar interests. The last of these groups are individual business networking groups. Sometimes, these are large professionally organized groups, like BNI, while most are locally run. In fact, my Whiskey Bid'ness "And Cigars" group I created in 2019 is specifically a social business networking entity.

Social media networks. There are several social media platforms in existence today. I am aging myself when I say that I started with Myspace, which still actually exists today. Today, the most popular social media platforms are LinkedIn, Facebook, Instagram, Twitter, TikTok, and YouTube. There are; however, many other ones. Each of these platforms serves specific audiences and provide different ways to reach that audience. Perhaps, if your expertise is in music, then Myspace may still be a valid platform for you to use. If your expertise is in cake decorating, then maybe Pinterest is your most important platform.

Cultivating social networks

I often tell small business owners that social media is no longer social when you own a business. The same is true when you embark on a journey of becoming unbelievably successful. When this is your focus, then social networks become a tool to share your expertise, so other people can recognize it. The remaining chapters in this part of the book talk about these ways. But, in this chapter this is all about building the right audience through the three social network types. This means that you should engage with and join those groups that serve your needs the best. When on social media, you want to connect with those people who have interests in your expertise, otherwise they will not be interested in you. Whether it is personal, professional, or social media, spend your time with purpose.

Chapter 42 Questions

1. When at work, what should you pay attention to and why?

2. What is the second most common professional social network?

3. What is the twofold mission of the Chambers of Commerce and Economic Development Foundation?

4. What are the three social network types?

Essay Question

Describe a professional social network that aligns to your Personal Strategic Plan and explain why it aligns with your plan.

Chapter 42 Notes Page

Use this page to capture notes in each Part and Chapter

Chapter 43
Professional Organizations

In Chapter 42, I discussed professional social networks. Professional organizations are part of that group. They afford multitude ways to increase your recognized success. These include business-aligned organizations and industry-aligned organizations.

My advice in this area is to get involved, as discussed in Part 7 of this book. There are many ways to do this. I group them into Participation and Contribution.

Participation. Like I said in Part 7, do not be just a joiner. Get involved with the organizations that you join that support your goals. The first step is to attend meetings and events. These organizations provide you with an opportunity to meet new people and network. This is an important first step to becoming a recognized unbelievable success. If people in business and industry do not know who you are, then how will they ever learn anything about you? Networking in professional settings is a definite skill. Networking is about building lasting relationships. Successful networking relies on four things:

1. A memorable leave behind.
2. Letting them talk.
3. Taking notes.
4. Following up.

<u>A memorable leave behind.</u> When you are meeting people in a professional setting, you should always have something to give the people you meet so they can remember you. Typically, this is a business card. How you present your card leaves as much of an impression as the card itself – maybe more. I was at a local business networking event and was talking to somebody. Two women walked up. One of them abruptly shoved her business cards in our face without a word. When we took them, the two women walked away to do this again to someone else. The guy I was talking to took a brief look at the card and tossed it on the ground. I do not know who these women were, but I noticed that his card was not the only one on the floor or left on tables. I hazard to guess that they did not get any business from that endeavor.

When I meet individually with a potential client or strong leadership contact, I like to take along a copy of my paperback, *Overcoming Organizational Myopia*. I will sign the title page and leave it with the person I met. Recently, I met with a new client. I started off by handing her a copy of my book, although I did not tell her that I wrote the book – first impactful event. She was thanking me while looking at the book, when she realized I had written the book – second impactful event. The next day I saw her, she told me she had started reading my book. That is when she realized I had signed the title page on the inside – third impactful event.

Make your leave behind as memorable and impactful as possible.

<u>Letting them talk.</u> When I meet with people at a business networking event, I like to ask them a lot of questions to get them to talk about themselves. If someone approaches me and asks me what I do before I can ask them, I respond with a question. I will ask them, "Well, that depends on what interests you. Are you interested in business coaching, whiskey, cigars, or horses?" This always makes for an interesting icebreaker, and I can explore any one of those topics with them. If they respond with, "None," then I quickly realize that we will have very little to talk about.

When I ask someone what they do for a living, I like to follow that up with deeper questions. "How long have you been doing that?" "What got you into that line of work?" "What is it that you like most about what you do?" By digging deeper into their life and taking a genuine interest, we start to form a definite relationship.

Along with asking questions, I have found significant value in introducing those whom I have met to others who might have an interest in what they do. This is a superconnector trait that I talked about in Chapter 17. You will find it very powerful when you selflessly connect someone else at a networking event.

<u>Taking notes.</u> Now, I am not suggesting breaking out a steno pad and writing down everything everyone says. That would be a bit much and probably weird. However, when I go to a networking event, I take a pen. After meeting someone and getting their business card, I will jot a couple of key notes on their card. I try to write down memory jogger words that help me remember the person I met and what they might be interested in. When you meet several people in a couple of hours, you can quickly forget who was who. So, it helps to have a few notes on everybody that you meet.

<u>Following up.</u> This is something that always amazes me – mainly because so few people do it! The same day or the day after, reconnect with the people who you met at the networking event. Do not wait – the longer you wait the less you remember about them and the less they remember about you.

Here is my typical follow-up routine. The first thing I do is send them a follow-up email. I thank them for meeting with me and I personalize the email based on my notes. I offer them a free copy of my recent book, *Business 2020*. Since I already have their email from their business card, I do not need to send them to the site to request to download the book (which captures their email address). I also let them know that I will reach out via social media to connect if they have active profiles. Then, I send them connection invites via Facebook and LinkedIn.

If you use any type of customer relationship management (CRM) system, then you should enter these people into your system. Without spamming people, I try to stay in touch.

Going to meetings and events gets you involved with professional organizations, but to take it to the next level, consider a leadership role in the organization. All these organizations are nonprofit in nature and survive and grow with volunteer leadership support (remember Chapter 41). One of the earned benefits of becoming a leader in a professional organization is building your recognized success. As a leader in an organization, you will learn a great deal about what is occurring in your business area. Plus, everyone will know who you are – especially if you are heavily involved and impactful. The bigger the organization, the more opportunity for visibility.

Most professional industry organizations have at least one annual event – typically a conference – that is open to the membership. These are like huge national or international meetings. Aside from them being a great way to engage with the organization, they also provide incredible learning opportunities. Like attending meetings, you have a great ability to broaden your network.

Contribution. Participation is a good way to engage and deepen with professional organizations. But, to really increase your recognition across an organization, there are four things you can do: publish, speak, teach, and build the organization's body of knowledge (BOK). In Chapter 44, I will discuss publishing. In Chapter 45, I will discuss speaking.

Many professional organizations provide learning opportunities to their members. Thus, organizations are always looking for knowledgeable people to provide some type of teaching program. This could be a webinar, short lunch-and-learn, a daylong workshop, or even a multi-day course. For the last two years, I have worked with a local Chamber's leadership development program. Every year they immerse 70 to 80 business leaders in a leadership lab. I provide a daylong Leading Change workshop for the participants.

Industry aligned professional organizations tend to have some sort of professional certification program. They might have several different programs and levels. The certification programs normally possess a BOK. A BOK is a set of concepts, terms, and activities that make up a profession. They highlight the core teachings and skills required to obtain a certain level of recognized certification. These organizations will regularly review and update their BOK, and this is normally done by knowledgeable members. When the Association for Change Management Professionals (ACMP) was created, they needed to build their initial BOK. I was asked to assist with the development of the BOK, which is now used to certify change managers in the organization.

Involvement in the right professional organizations can be very influential toward your professional and personal recognition. Additionally, the earned benefits are extremely valuable. On your journey to becoming unbelievably successful, gaining recognition via your involvement with these organizations is a very good idea.

Chapter 43 Questions

1. What are the four things successful networking relies upon?

2. What is a business card considered in successful networking?

3. What can you take notes on at a networking event?

4. What is contribution?

Essay Question

Describe one networking activity that you could do now or would like to be able to share with others in your profession.

Chapter 43 Notes Page

Use this page to capture notes in each Part and Chapter

Chapter 44
Published Author

A sure-fire way to demonstrate your expertise is to become a published author. When I built my Personal Strategic Plan (see Part 2), I determined that I needed to become a published author. Over 20 years ago, this meant to me that I needed to have a physical book published. Electronic books (e-books) and e-book readers barely existed then. When I created my plan, the Kindle e-book reader was not even launched until five years later. Audio books were not even a concept, like they are today.

I learned, over the years, that being a published author meant more than just publishing a book. In fact, there are many ways to be recognized as an unbelievable success through publishing, which do not require one to publish an actual book.

An important point to remember about publishing anything is "currency." The main entity that recognizes authors is school – specifically college. Authors are often cited for their recent work; especially if it is good. Many schools want more current materials researched and the rule of thumb is no more than five years old. Some older material is fine, especially if it is foundational in nature, but it is good to keep published materials more current and up to date. This means that you cannot just publish something once and be good. No! What I learned is that you need to always be publishing and updating what you previously published.

Publishing is a journey in itself. It starts with some very basic activities and eventually works its way up to having several books in mainstream media. It is estimated that over 80 percent of people in the world desire to write and publish a book, although many never realize their dream. If you desire to be a recognized unbelievable success, this should be one of your goals – and not just one thing published.

Getting started. The first step to publishing is to start small. There are three ways you can do this. For a nonprofit organization, you can create a regular newsletter or write for one that already exists. You can create and post regular content on social media. And you can create your own blog. These are low-entry and low-cost options to get your writing juices flowing. The first thing you might struggle with is what to write about. So, starting with simple publishing avenues makes it easy to test out various subjects. When you are writing for a small newsletter, the topics tend to be very focused. Usually, a blog has some kind of theme that you stick to. Some people simply write about their life. Focus on your ikigai from Chapter 4 when determining topics.

In AFSA, while stationed at Vandenberg Air Force Base in California, I started a monthly newsletter. I put the whole thing together, had it printed, folded every one of them, stuffed them in envelopes, and mailed them to all the members. For two years I ran that newsletter – a very effective communications tool. Nowadays, this type of communication is typically emailed or posted online. For the next 13 years I continued some form of regular newsletter communication with every AFSA organization I was in.

In 2011, I started two blogs and a digital magazine. By 2012, I was also guest writing for two other blogs. For several years, I regularly wrote and published work in this manner. Also, in 2012, I published my first book. It was a post-apocalyptic sci-fi fantasy called, *One Dead Marine*. I published the book as a learning experience.

In 2016, I learned leveraging social media as a publishing medium. I started with Facebook and expanded to LinkedIn. My first business book, *Overcoming Organizational Myopia*, was published in 2019 – it took me 10 years to write, edit, and publish that book.

My publishing journey started with a simple newsletter – two pages every month – and evolved over time to regular posting on LinkedIn. In *Good to Great*, Jim Collins talks about the flywheel concept. When you start something, at first it is hard, and it takes a lot of time and work. But, if you stick with it, it gets easier and easier. My first business book took 10 years to write, edit, and publish. My second business book took four months. I have learned how to do this faster, and it has become much easier.

Writing for others. As I talked about, I was a guest blogger for several years. In 2019, I joined the Forbes Coaches Council and have been published over 100 times. Also, I have written monthly for the *Global Business Playbook* and *Authoritti 5.0*. While writing this book, another forum was actively recruiting me. By writing for others, you only have to worry about writing the material. When you write for yourself or your organization, then you must worry about everything.

Although I have never done this, the professional organizations you belong to probably have publications you can write for. Sometimes these are simple articles that just have to meet basic criteria. Others might be peer-reviewed research papers, which are much more difficult to put together. This is a way to write for others, which I have not yet employed.

Writing a book. There are a lot of things that go into writing and publishing an actual book. It is a long process, which speeds up with use. There are four important questions that you should answer before you start writing.

1. Why?
2. When?
3. What?
4. Who?

Why? The first question to ask yourself, is why you are writing a book in the first place. I have emphasized the importance of establishing your purpose upfront throughout this book. It is no different when it comes to writing your book. When you know why you want to write a book, it frames everything else about the book. A helpful tool is to look at the six motivators that I described in Chapter 30.

My first book was simply a pilot effort – a test. I wanted to see what the process was like when it came to writing and self-publishing a book. I never cared if anyone, except my closest friends and family, ever read it. My second book was written as a business card. No kidding! I wanted to be able to give someone my book that demonstrated my knowledge and capability more than a business card ever could (remember Chapter 43). I have probably given out as many copies of my book as people have actually bought. My third book was designed to get out into the public quickly and get into as many business owners' hands as possible during and immediately after COVID. Therefore, it was created as a free PDF available for download. The idea for *Becoming Unbelievably Successful* hit me like a ton of bricks. I realized one day, in early July 2020, that things in my life would have been incredibly different if I had read a book like this in high school or even in college.

When? This question brings to light whether this really is the right time for you to write a book. Writing, editing, publishing, and marketing a book takes a great deal of effort. When you know exactly what you want to say, the words simply flow, but there will be times where you stare at an empty page and have no idea what to write. If your life is really busy with work, family, school, etc., then right now might not be the right time to start.

What? A great number of people want to write a book. However, many of them have no clue what to write about. Remember in Part 2 of this book when I shared my goal area of becoming a published author? I had no idea what I would write about. So, if you do not know what you want to write about, then now is not the right time to start writing.

So, how do you learn what to write about? The first step is to break out your work around your ikigai from Chapter 4 and look at all the stuff you listed. Within all those things are a great deal of potential topics just waiting to be written about.

Who? This last question is probably the most important and impactful question to ask yourself. Who are you writing your book for? For many people, who I have talked to about writing a book, the most common answer I hear is, "Everyone." No, sorry, wrong answer, try again. Writers need to be laser-focused on who they are writing their book for. Sure, "anyone" can pick your book up and read it, but specifically who needs to read it?

This book, *Becoming Unbelievably Successful*, was written for me – the high school me. As I looked back on my life, I realized the things that happened and what I did or did not do about them. Today, I see me all over the place – people without purpose, vision, or drive. I know there are those in high school and college today that know exactly what they want out of life. But I also know there are many others who do not! This book is for them. It is a book that I hope sparks something in them that makes a difference in their lives. When writing a book, know exactly who you are writing it for.

Plan out the writing of your book

When I started thinking about writing a book, I could think of only one way to do that – write it myself. However, this is not the only way.

When I was a kid, I loved to read fiction. I devoured swords and sorcery fantasy novels. But I also love to read *The Hardy Boys*. Frank and Joe Hardy were created in 1927, and I loved those guys! I amassed quite a collection of hardback books, trying to get every one of the books for my collection. Imagine my surprise when I learned that the author, Franklin W. Dixon, had not written all those books! In fact, *The Hardy Boys* mystery books I loved so much were all written by several different ghostwriters.

Today, many books are written by professional "ghosts" (as they call themselves). These people can be very good at capturing your thoughts and putting them into a book, written under your name. Like many songs sung by singers that are not written by the artists, many books are not written by the authors. Today, ghostwriting is big business, and many ghostwriters know how to publish and market your book as well.

Have you ever heard of the phrase, "It takes a village?" Well, this is another way to write a book – get others to help you. Many books are written by more than one person; some are written by many. If you have a concept, you can enlist the help of one or more people to write your book. Sometimes, you might be a contributor to someone else's book. In 2005, I became a certified Master Speechwriter, working with Joan Detz. Detz was writing a book and she asked me to provide a written recognition speech for that book. You too can bring together several writers to collaborate on your book. In 2022, I worked with EBR, to bring together six other authors and publish *Lessons in Life Long Learning*.

Once we know that we want to write a book, there are several things you need to do to make your book a reality – no matter what writing route you take. These five things are called ideation, research, brainstorming, testing, and outlining.

Sometimes I see something, and it triggers an idea. Sometimes I might read something, and it sparks a thought. I might be talking to someone, and I am hit with inspiration. This is where ideation starts. My second article with the *Global Business Playbook* was called *Drive 4 Success*. I was driving to work one day and someone on the highway cut over several lanes to exit without even signaling. I knew a guy once that would comment about people like that, saying, "They're alone in this world." As I thought about this driver's actions, I started to think about the behaviors of many – no, all – drivers on the road. Were they just a reflection of their behaviors at work? Bam! Ideation!!!

When you have an idea, write it down and file it away on your hard drive. You may not address that idea again for years – you might jump on it right away. But whatever you do, do not lose it. When you decide to follow your idea, now comes the process of fleshing it out. Start researching the topic – remember Chapter 31? Brainstorm ideas alone or with others. I like to write small posts about the concepts I am thinking about and get feedback from my social community. I also test out parts of a book with my social audience. But you can test out your ideas in many different ways. Most importantly, do not write in a vacuum. Make sure your messages resonate with others – especially your target audience. My book idea, which I talked about above, started as a short blog, recently made its way into an expanded article, and I plan on turning into a full book someday.

The third way is to simply look at what everyone else is writing about and see if that jogs ideas. Many people write about the same things and only put their slant on the topic.

As you continually go through this process, an outline will start to form. You will start to lay things out in logical order. To better understand the layout of a book, look to the ones that others have written. Also, there is good advice from the top self-publishing sites, such as Kindle Direct Publishing, Lulu, and BookBaby. It is best to have a really good outline before you start to write. Otherwise, your book will seem disjointed. You will always continue updating your outline as you write, but I recommend trying to lock-in most of the outline early.

Most of your time-consuming work will probably be in the writing and editing cycles. Typically, you create a rough draft that receives a massive edit. The second and third drafts refine your manuscript. Before you go to publish you will do one final edit to ensure everything is ready and looks good. Unfortunately, errors still have a way of being missed by many eyes and show up in the final published product.

When I started writing, I always started with a template with a specific format. However, I found it hard to not screw up the format as I wrote and edited my work. Now, I write with very little formatting and then go back and format the book in my second or third draft. Every time you edit your work, you will mess something else up – just keep an eye out for it.

The last step in publishing a book is to decide how to get your work published. Also, you must decide what formats (hardcover, paperback, e-book, or audio) you will publish your work in. There are basically three ways to publish a book: 1) as a PDF, hosted at your own web-based location for download or to send to people; 2) self-publish through one of the many self-publishing services available; or 3) through a publishing house. Although this is the last step to publishing, you should start considering your options much earlier in your journey.

Although publishing an actual book is the pinnacle of success recognition, there are many ways to be recognized through the written word. Consider recognition of your expertise through publishing as part of your journey to becoming unbelievably successful.

Chapter 44 Questions

1. What is "currency?"

2. What percentage of people in the world want to publish a book?

3. What are the four important questions you must answer before writing a book?

4. What is a "ghost?"

Essay Question

If you were to publish a book, describe what it would be about.

Chapter 44 Notes Page

Use this page to capture notes in each Part and Chapter

Chapter 45
Public Speaker

Another way to prove to others your knowledge and expertise on a subject is by presenting what you know to them. Many people give work presentations regarding things they know every day. However, it can be a little different getting in front of an audience that you do not know.

When people hear the words "public speaker," this creates a vision of thousands of people in an auditorium, listening to one expert up on stage. Although this might be the pinnacle of public speaking, it most certainly is not the norm. Like becoming a published author, becoming a public speaker is a journey of speaking to the public.

Before we discuss the journey, let me make another plug for Toastmasters International. Once someone is 18 years old, they are eligible to join Toastmasters. A Toastmasters club is one of the safest, most welcoming experiences to learn to speak in public. You are with people who want you to succeed. As soon as you are eligible, I recommend you join a local club in your area.

Everyone will be forced to take a speech class at some point in school – it might be high school, college, or both. Just expect it. However, most people really start speaking in front of other people at work. Unless you run for class president, join a debate team, or get into theater classes, work will probably be your first true immersion into public speaking. Many people avoid promotions at work because the job requires them to speak. So, if you plan to be successful, this is one phobia that you need to get over!

Social media is the next step on the speaking journey. This is not silly TikTok videos – I am talking about creating and posting short, informative, and engaging videos that promote your professional success. My friend on LinkedIn, Julie Hruska, is excellent at this. I am not saying that they cannot be fun and humorous, but they should have a purpose. Many people think that shooting a quick two-minute video and posting it online is easy. They are wrong! Many people try, and they struggle before they finally do it. Over time it gets easier and easier for people to do this. YouTube is a great place to better share your knowledge. Sometimes it is simply you recording over a slide presentation, and sometimes it is you on camera. This type of approach helps you get comfortable in front of the audience and is easy to do with today's technology.

In Chapter 43, I talked about the importance of getting involved with professional organizations. These organizations are always looking for public speakers for meetings and conferences. Typically, I will speak at least 20 times with local organizations, every year. Find the person in your organization that schedules speakers and sign up – trust me, they will appreciate it. If you are good, you will find yourself asked back, and you will be asked to speak at other venues. If you take on a leadership role in an organization, you will often find yourself speaking as part of your role.

Experience is the best teacher for someone to become a good public speaker. In Chapter 28, we discussed ways to communicate better. But, actually doing it is what will make you a better speaker. The best public speakers know their material so well that they do not need notes or to memorize their presentations – they speak off-the-cuff. The best can command an audience's attention and get them engaged. And the very best seamlessly leverage audio and visual technology to share their message.

Those who avoid facing their fear of public speaking will never fully realize their unbelievable success. Embrace this skill and learn how to "own the room."

Chapter 45 Questions

1. How old do you have to be to join Toastmasters International?

2. Where is a good place to post video presentations?

3. What typically happens when you take on a leadership role in a professional organization?

4. What will make you a better public speaker?

Essay Question

Describe a situation where you had to speak before an audience and how it went.

Chapter 45 Notes Page

Use this page to capture notes in each Part and Chapter

Chapter 46
Awards and Recognitions

The last aspect of becoming a recognized unbelievable success is through formal awards and recognition.

When I was in the Air Force, at my first assignment, I was put in for an award called the "Squadron Airman of the Month." I did not know anything about the award, but when I competed, I won. It was not much of a big deal because I never competed for awards in the past. The three monthly winners for the quarter then went on to compete for "Squadron Airman of the Quarter." I won that award as well. Every squadron's Airman of the Quarter then competed for the "Wing Airman of the Quarter." I went on to win that award as well!

Now, I had no idea what this meant until it happened. This award suddenly opened up all kinds of opportunities for me. Different departments in my squadron were fighting over me to come work for them. One of my mentors told me that everything would change. The biggest thing this did was open my eyes to the importance of winning awards and recognition on the road to unbelievable success. Not because of the award itself, but the visibility that would come with the recognition.

At my second assignment, I took over a role as the Executive Staff Noncommissioned Officer. However, I filled this role as an airman because of a letter of recognition that was sent to my new commander. One of my responsibilities in that position was to respond to applicable award submissions. There were over 50 award requests that would occur every year. Many of them we received so late that we might only have a day or so to respond. The key thing I learned was that few ever responded to these awards. I started to get proactive with the awards and I would ensure the squadron was ready when the request came down. It was not long before our unit and our people were winning these awards on a regular basis.

When I worked with USAA, they had a strategic performance measure based on awards and recognition. However, the important thing to remember is that the company would normally have to submit (put themselves in the running) for these awards. I have seen this with every company I have worked with.

The moral of this story is that awards and recognition are what shout your success from the rooftops, and you must be the driver when it comes to competing for them. On your journey of becoming unbelievably successful, seek out and compete for awards and recognition when you are deserving of them.

Chapter 46 Questions

1. What was the key thing the author learned about awards at his second military assignment?

2. What happened when the author won the Wing Airman of the Quarter?

3. What was the moral of this chapter?

4. What was the first award the author won in the military?

Essay Question

Describe an award or recognition that you, or someone you know, has received.

Chapter 46 Notes Page

Use this page to capture notes in each Part and Chapter

Part 8 Questions

1. Why are awards and recognition important?

2. What is meant by "not writing in a vacuum?"

3. What is "no longer social" when you own a business?

4. Why is making and posting professional video presentations good?

Essay Question

Why is being recognized for your success important?

Part 8 Notes Page

Use this page to capture notes in each Part and Chapter

JOHN KNOTTS

Part 9
Becoming Unbelievably Successful

"Do not judge me by my successes.
Judge me by how many times I fell down and got back up again."
~ Nelson Mandela

On July 11, 2020, I started the effort of putting this book together. I did not start writing anything until July 27, 2020. On September 6, 2020, I formally wrote this last part of the book. In 43 days, I wrote this entire book!

Over 20 years ago, I knew I wanted to become a published author. This was one element of my Personal Strategic Plan to become unbelievably successful. This is now my fifth published book, along with many other publishing successes.

However, this will not be my last book. In fact, there are at least 16 future business titles listed in the back of this book.

See, this book is not about how to "be" an unbelievable success, it is about "becoming" unbelievably successful. This book is about the journey, not the destination.

I, personally, am not an unbelievable success. But I am well on my way. The important thing to remember is that it is your journey and no one else's. Never let anyone else define what success looks like for you! This only makes you live in their shadow. You, using this book as your guide, define what your success looks like and how you will get there.

Most of this book has focused on the things that hold you back from unbelievable success. Whether it is a lack of belief in yourself, the wrong mindset, being overwhelmed with stress, a lack of motivation, or many other potential things, it is only you that holds you back!

What is unbelievable success?

Unbelievable success is you becoming unbelievably successful. It is about embarking on a purposeful journey and getting closer to your vision every day. Then, everything you do that moves you forward – even the failures – is a success.

This is how you stop being a human being, and start being a human doing! For 35 years of my life, I was successful at times and unsuccessful at others. But that was without purpose and direction – it was akin to dumb luck! "Becoming Unbelievably Successful" is your guide to eliminating dumb luck.

Follow this guide!

Discover your purpose – your ikigai.

Build your Personal Strategic Plan.

And use the tools and tips from throughout this book to become unbelievably successful!!!

Happy journey.

John R. Knotts, Jr.

Part 9 (and end of book) Notes Page

Use this page to capture notes in each Part and Chapter

Becoming Unbelievably Successful Glossary

Below is an alphabetical list of key terms or words found in *Becoming Unbelievably Successful*, with short explanations.

Format Example:
[Glossary Item]: [Description].

5S: an approach to assess everything in a given space and removing what is not necessary.

Abundance Mindset: belief that giving away means more will come in return.

Active Listening: ability for a listener to fully concentrate on, respond to, and remember what was said.

Agile: approach to project management.

Agile Perfectionism: striving for perfection, not to be perfect.

BHAG: Big Hairy Audacious Goal; goals that stretch a person to aim high.

Business Strategic Plan: assessment of a business, then creation of targets and an implementation process.

Business Transferable Skill: a capability that can be used in many roles.

Change Management: effectively preparing, supporting, and equipping people for change.

Defensive Mindset: belief in a need for be self-protective.

Deliberate Success: making a concerted effort to constantly focus on building yourself, and your successes, every day.

Emotional Intelligence (EQ): an ability to understand and manage personal emotions.

Extrinsic Motivator: motivation from the world; typically tangible; usually produces short-term results.

Extrovert: a person who draws energy from others.

Fixed Mindset: belief that capabilities, intelligence, and talents are set in stone and cannot be changed.

Flowcharts: process maps, lean value streams, process charts, and flow diagrams.

Gap Analysis: assessing performance to identify whether objectives are being met.

Glossophobia: fear of public speaking.

Goals (Goal Areas): a broad area of objectives, initiatives, and actions that move the company closer to its vision.

Growth Mindset: belief that capabilities, intelligence, and talents can be developed.

Ikigai: a Japanese concept known as "a reason for being" – having a direction or purpose; "Iki" roughly meaning Life; and "Gai" roughly meaning value.

Intelligence Quotient (IQ): an assessment of intelligence scored from standardized tests.

Intrinsic Motivator: motivation comes from inside; much less tangible in nature; usually produces long-term results.

Introvert: a person who derives energy from within.

Imposter Syndrome: a mindset that you cannot reach success.

Law of Action: a philosophy that states that you must take action for action to occur.

Law of Attraction: a philosophy that your actions (positive and negative) will bring about equal experiences.

Law of Belief: a philosophy that whatever we fully believe in, eventually becomes our reality.

Law of Cause and Effect: a philosophy that nothing happens without an equal reaction.

Law of Compensation: a philosophy that your efforts come back to you in different forms matching the same energy with which we performed the actions.

Law of Correspondence: a philosophy that there is an equal relationship between the positive and negative world.

Law of Divine Oneness: a philosophy that we are all connected to one source.

Law of Gender: a philosophy that everything has its masculine and feminine energies.

Law of Gestation: a philosophy everything must go through a period during which it is conceptualized and actualized.

The Law of Perpetual Transmutation of Energy: a philosophy that everyone has the power to change the conditions within their life.

Law of Polarity: a philosophy that everything is on a continuum and has an opposite.

Law of Reciprocity: a philosophy that when someone does something nice for you, you have a deep-rooted psychological urge to do something nice in return.

Law of Relativity: a philosophy that everything in the physical world is made real by its relationship to something else.

Law of Rhythm: a philosophy that energy is like a pendulum, flowing left and right.

Law of Vibration: a philosophy that everything is energy, and all energies vibrate at certain frequencies.

Lifestyle Business: a business where you earn a decent living doing whatever it is you enjoy doing.

Leaderment: a combined effort as a manager and a leader.

Lean Six Sigma: a methodical process of systematically improving performance.

Likert Scale: a psychometric scoring methodology, typically used in scoring survey responses.

Locus of Control: a person's perception of the control they have over their actions.

Mastermind Principle: people working in perfect harmony, to reach a definite purpose – when two or minds come together, the mastermind forms.

Memory Mastery: things you can do to improve your ability to remember important information.

Mindfulness: being self-aware in the moment; being fully present.

Mindset: a set of attitudes, assumptions, methods, or notions held by someone.

Mission: what you do; where you focus.

Mnemonics: a pattern of letters or words that help people remember information.

North Star: your purpose; vision; where you are going in life.

Personal Strategic Plan: a structured method of personal planning, including an individual mission and vision.

Process Improvement: a very tactical response to dealing with problems in your operation.

Process Management: taking a program-based view of continuous process improvement in an organization.

Productive Mindset: belief in a need to share and expand thoughts with others.

Project Management: ability to assess and implement information, tools, and techniques to deliver value.

Purpose Venn Diagram: a pictorial display that shows where work takes place, used to find balance.

Relationship Management: an ability to work with others through strong social awareness and self-management.

Scarcity Mindset: belief that a person does not have enough, so does not give.

Self-actualization: achieving the fullest potential; the top of the Maslow's Hierarchy of Needs pyramid.

Self-awareness: understanding yourself on a deep level; actively recognize your personality, your feelings, what motivates you, and what you believe in.

Self-care: initiating regular activities that promote positive mental, emotional, and physical health.

Self-efficacy: a person's belief in their ability to reach goals.

Self-management: an ability to recognize triggers and drivers as they occur and manage your responses to them.

SMART Goal: a goal that includes five pieces; Specific, Measurable, Attainable, Relevant, and Time-bound.

Social Awareness: ability to tune into what is happening around you.

Superconnector: a person, group, or technology who holds the trust of a large group of people and has a means of reaching out to them directly.

Theory of Inventive Problem Solving TRIZ): a theory and process for analyzing and solving problems.

Universal Law: 15 laws that people consider to be universal truths.

Venn Diagram: a pictorial display that shows relationships between sets of items or information.

Psychopathology of Normality: the average space where people function for much of their life.

Shuhari: an ancient Japanese martial arts term that is an approach to learning and growth.

Structured Lifelong Learning: purposeful approach to self-directed growth.

Values: principles to live and operate by.

Vision: aspirations and direction.

Zone of Comfort (Comfort Zone): a state of mind where a person is typically without anxiety and minimal risks.

Zone of Fear (Fear Zone): a state of mind where self-confidence is lacking, an uncomfortable place found immediately after leaving the comfort zone.

Zone of Growth (Growth Zone): a state of mind where a person finds a high level of success and purpose.

Zone of Learning (Learning Zone): a state of mind where a person is willing to explore new skills and abilities.

Becoming Unbelievably Successful Subject Index

Below is an alphabetical list of subjects mentioned in *Becoming Unbelievably Successful*, indicating where in the work they are referred to.

Format Example:
[Subject]: [Page Numbers]

#
5S: 138, 154-156

A
Abundance Mindset: see Mindset
Agile: 66
Agile Perfectionism: 125

B
Business Transferable Skill: 164

C
Change Management: 163, 185-186
Comfort Zone: see Zone of Comfort

D
Defensive Mindset: see Mindset
Deliberate Success: 4

F
Fear: 3, 127, 185-186, 189-190, 226-227, 233, 237, 240-241, 297
Fear Zone: see Zone of Fear
Fixed Mindset: see Mindset
Flowchart: 202-203

G
Goal Area: 34, 43, 55-56, 60-63, 72, 143, 165-167, 195, 231-232, 267, 279, 291
Goal: see Goal Area
Growth Mindset: see Mindset
Growth Zone: see Zone of Growth

I
Ikigai: 11, 23-24, 27, 51-52, 60, 79, 99, 231, 289, 291, 307
Imposter Syndrome: 98, 236

L
Law of …: see Universal Law
Leaderment: 178-181, 271
Lean Six Sigma: 104, 200
Learning Zone: see Zone of Learning
Likert Scale: 26, 80, 83
Locus of Control: 33, 79, 83-84, 98, 150

M
Mindfulness: 98, 116
Mindset:
    Abundance Mindset: 83, 97-98, 147
    Defensive Mindset: 97-98
    Fixed Mindset: 97-99
    Growth Mindset: 97, 99
    Productive Mindset: 97
    Scarcity Mindset: 97-99
Mission: 60, 172-174, 179, 272, 280

P
Personal Strategic Plan: 11, 15, 20, 24, 34, 41-43, 51, 57, 60-61, 67-68, 71, 80, 84, 93-94, 97, 107-108, 112, 120, 135-139, 143, 165, 168, 172, 179, 185, 189, 195-187, 200, 224, 226, 231-232, 249-250, 289, 307
Process Improvement: 23, 103-106, 112, 127, 138, 175, 200-205, 250
Process Management: 104, 200-205
Productive Mindset: see Mindset
Project Management: 195-197
Program Management: 195-197

R
Relationship Management: 91-94, 116

S
Scarcity Mindset: see Mindset
Self-awareness: 91-92, 98, 129
Self-actualization: 11, 27, 32-35, 43-44, 51, 83, 163, 259-260, 267
Self-care: 116, 135-156, 164
Self-efficacy: 33, 79-84, 98, 236
Self-management: 91-94, 129
Shuhari: 44, 111-113
SMART: 231-233
Social Awareness: 91-94
Stop, Challenge, and Choose: 99-100
Structured Lifelong Learning: 67, 81, 97, 103-108
Superconnector: 122, 285

T
Toastmaster: 20, 53, 55, 57, 61, 121, 190-191, 267, 296

U
Universal Law: 38-44
    Law of Action: 38-40
    Law of Attraction: 11, 38-40, 52, 212
    Law of Belief: 38, 44
    Law of Cause and Effect: 38, 40, 98
    Law of Compensation: 38, 40, 83, 98, 181
    Law of Correspondence: 38-40
    Law of Divine Oneness: 38, 40
    Law of Gender: 38, 44
    Law of Gestation: 38, 41
    The Law of Perpetual Transmutation of Energy: 38, 41
    Law of Polarity: 38, 43-44, 97
    Law of Reciprocity: 38, 42-43, 98
    Law of Relativity: 38, 42, 225
    Law of Rhythm: 38, 44
    Law of Vibration: 11, 38-39, 41, 93

V
Values: 93, 172, 174-175
Venn Diagram: 23-24, 27
Vision: 29, 40-43, 60, 79, 99, 103-104, 136, 143, 172-174, 178-179, 185-186, 195, 208, 231-233, 245, 291, 296, 307

Z
Zone of Comfort: 7-8, 232, 240, 249
Zone of Fear: 7-8, 240
Zone of Growth: 7-8, 240
Zone of Learning: 7-8, 240

Becoming Unbelievably Successful Bibliography

Throughout this book, I have referenced various different books, videos, articles, and movies that have guided my journey to unbelievable success. Additionally, there are many books that I have read, but are not mentioned, but I still think are important. In keeping with the concept of lifelong learning in Chapter 14, here is an exhaustive list of those items mentioned in this book or those I feel are important to your journey to becoming unbelievably successful.

Format Example:
Title (DATE). Author(s).
Website (if applicable).

7 Habits of Highly Effective People (1989). Stephen R. Covey.

A Theory of Human Motivation (1943). Abraham H. Maslow.

Agile Software Development (2001). Alistair Cockburn.

Animal Farm (1984). George Orwell.

Atlas Shrugged (1957). Ayn Rand.

Atomic Habits: An Easy & Proven Way to Build Good Habits & Break Bad Ones (2018). James Clear.

Becoming Unbelievably Successful (2022). John Knotts.

Big (1988).
https://www.imdb.com/title/tt0094737/.

Black Swan (2018). Nassim Taleb.

Born to Win: Transactional Analysis with Gestalt (1971). Dorothy Jongeward and Muriel James.

Business 2020: The Business World After COVID-19 (2020). John Knotts.
https://bit.ly/GetBusy2020/.

Breaking the Habit of Being Yourself: How to Lose Your Mind and Create a New One (2012). Joe Dispenza.

Breaking Your Intelligent Process Automation Paradigms (unpublished). John Knotts.

Cumulative Advantage: How to Build Momentum for Your Ideas, Business and Life Against All Odds (2021). Mark Schaefer.

Curious (2015). Ian Leslie.

Don't Sweat the Small Stuff and It's All Small Stuff: Simple Ways to Keep the Little Things from Taking Over Your Life (1997). Richard Carlson.

Driving 4 Success (2020). John Knotts. https://globalbusinessplaybook.com/article-archive/driving-4-success.

Drive: The Surprising Truth About What Motivates Us (2009). Daniel Pink.

Execution: The Discipline of Getting Things Done (2002). Lawrence Bossidy and Ram Charan.

Essentialism: The Disciplined Pursuit of Less (2014). Greg McKeown.

Feel the Fear and Do It Anyway (1987). Susan Jeffers.

From Lucky to Smart: Leadership Lessons from QuikTrip (2008). Chester Cadieux.

Getting Things Done (2001). David Allen.

Good to Great: Why Some Companies Make the Leap...and Others Don't (2001). James C. Collins.

Global Business Playbook (n.d.). http://www.globalbusinessplaybook.com.

Grit: The Power of Passion and Persistence (2016). Angela Duckworth.

Habits of Health Transformational System (2019). Dr. Wayne Scott Anderson.

Hardwiring Excellence: Purpose, Worthwhile Work, Making a Difference (2004). Quint Studer.

Hogan's Heroes (1965 – 1971). https://www.imdb.com/title/tt0058812/.

How Good Do You Want to Be? (2007). Nick Saban.

How to Win Friends and Influence People (1936). Dale Carnegie.

Influencer: The Power to Change Anything (2007). Joseph Grenny, Kerry Patterson, David Maxfield, Ron McMillan, and Al Switzler

Jonathan Livingston Seagull (1970). Richard Bach.

Leaders Eat Last (2014). Simon Sinek.
Lessons in Life Long Learning (2022). John Knotts.

Limitless: Upgrade Your Brain, Learn Anything Faster, and Unlock Your Exceptional Life (2020). Jim Kwik.

Lincoln on Leadership: Executive Strategies for Tough Times (1992). Donald T. Phillips.

List of Forgotten Realms Novels (2020). Various Authors. https://en.wikipedia.org/wiki/List_of_Forgotten_Realms_novels.

List of Shannara Book Series (2020). Terry Brooks. https://shannara.fandom.com/wiki/List_of_Shannara_Book_Series.

Lord of the Flies (1954). William Golding.

Make Your Bed (2017). Admiral William H. McRaven. https://youtu.be/GmFwRkl-TTc.

Man's Search for Meaning (1946). Victor Frankl.

Mind Power Into the 21st Century: Techniques to Harness the Astounding Powers of Thought (1996). John Kehoe.

Mindset: The New Psychology of Success (2006). Carol Dweck.

Mr. Magorium's Wonder Emporium (2007). https://www.imdb.com/title/tt0457419/.

Mr. Shmooze: The Art and Science of Selling Through Relationships (2005). Richard Abraham.

New Brand Leadership: Managing at the Intersection of Globalization, Localization and Personalization (2015). Larry Light.

On Writing: A Memoir of the Craft (2000). Stephen King.

One Dead Marine (2012). John Knotts.

Opportunities (1981). Edward de Bono.

Outliers: The Story of Success (2018). Malcolm Gladwell.

Our Iceberg is Melting: Changing and Succeeding Under Any Conditions (2006). John Kotter and Holger Rathgeber.

Overcoming Organizational Myopia: Breaking Through Siloed Organizations (2019). John Knotts.

Prepared: What Kids Need for a Fulfilled Life (2019). Diane Tavenner.

Principles (2017), Ray Dalio.

Process Improvement Guide, Second Edition: Quality Tools for Today's Air Force (1994). Susan Holmes.

Psychology Review (n.d.). https://www.apa.org/pubs/journals/rev.

Range: How Generalists Triumph in a Specialized World (2016). David Epstein.

Rich Dad Poor Dad (1997). Robert T. Kiyosaki.

Self-Directed Learning: A Guide for Learners and Teachers (1975). Malcolm Knowles.

Self-Leadership: How to Become More Successful, Efficient, and Effective from the Inside Out (2012). Ana Lucia Kazan and Andrew Bryant.

Smokey and the Bandit (1977). https://www.imdb.com/title/tt0076729/.

Start With Why (2009). Simon Sinek.

Stop Jumping To Do (unpublished). John Knotts.

Strengths Finder 2.0 (2007). Tom Rath.

The 10X Rule: The Only Difference Between Success and Failure (2011). Grant Cardone

The Alchemist (1988). Paulo Coelho.

The Art of War (5th Century). Sun Tzu.

The Catcher in The Rye (1945). J. D. Salinger.

The Diamond Cutter: The Buddha on Managing Your Business and Your Life (2000). Geshe Michael Roach and Lama Christie McNally

The EQ Difference: A Powerful Plan for Putting Emotional Intelligence to Work (2004). Adele B. Lynn.

The Fountainhead (1943). Ayn Rand.

The Great Gatsby (1925). Scott F. Fitzgerald.

The Hardy Boys (2020). Franklin W, Dixon. https://en.wikipedia.org/wiki/The_Hardy_Boys.

The Inner Game of Golf (1981). Timothy Gallwey.

The Law of Success (1928). Napoleon Hill.

The Lean Startup (2011). Eric Ries.

The Little Blue Book: United States Air Force Core Values Handbook (1997). United States Air Force.

The Memory Jogger II (1994). Michael Brassard and Diane Ritter.

The Motive (2020). Patrick Lencioni.

The One Thing: The Surprisingly Simple Truth Behind Extraordinary Results (2012). Gary W. Keller and Jay Papasan.

The Organism: A Holistic Approach to Biology Derived from Pathological Data of Man (1939). Kurt Goldstein.

The Power of Nice: How to Conquer the Business World with Kindness (2006). Robin Koval.

The Power of TED (2005). David Emerald Womeldorff.

The Project Method (1918). William Heard Kilpatrick.

The Ride of a Lifetime: Lessons Learned from 15 Years as CEO of the Walt Disney Company (2019). Robert Iger.

The Richest Man in Babylon (1926). George Samuel Clason.

The Secret (2006). Rhonda Byrne.

The Subtle Art of Not Giving a Bleep: A Counterintuitive Approach to Living a Good Life (2016). Mark Manson.

The Total Money Makeover (2003). Dave Ramsey.

The Wizard of Oz (1939). https://www.imdb.com/title/tt0032138/.

Theory of Inventive Problem Solving (TRIZ). https://en.wikipedia.org/wiki/TRIZ.

Think and Grow Rich (1937). Napoleon Hill.

Think Big Take Small Steps: Overcoming the Five Reasons Strategies Fail (unpublished). John Knotts.

Unshakeable: Your Financial Freedom Playbook (2017). Tony Robbins and Peter Mallouk.

What I Learned from 100 Days of Rejection (2015). Jia Jiang. https://www.ted.com/talks/jia_jiang_what_i_learned_from_100_days_of_rejection.

What Would You Do If You Weren't Afraid? (2020). Borja Vilaseca (in Spanish).

Who Moved My Cheese? An Amazing Way to Deal with Change in Your Work and in Your Life (1998). Spencer Johnson.

Why We Sleep: The New Science of Sleep and Dreams (2017). Matthew Walker.

Willy Wonka and the Chocolate Factory (1971). https://www.imdb.com/title/tt0067992/.

Your Network is Your Net Worth: Unlock the Hidden Power of Connections for Wealth, Success, and Happiness in the Digital Age (2013). Porter Gale.

You Are the Placebo (2014). Joe Dispenza.

Becoming Unbelievably Successful Acronyms

In this book, several acronyms were used. Here is a complete list of all of them used in the book.

AAC	Airmen Activities Coordinator
ACMP	Association of Change Management Professionals
ADKAR	Awareness, Desire, Knowledge, Ability, and Reinforcement
AFSA	Air Force Sergeants Association
AMA	American Management Association
APA	American Psychological Association
ASQ	American Society for Quality
B2B	Business to Business
B2C	Business to Customer
BHAG	Big Hairy Audacious Goal
BOK	Body of Knowledge
CEO	Chief Executive Officer
COO	Chief Operating Officer
CRM	Customer Relationship Management
COVID	Corona Virus Disease
CX	Customer Experience
DEAL	Delegate, Eliminate, Automate, and Leverage
EBR	Executive Book Review
EQ	Emotional Intelligence
FEAR	False Evident Appearing Real
GPA	Grade Point Average
GPRA	Government Performance Results Act
HUA	Heard, Understood, Acknowledged
ITIL	Information Technology Infrastructure Library
IQ	Intelligence Quotient
JEEP	Just Educated Enough to Pass
Leaderment	Leadership and Management

NP	Nonproductive time
NPR	Nonproductive yet Required time
NPV	Nonproductive yet Valuable time
OECD	Organization for Economic Co-operation and Development
P	Productive time
PMI	Project Management Institute
PMP	Project Management Professional
POW	Prisoner of War
RV	Recreational Vehicle
USAFE	United States Air Forces in Europe
VUCA	Volatile, Uncertain, Complex, and Ambiguous

About the Author

John Knotts is a personal and professional business coach and consultant with over 25 years of experience in military, non-profit, and commercial businesses. He has an extensive background in strategy, change, process, leadership, management, human capital, training and education, innovation, design, and communication. He believes strongly in a holistic and no-nonsense approach to establishing operational excellence.

A 21-year Air Force Veteran and former consultant with the top-rated consulting firm, Booz | Allen | Hamilton, John recently held several internal strategic roles with the United Services Automobile Association (USAA). John also owns his own consulting business, Crosscutter Enterprises, with which he has sharpened the saw since retiring from the Air Force in 2008. He has been very involved in several non-profit organizations since the early 1990s.

John is a Doctoral student in the field of Industrial and Organizational Psychology. He holds a Master's Degree in Quality Systems Management from the National Graduate School and his Bachelor's is in Management from the American Military School. He has a Lean Six Sigma Master Black Belt from Smarter Solutions, a Master's-level certification as a Change Management Advanced Practitioner from Georgetown University, and Change Management certification from Prosci. Additionally, he has had extensive training and education in Information Technology Infrastructure Library (ITIL), project management, and agile methodologies.

John boasts an extensive writing, speaking, facilitating, and teaching background. In the Air Force, he was instructor certified, and taught hundreds of classes in many areas. He is an Advanced Toastmaster with experience in ten different clubs in Europe and the United States. John is also a certified Master Speechwriter, studying under Joan Detz, professional speechwriter, and coach. As a Master Black Belt, he developed and led numerous process improvement and process management courses. For both the National Graduate School and Hallmark University, John has been an Adjunct Faculty member. John previously published a fictional novel, *One Dead Marine*, a business book, *Overcoming Organizational Myopia*, and has been an avid blogger. He is an active invitation-only member with Forbes Coaches Council and was a Strategist with the Global Business Playbook.

John and his wife, Lori, enjoy horses, golf, reading, writing, and traveling. Together, they own Fine Print Farms, an equestrian destination in the Texas Hill Country. They also are the founders of two equine-related non-profits. The first is Hill Country Eventing Foundation, designed to support and promote the equestrian sport of Eventing in the Texas Hill Country and South Texas. The second, a true passion of Lori and John's, is Reckless Rangers Veteran's Equitherapy. Through this program, they provide free equine-based learning and therapy to veterans dealing with post-traumatic stress.

John invites you to **Connect** with and **Follow** him and his business endeavors through social media platforms such as:

- LinkedIn: www.linkedin.com/in/successincubator/
- Facebook: www.Facebook.com/john.knotts1/
- Twitter: www.twitter.com/johnrknotts/

Interested in further discussing this topic with John? Want him to come to your organization? Looking for a speaker with lots to share? Email John today at John.Knotts@crossctr.com and let him know how he can help.

Related Works

Overcoming Organizational Myopia: Breaking Through Siloed Organizations, was John's initial business work, highlighting the many areas of expertise he has employed to deal with siloed organizations. This book formed the initial platform for several future business titles that will be related to the nine areas addressed in the book.

Business 2020: The Business World After COVID-19, was created as a free resource for business owners to prepare for and weather the next pandemic-level event that impacts their business.

Lessons in Life Long Learning, was created by John for EBR. He brought together seven authors from the Board and Faculty to provide their views on lifelong learning.

You can find all current and upcoming publications at https://www.crossctr.com/.

- *Becoming A Better Leader and Manager*
- *Corporate Epidemic: Toxic Leadership and Undead Businesses*
- *Getting Ahead in the Corporate World*
- *Choices We Have – Decisions We Make*
- *Think Big Take Small Steps*
- *Becoming A High Performing Organization*
- *Organizational Commitment: Your Employees Can Be Heroes Too*
- *Employee Engagement in Four Steps*
- *Stop Jumping To Do: A PDCA Approach to Project Planning and Problem Solving*
- *Building a Culture of Continuous Improvement*
- *Getting Good @ Process Improvement*
- *Experience-based Operational Excellence*
- *Breaking the Intelligent Automation Paradigm*
- *Ready…Set…Change: Change Management is Dead, Long Live Change Readiness!*
- *Maturing Your Document Domain*
- *A Formula for Innovation*
- *Building a Future-Ready Business*
- *Start, Grow, Scale, and Improve Your Business*

Becoming A Better Leader and Manager

Leaderment® and Leader Youniversity®

True Leadership is a dying art. The great leaders of the past, George Washington, Winston Churchill, Alexander the Great, Martin Luther King, even Adolph Hitler, are now few-and-far between. Some successful leaders, such as Steve Jobs, have risen to an iconic status. But have they been truly great leaders or were they just successful at running something?

Often, the skills a leader needs are inconsistent with those needed by a manager. I believe that if you are not a good leader, you will also not be a good manager, and, if you are not a good manager, you will also not be a good leader. It is my contention that those who apply both talents expertly demonstrate what I call, "Leaderment." This is the expert combination of the skills required for Leadership and Management.

Leaderment is a master-planned series of six volumes that culminate in a certification from the Leader Youniversity. This certification program is comprised of a set of five workbooks; each containing specific tools designed to improve your leadership and management skills.

Leaderment: *Becoming A Better Leader and Manager*, will be available through traditional book channels (printed and e-book). The five Leaderment workbooks, are part of the Leader Youniversity and will only be available upon registration for completion of the leadership certification program.

Corporate Epidemic: Toxic Leadership and Undead Businesses

Bad Leadership is Becoming an Epidemic!

Everywhere I look, I see evidence of bad leadership. The most prevalent problems are leadership apathy and leaders that lack accountability, the "it's good enough" leaders and the leaders who are "just getting by."

"Why are we seeing this," you ask yourself?

Bad leaders hire and promote bad people. And, unfortunately, bad leadership is not just destroying corporate America, but it is doing it at a record pace; the effects of which will extend far into the future.

These leadership charlatans are building armies of apathy whose members will follow in their footsteps. If you are someone who gets things done, you are kept in a position to get things done because bad leaders do not want you in a leadership position – you threaten them!

No wonder more than 70 percent of employees are disengaged at work. Who would not be with such a depressing and disheartening leadership outlook? Do you really have to be lazy and barely competent to get ahead?

Bad leaders are running rampant in corporate America and the undead companies they lead are foundering. Is there nothing that can be done?

Getting Ahead in the Corporate World

Getting Ahead in the Corporate World is like driving. There are five types of drivers on a multi-lane business highway.

The first type of driver is the slow poke who picks a lane and drives under the speed limit. This type is happy not getting ahead fast.

The second is the one who always takes the fast lane and stays there, riding the tail of the person in front of them, hoping that person will move over or go faster. Someone else going even faster always ends up in that lane and eventually comes up to ride the second driver's tail.

The third type of driver thinks the road was put there just for them. They use every lane on their commute, travelling as fast as they can. They are dangerous, and they switch lanes often, cutting others off.

Then, there is the risk taker type of driver, who sees the traffic and gets off the highway onto side streets, hoping to pass that traffic and re-enter ahead of others.

The last type is the methodical driver. These people stay at a safe speed limit for the road conditions, travel in the slower lanes, only pass when necessary, plan their routes, and are ready for the trip's end well in advance.

What type of driver are you?

Choices We Have – Decisions We Make

Every day – at work and at home – we are faced with choices. Some of these choices are big decisions, while others are as simple as, "Do I want fries with that, or do I want a salad?" Have you ever stopped to consider the variety of options you need to respond to and how your response to these options is formulated?

Sometimes, we simply jump to our decisions – we do not look before we leap. At those times, it is not until after making the decision that we really examine the choices we had and the ramifications of our decision.

We are, ultimately, faced with three possible decisions to the choices presented to us. Sometimes, following the decision we make for one choice, we have to then make another decision based upon that first decision, and so on. The decisions to each choice are, Easy, Normal, and Hard.

Our lives are made up of choices and decisions. Simple things such as:

- Easy: Should we eat fast food, which is cheap and easy, but tends to be bad for us.
- Normal: Do we eat at a nice restaurant, which generally has better choices and food, but costs more.
- Hard: Do we take the time and effort to purchase food at a grocery store or other outlet, where we get more for our money, but then must prepare the food, which takes time and effort.

We are faced with hundreds of these decisions throughout the day. We often make these decisions without putting much thought into the choices available to us. Making better and more informed decisions – in our daily lives and in our business lives – can be done using a simple approach outlined in this book.

Think Big Take Small Steps

Proper Strategic Planning is the Most Important First Step for Any Organization.

FORTUNE Magazine, in 1999, published the article *Why CEOs Fail*, which stated, "70 percent of all strategies fail to achieve their desired results and 30 percent fail to achieve anything at all." Planning, specifically strategic planning, tends to fail for many reasons. These reasons can be grouped into five specific categories that can be placed into a structured and systematic process of planning to ensure success. They are:

- Executable Focus
- Strategic Framework
- Traceable Implementation
- Rigor and Accountability
- Communication

Leadership must own this process. If leadership passes this strategic planning initiative over to others, even if they satisfy all five categories during their strategic planning activities, the organization's planning will always fail.

Think Big Take Small Steps is a no-nonsense strategic planning guide that takes away the mysticism and confusion surrounding strategic planning. It breaks the planning process down into three simple and easy-to-follow phases that include those five categories listed above. This book demonstrates how to create winning strategies and turn them into executable and trackable strategic plans.

Becoming A High Performing Organization

Over the years, I have worked with many businesses – nonprofits, government, and corporations. Many organizations ascribe to the statement made by Voltaire, "Perfect is the enemy of good." What Voltaire is saying is that achieving absolute perfection becomes increasingly inefficient because the increasing effort results in diminishing returns. Essentially, good is good enough. This is something I am simply not able to believe.

Every organization can become a high performing organization. The common belief in business is that there is a finite pie, and each company fights for a piece of this pie. I believe that the existence of the pie is a falsehood. If you are a high performing organization, and deliver goods and services in a quality manner, worrying about your "piece of the pie" is a waste of time and energy. To succeed, do not focus on this nonexistent "pie", rather, focus on being the best you can be.

The problem is organizations simply do not know how to become high performing. There are slews of books and research on the subject, but somehow, how to become high performing often alludes organizations. Perhaps, it is because they choose to believe Voltaire and the countless others who caution against setting goals too high. Thus, this holds everyone back in the belief that achieving your best simply is just too hard or even unattainable.

Becoming a High Performing Organization provides you with the tools to put all that nonsense behind you. This work and its associated products are designed to eradicate the myths that hold organizations back with easy-to-follow formulas to become the high performing organization you desire.

Organizational Commitment: Your Employees Can Be Heroes Too

There is a fable about a chicken, a pig, and breakfast. The fable says the chicken is fully dedicated to providing breakfast because she works hard to provide the eggs. The pig; however, is fully committed to providing breakfast because he gives his life to provide the bacon. In a sense, the pig is breakfast's hero, sacrificing his life for the mission – the ultimate in organizational commitment.

Research on organizational commitment often describes it as, "The employee's psychological attachment to the organization." The works of Meyer and Allen segregate organizational commitment into three components – affective, continuance, and normative. In *The Art of Winning Commitment*, Dick Richards states that there are four forms of commitment: 1) Political, 2) Intellectual, 3) Emotional, and 4) Spiritual.

Although the above definitions categorize the concept of organizational commitment, they do little to e-plain what this type of commitment really is. In fact, there is little established work that pinpoints what organizational commitment is, or more importantly, how to cultivate it in the workplace. In other words, these definitions are incomplete and flawed.

In *Organizational Commitment*, we develop a new definition, consisting of a demonstration of dedication, loyalty, and sacrifice to an organization. It is the demonstration of these three basic tenants, regardless of the organization's type, that constitutes organizational commitment. By understanding and applying this new definition, you learn how to help your employees become fully committed heroes.

Employee Engagement in Four Steps

For the last ten years, businesses have focused on employee engagement and the cost associated with a lack of engagement to businesses. Virtually any report or study on engagement points out that about 85 percent of employees in the U.S. are not engaged at work. This is costing businesses over $500 billion a year.

Although the nomenclature is different, this employee-focused issue has not really changed since before the 1930s when the emphasis was on employee satisfaction. In the 1980s, the emphasis turned to organizational commitment. Regardless of what it is called, the same business issue has not changed since researchers started studying and quantifying it more than 70 years ago.

However, engagement is the term that confuses managers the most. What is being measured is how employees feel about their jobs. This is difficult for companies to manage to. So, they do what they think will work and manage to single items that received low scores on an engagement survey.

Employees are, essentially, engaged by four things at work: organization; communication; development; and quality. For some reason, it is not obvious to organizations that this is where employees' focus lies. Thus, these four things become some of the major problem areas in many companies.

Employee Engagement in Four Steps covers these four areas in-depth to help any organization understand and improve its employee engagement.

Stop Jumping To Do: A PDCA Approach to Project Planning and Problem Solving

We are faced with a task...

Our boss says one of these things to us: "I need 'x' done."; "Our product is not selling as well as we expected."; "In our annual strategy meeting we were assigned a strategic objective."; or "Something is wrong in our process, and we are really not sure why."

Every day, millions and millions of people around the world are facing a task – something that needs to get done. This usually takes the form of a project or problem to be solved.

It is in our human nature to solve problems. We jump right in and do the thing we are tasked with; or fix the problem. However, all too often, the work we do fails to achieve the objectives we set out to make happen.

Why?

Because we are "Jumping To Do."

It was several years ago that I stumbled upon a relatively simple, yet extremely effective method I could use to implement any strategic plan. What I quickly realized was that this approach was the answer to any project-based challenge anyone is faced with today.

As stated, we want to solve problems, fix things, and implement projects. What I am going to provide to you in this book is a basic and simple planning tool that:

- Is easily repeatable
- Ensures project success
- Allows for simple timeline planning
- Takes less than an hour to complete

Building a Culture of Continuous Improvement

A culture of continuous improvement provides any company with a significant advantage in the marketplace. But do not take my word for it! An example is Corus, a customer focused, innovative solutions-driven company, which manufactures, processes, and distributes steel and aluminum products and services to customers worldwide. Corus is already seeing the benefits of continuous improvement with:

- Reduced process waste
- Improved product quality
- Reduced re-work time
- Faster response times
- Driving costs down
- Retaining and gaining customers

Building a culture of continuous improvement is not easy and can take a considerable amount of time. However, it is achievable, and results will be felt within months, if not weeks, of seriously embarking on a journey to continuous improvement. Deciding to move toward a culture of continuous improvement means becoming more strategic about how you manage your day-to-day operations. This is not about putting a few changes in place and calling it "good."

Over the past 25 plus years, I have developed a model for building this type of culture. This model centers on a strategy designed to build this type of culture in your organization. The strategy involves an equal portion of measuring, improving, and changing work. This model is fueled by a certain level of employee commitment and innovation.

Learn about it in my upcoming book.

Getting Good @ Process Improvement

Process improvement certification programs today have become watered down. People who receive a certification are educated just enough to pass. Organizations are filling up with employees with certifications. But are they really any good at process improvement and do these certifications even mean anything?

How do you get really good at improving processes?

Explore a multitude of ways to become better at improving processes in *Getting Good @ Process Improvement*. In this book, we will explore:

- External versus Internal and In-person versus Online
- With Project versus Without and Actual Project versus Simulation
- Formalized Training and Coaching versus Seat-of-your-Pants
- Testing versus No Testing
- Continuing Education Requirements
- Official Position versus Additional Duty
- Relying on Common Sense, Algebra, and Statistics
- Systems Thinking, Gap Analysis, and Bridge Building
- Being A Four-Year-Old – Asking Why
- Carrying a Big Toolbox
- Knowing the Difference Between Lean and Six Sigma
- Facilitation Like A Champ
- Thinking Like A Project Manager
- Alignment to Strategy
- Measure to Improve – the Measurement Cycle
- The Power of Go See and Digging Up Roots

Experience-based Operational Excellence

An experience is a direct observation of, or participation in, events as a basis of knowledge. Experience occurs when an individual has been affected by, or gained knowledge through, direct observation of or participation in an event. Each individual's experience is filtered by his or her practical knowledge, skill, and training. Thus, two people can experience the same thing and have very different reactions.

Customer experience (CX) is something a customer personally encountered, experienced, or lived through with a certain company. It is the product of an interaction between a company and a customer over the duration of their relationship. This interaction includes the attraction, awareness, discovery, cultivation, and advocacy of the customer, and purchase and use of a service by that customer. This is what his or her opinion of the organization is based on.

Many companies today only focus on the "touchpoints" – the critical moments when customers interact with the company relative to its provision of a product or service to that customer to establish the customer experience. This is often depicted in marketing as an experience map. Customer experience is more than just touchpoints! All parts of an organization affect the customer. An emphasis on Operational Excellence within a company, as the driver of the customer experience, is important to carefully consider.

Breaking the Intelligent Process Automation Paradigm

A process is nothing but a series of step-by-step tasks that begin with some type of request and end with the fulfillment of that request. Processes come in many shapes and sizes. The concepts of process management and process improvement have been around for hundreds of years.

Process automation in manufacturing began in the first Industrial Revolution. Intelligent Process Automation is a mindset and thought process of moving from a fully-manual process to a fully-automated solution.

This book outlines how to overcome the Five Paradigms of Intelligent Automation.

- Paradigm of the Shiny Object
- Paradigm of the Virtual Employee
- Paradigm of Done
- Paradigm of Tactical
- Paradigm of Ownership

Ready…Set…Change: Change Management is Dead, Long Live Change Readiness!

Since the 1940s, businesses have focused on change resistance and the management of change resistance. Companies and consultants are cashing in on the "Change Management" craze, but are we too late? Is that what we really ought to focus on? Change is constant and the speed of change is ever-increasing. Is it that we are too late to manage change or is there simply too much change to manage?

In today's business world, if you are managing change, you are too late. To be successful, businesses must be able to change quickly and change often. They need to be ready for change and view it as part of their daily existence.

Stop Managing Change

Start Building Change Readiness!

Ready…Set…Change talks about change, change management, and change readiness and takes the audience through the steps to become a Change Ready Business.

Maturing Your Document Domain

Document Management has become one of the most elusive business concerns of the information age. Businesses that aggressively seek to improve operations are now finding that they ignored their document production and management engine while they focused on improving products and services.

For many companies, the "document" has been looked at as a "necessary evil" and its development and delivery improvement has not kept up with improvements to the products or services. However, the number and size of documents are growing, and, for most companies, they are one of the most important as-sets a company has.

Many forward-thinking organizations make the mistake of believing that when they move to a digital platform, the "document" will go away. This is because, more-and-more, the physical document is being phased out for an electronic representation and organizations fail to understand that documents, tangible or not, are critical.

Documents, in various forms, still exist and are becoming harder and harder to manage, or their appropriate management is simply being ignored. Over twenty years ago, physical documents were simple, but today, the document can be a myriad of things: an email, a PDF, and image, a text message, a chat stream, a social media post, and even more.

This book provides a strategic model for evaluating an organization's end-to-end document management process, developing a road map to improve it, and measuring those improvements.

A Formula for Innovation

Vince Lombardi once said, "It is time for us to all stand and cheer for the doer, the achiever – the one who recognizes the challenge and does something about it." The thing that differentiates between a "human being" and a "human doing" is our ability to act in innovative ways in the face of adversity.

Plato, in his work, The Republic, said, "Necessity is the mother of invention." Necessity may be the mother of invention, but innovation is the foundation of overall positive change, and change requires more than simple necessity for it to occur.

Between the two – innovation and invention – there are arguably common themes. In this book, I explain the formula that exists for true innovative thought. This formula, not easily defined, is made up of several variables.

The Encyclopedia defines innovation as the introduction of new ideas, goods, services, and practices, which are intended to be useful. The main driver for innovation is often the courage and energy to better the world. When you take a more in-depth view of innovation, especially regarding invention, there are numerous variables that impact the activity.

A Formula for Innovation explores and explains the formula for true innovative thought, how to use it, and how it can influence your organization and business.

Building a Future-Ready Business

The world is changing fast.

What was yesterday's cutting-edge technology is now a clunky relic of the past. It is no secret that the world is changing, and the businesses that can adapt to those changes are going to be the ones that succeed.

In fact, there is a growing consensus among business leaders that being "future-ready" is one of the most important considerations you can make when building a new business or improving an existing business.

What does future-ready mean?

Future-ready means being able to adapt when things change, which, if evidenced by the last few years, will occur! The key to being future-ready is being flexible enough to pivot as necessary.

This book is designed as a roadmap to becoming future-ready. Continuously leverage this as a guide for your business.

Start, Grow, Scale, and Improve Your Business

Every business is fraught with challenges from the very start of their journey to the very end. These challenges are very system-driven and cannot be solved with just one tactic.

Start, Grow, Scale, and Improve Your Business is a single book with four follow up books to fully explain how to start a new business, grow it in revenue, scale it to meet and facilitate its growth, and improve it for efficiency and effectiveness.

These books will be borne out of years of working with startups to Fortune 100 companies and a multitude of business articles and blog posts over the years.

www.ingramcontent.com/pod-product-compliance
Lightning Source LLC
Chambersburg PA
CBHW080410170426
43194CB00015B/2770